Women Serving God

My Journey in Understanding
Their Story in the Bible

JOHN MARK HICKS

WOMEN SERVING GOD
My Journey in Understanding Their Story in the Bible

Cover Artwork (18x24 oil on canvas) by Dr. Heather Heflin Hodges, Dallas,Texas:

> "The Open Door" was a response to and celebration of the first time Heather heard a woman preach the gospel. That person was Dr. Sara Barton, the first woman to preach a keynote message from the main platform of the Pepperdine Bible Lectures (May, 2015). "The Open Door" of Stauffer Chapel says to both women and men, "Welcome, the door is open to all."

Cover and interior design: Strong Design

Printed in the United States of America

Responses from Readers

As a woman who preaches, I am often asked for resources that address biblical teachings about women's leadership in public assemblies and church ministries. John Mark Hicks has written a book I will recommend to those who agree and disagree with me on this important matter. He is detailed, fair, and vulnerable about his own journey and our collective journey in Churches of Christ. I recommend John Mark as a trustworthy guide.

Dr. Sara G. Barton, *University Chaplain,*
Pepperdine University, Malibu, CA.

Both Scripture itself and all who read it are bound up in cultural contexts, meaning(s) of words, and presumed behaviors. Thus, ancient texts are notoriously difficult to read and interpret. "Neutrality" and "objectivity" are not possible, so the best we can offer is a good-faith attempt at fairness and teachability. John Mark Hicks traces his journey along a path I know only too well in explaining his movement from a dogmatic reading of passages on female roles in the church to a full participation reading of those same texts.

As one who has made the same journey from arguing for radical limitations on my sisters in Christ to affirming all the biblical rights for them I would claim for myself, I cringe to look back to those earlier times—some of which are documented here and may have influenced John Mark. The option of time in which one could be challenged, get extra tools for research, and benefit from communal discernment is a gift of divine grace. Are all questions on the subject settled now? Hardly! But the joy of wrestling with them and the humility fostered by looking back are additional gifts for which to be thankful. John Mark's humble work here will help others with their own inquiries.

Dr. Rubel Shelly, *educator, minister, author.*

In this second volume of a three-part series, John Mark Hicks invites readers to reexamine practices of gender exclusion in Churches of Christ. With characteristic depth, rigor, and generosity, Hicks offers his own journey toward embracing the inclusion of women's voices in the assembly. Hicks writes with a familiarity of Restoration Movement history that few can boast, with an accompanying dedication to searching the scriptures. Readers will find in these pages, not only a compelling story of transformation and growth, but an invitation to deepen their faith in God, who is still at work in our midst.

Amy McLaughlin-Sheasby, *Instructor in the Department of Bible, Missions, and Ministry, Abilene Christian University.*

This book is a wonderful addition to the conversations about women's roles in the church. Readers will appreciate Hicks's honesty as he recounts his journey on this topic, benefit from his careful historical work as he describes how earlier Restoration Movement leaders addressed these matters, and profit from his detailed treatment of the key Scriptures under question. Churches should be studying this issue, reading this book, and making changes in their practice.

Dr. Ken Cukrowski, *Interim Dean of the College of Biblical Studies, Abilene Christian University*

John Mark Hicks prayed Psalm 119:32, "enlarge my understanding," and through the course of many years, in-depth Bible study, and listening to women, God accomplished just that within him on the subject of women in the Body of Christ. The breadth of this journey is detailed in *Women Serving God* in a way that is compassionate to his former self, but also boldly teaches the contemporary church his current understanding directly from the text. Hicks sheds redeeming light on the most cited passages, 1 Corinthians 14 and 1 Timothy 2, with thorough exegesis and helpful charts. But he also invites the church into the broader arc of scripture where we find many forgotten [or unknown] women in God's service-an arc that extends through our time into the eschatological age in which we participate through the Spirit even now.

The gravity of how this truth should inform our current practice undergirds *Women Serving God*. This is a one of a kind resource for the church in a critical time, not only because it exegetically explores the full humanity of women in the church through all of the relevant passages, but also because it includes insight into the moral consequence of the current practice that denies women a voice. Hicks's line, "I sensed the book hurt her in some way," lands like an anvil on the prepared heart. Female contributors graciously explain why female inclusion is a moral issue, a Gospel issue, supported by the culture of God's Kingdom established at Eden. If Churches of Christ have ears to hear and needs a singular, credible resource to aid their obedience to God's Word on women, this is it.

Tiffany Mangan Dahlman, *Minister at Courtyard Church of Christ, Fayetteville, North Carolina*

This book is a gift to twenty-first century Churches of Christ. Part autobiography, part history, part exegesis, and part biblical theology, Hicks's exploration of the Bible's teachings on the role of women in congregational gatherings offers several invaluable components. Hicks provides a close reading of the key texts, delineating the interpretive options taken by leading writers from Churches of Christ and from other traditions. But he always reads individual passages through the lens of a biblical theology rooted in the story of God from creation to new creation, demonstrating how a theological hermeneutic enriches our reading of the Bible. Hicks's deep respect for Churches of Christ emerges on every page, especially as he helps readers understand the diversity in their history of interpreting these texts. In the end, Hicks persuasively argues that the story of God we find in the Bible is one in which God equally gifts women and men to participate in the gathering of God's people. Hicks's accessible book on this urgent matter deserves careful attention from leaders among Churches of Christ.

Dr. James L. Gorman, *Associate Professor of History, Johnson University*

Interweaving careful study of the biblical text and its historical context with a candid and often vulnerable account of his own journey toward inclusion, John Mark Hicks makes a compelling argument for the participation of women in the assembly. This book will be an invaluable resource for leaders among Churches of Christ desiring to study this topic anew and take the next faithful step.

Lauren Calvin Cooke, *Ph.D. student, Emory University*

One of the most trusted theological voices in my education formation has given us another gift with this new book. John Mark Hicks reminds us that any discussion of how women and men serve together in the church must begin with the power of our baptismal identity. That is, do we believe that the Holy Spirit equally equips both women and men to carry out Jesus's message of reconciliation? Dr. Hicks is a trusted guide in navigating the depth of scripture and the complexity of our cultural moment. Drink deeply from this well!

Dr. Joshua Graves, *Otter Creek Church, Brentwood, Tennessee*

This is the book I've been waiting for—a scholarly and pastoral examination of the full participation of women in the life of the church. Building on his earlier work, *Searching for the Pattern*, Hicks describes his journey that sounds so familiar to many of us. With generosity of spirit for his religious heritage, he wrestles with both the sweeping narrative of scripture and the individual texts that are pertinent. This work will bless churches—both as an example of how we are to read scripture and as a call for the complete sharing by men and women in our life in the Spirit.

Mike Cope, *Director of Ministry Outreach, Pepperdine University*

Dedication

For my mother, Edith Lois Hicks,
whose intelligence, wit, and faithfulness
taught me so much about life and serving God,
and whose patience and love formed me in profound ways.

Table of Contents

Preface

This is my journey. It may not reflect anyone else's experience. That's okay. None of us are exactly the same. But perhaps my journey may shed light on your own. I'm sure yours would illuminate mine.

This is the second in a series of three books. The first, *Searching for the Pattern*, explored the question of hermeneutics. This book investigates the participation of women in the assembly. The third will address questions about leadership and church organization.

I tell this story because in recent years I have been asked numerous times to recommend books, articles, podcasts, and videos that explore the Bible's teaching about women in ministry. This book is a specific response to the sorts of requests I regularly receive in the context of churches of Christ.

There are many substantial and credible explorations of this subject at both the popular and academic level from different perspectives. Sometimes they engage the understanding of biblical texts in profound ways, and others helpfully address emotional bewilderment, traumatic wounds, and practical problems.

As an extension of my book *Searching for the Pattern* (2019), I write in the context of my *adoration* of God, my *commitment* to Scripture, and my *love* for churches of Christ. As you read this book, I hope you will remember the gratitude, heart, and grace I have for churches of Christ evident in *Searching for the Pattern*. At the same time, this is my journey through a deeply emotional, personal, and thorny subject. My intention is to write with respect, love, and kindness as I describe and assess various positions.

Within the worshipping assemblies of churches of Christ, the voices of women are typically silent and their visible leadership is absent. This book is my journey (1) from the *exclusion* of the voices of women and their leadership in the assembly (2) to a *limited inclusion*, and finally (3) to the *full inclusion* of those voices and their leadership in the assembly.

While most who grew up in churches of Christ will understand why I focus on the assembly, some will question whether my scope is too narrow. Are there no other dimensions of society, church, and family where women serve God? *Yes, of course, there are.* I do not diminish that service one iota. I focus not only for the sake of brevity but also to address the question that is, in my experience, the most pressing one for most people.

Larger questions will come into play as I explore how women served God throughout Scripture. Yet, my purpose is not comprehensive. My focus will return to the assembly because it is often the church's most public witness. Moreover, the assembly, whether right or wrong, is also central to the identity of churches of Christ and its historic practices. *Most importantly, the public assembly is* **one** *of the last bastions of the exclusion of women among churches of Christ.* There are other spaces where women are restricted (like elders), but I will not address those in this book. *Even if the eldership is limited to men, this does not necessarily entail women cannot fully participate in the assembly* any more than male elders restrict men who are not elders from full participation.

Neither will I address questions about the relationship between husbands and wives (e.g., 1 Peter 3:1–6; Ephesians 5:22–33; Colossians 3:18) except only in tangential ways because my focus is on the assembly.

My goal is to describe as simply but as thoughtfully as I can my own journey regarding the assembly. For this reason, I decided to forego documentation through footnotes. My hope is that the book will contain its own justification. Many judgments, however, are based on specific research in ancient culture, lexical studies, the history of movements, and fuller discussions in the literature. In those situations I have noted appropriate resources. Whenever I cite a name, you can find it in "Works Referenced" at the end of the book.

Though I have occasionally written on this topic, I know I must listen to other voices than my own gender. Consequently, I asked three female servants of God to meet with me every other week over a period of three months in order to discuss this material. I also asked Claire, Jantrice, and Lauren to write responses to the manuscript. I am deeply grateful for their assistance.

I also asked some male servants of God who held more conservative positions than I to walk with me. They also met with me every other week over a period of three months. I am deeply grateful for their assistance.

I hope the book reflects the wisdom of these two groups. Hopefully, this communal discernment has helped produce a patient, careful, and sensitive engagement with this deeply emotional and often divisive topic. Of course, I alone am responsible for the book's content.

In addition, I asked Bethany Joy Moore to contribute a brief piece about growing up in churches of Christ as the daughter of a preacher. She is now a graduate student in theology because her parents respected her journey and encouraged her participation at home and other settings even though she was not permitted to lead at her congregation.

I want to faithfully listen to the story of God in Scripture and understand how it invites the assembled people of God to rehearse that story. I want to apply it to the specific questions about the voices of women and their visibility in the worshipping assembly. I am committed to the God who sent Jesus the Messiah by the power of the Spirit. I confess that Scripture bears witness to God, guides our understanding of God, and equips us for ministry in service to God. I submit all my thoughts to the teaching of the apostles and prophets.

The specific question this book addresses is: *does God invite women to fully participate through audible and visible leadership in all the assemblies of the saints where men and women are gathered to glorify God and edify each other?*

May God bless our journey together.

Foreword:
Three Prominent Positions

Though I have adopted each of these views at different times throughout my life, I do not advocate for any position in this foreword. My goal is to further mutual understanding. I describe three typical positions and their reading strategies for grounding their understanding in Scripture. I attach neither a pejorative nor an affirming meaning to any of these descriptions.

NO LEADERSHIP IN THE ASSEMBLY

A strong principle of male leadership means women should not have any leading voices or presence in the assembly. This not only excludes reading Scripture, preaching, or presiding at the table but also making announcements, audibly requesting prayers, voicing a prayer, asking questions, passing the communion trays standing, or testifying about an answered prayer. Women may not audibly or visibly lead the assembly in any way. Consequently, there are no women's voices in the assembly other than singing with the congregation or their baptismal confession.

There are some variations within this category. For example, in some African American congregations women are encouraged to make prayer requests or offer testimonies in the assembly.

This is an historic position among churches of Christ. For example, David Lipscomb believed women should not speak when the whole church was publicly assembled. However, they did encourage women to teach men, women, and children privately in classes or small groups at the building and in their homes. They distinguished between public and private settings. However, most contemporary practitioners do not permit women to teach Bible classes or small groups that include men.

In the past, this perspective excluded women from any kind of public speaking and public leadership of any organization whether social or in the church. It also objected to their entrance into some professions (e.g., lawyers or medical physicians). Many believed the order of creation applied not only to home and church but also to society.

What kind of hermeneutical strategy grounds this theology? Every biblical text is a timeless norm to which every culture must conform. Scripture is absolute and is never relative to or dependent upon the circumstances in which they are written except those that apply to dispensational distinctions (e.g., "Mosaic Law" in contrast to "New Testament" [only those in Acts and the Epistles] instructions) or are *explicitly* identified as temporary or culturally relative.

As a result, 1 Corinthians 14:34–35 and 1 Timothy 2:12 are understood as timeless statements of God's intent for women in public assemblies of the church. These explicit directives, grounded in God's creation of man as the head of woman, are part of the requirements for a faithful church.

2. ## LIMITED LEADERSHIP IN THE ASSEMBLY

Male headship is understood in terms of responsibility rather than authority. Men are not empowered to order women to conform as much as men are accountable for the spiritual health of the community. Men, as Christlike "heads," should serve, empower, and sacrifice for women. Consequently, it recognizes many historic practices as too restrictive because they deny women the freedom God permits and encourages.

This group is more open to leadership by women in the assembly since not every form of leadership carries a headship function. For example, when Scripture is read, the authority lies in the text; when prayers are prayed, this serves the community rather than exercising authority over it; and whoever passes the trays, serves the community rather than standing over it.

There are a wide range of applications within this group. Some are fairly limited in this permission while others encourage a broad inclusion, including exhorting the church, teaching in its theological schools, and teaching men in Bible classes at the building. Some encourage the participation of women in the assembly in every way except as preaching ministers and ruling elders.

Historically, this was the practice of some churches of Christ. Many congregations in the nineteenth and early twentieth centuries regarded the participation of women as both a privilege and a right. They encouraged women to pray, read Scripture, lead singing, and exhort the church, though preaching and ruling as elders were not permitted.

Male headship is a key principle, but it does not exclude women from all leadership functions in the assembly. For example, 1 Corinthians 11:2–16 addresses an assembled community where women audibly prayed and prophesied while, at the same time, they honored their heads. Male headship does not deny women all forms of leadership. This means women may have a voice in the assembly as long as they honor their heads when they do so.

The principle of headship is rooted in creation. The original vision for humanity included male headship, which is played out in the history of God's people (priests are men, Jesus called only male apostles in his ministry, and only men served as elders in the early church). At the same time, women are invited to exercise their gifts in the assembly as long as male headship is honored.

FULL PARTICIPATION IN THE ASSEMBLY

This position opens all functions in the assembly to women according to their gifts while giving due attention to cultural sensitivity and deference to local customs or traditions for the sake of the gospel (e.g., Christians in Iran).

While some couch this primarily in the language of rights and justice, others frame it in the light of gifts and privileges. Some emphasize both. The inclusion of women's gifts is for the common good of the body. If the Holy Spirit has gifted women in particular ways, then the Spirit calls the church to use these gifts for the edification of the body.

To what degree cultural sensitivity comes into play is differently handled. On the one hand, some assert a kind of justice which demands inclusion irrespective of local customs and subcultures. However, others affirm, for the sake of love and unity, a more delicate approach that calls for mutual formation toward the goal of full inclusion. This acknowledges that the cultural path to equality in some congregations is a long one. In some cultures, it is practically unimaginable.

On the other hand, the cultural situation in the United States calls for the full inclusion of women. Unlike many ancient contexts, the inclusion of women is not a cultural scandal today. Rather, the exclusion of women is a cultural scandal in the United States.

Scripture points us beyond its own circumstances and specific applications through seed texts (e.g., Galatians 3:28), paradigm shifts in the story (e.g., the pouring out of the Spirit on women in Acts 2), and the original vision of full mutuality in creation fulfilled in new creation (Genesis 1–2). The church is new creation. This captures the original vision of creation itself and moves us into a new age where men and women are both fully empowered and gifted for ministry and service in the assembly of God as an expression of the priesthood of all believers.

CONCLUSION

I imagine within many, if not most, congregations of the churches of Christ all three positions are represented. *Our first task is mutual understanding.* This is where we begin. We must first listen attentively. Do I understand what the other is saying, how they read Scripture, and what their desire for the church is in love and unity? We cannot talk if we do not first listen.

PART 1

How I Once
Read the Bible

*For you, O Lord, are my hope,
my trust, O LORD, from my youth . . .
O God, from my youth you have taught me,
and I still proclaim your wondrous deeds.*

Psalms 71:5, 17

I pray those words.

The Psalm affirms what I have confessed my whole life. I have proclaimed God's mighty works and trusted in what God has done, is doing, and will do to secure my hope. I have always trusted God, though I have had seasons of doubt and deep lament. I learned the "wondrous deeds" of God in my youth. I honor my parents, the congregations in which I grew up, and Freed-Hardeman University for forming my faith.

This is what churches of Christ have always believed. We proclaim the "wondrous deeds" of God. We have sung them, prayed them, preached them, and named them at the table of the Lord in our assemblies. This is our shared faith. We have sought to faithfully obey God as revealed in Scripture. I share that commitment.

THE BLUEPRINT HERMENEUTIC

We valued simplicity and emotion-free objectivity. We thought the instructions in the Bible were clear. We were committed to following what God said.

This included how we worshipped as a congregation. For example, Acts 2:42 provided the basic content of our assemblies. "They continued steadfastly in the apostles' teaching and the fellowship, the breaking of bread and the prayers." We followed the apostolic pattern when we gathered every Sunday: (1) teaching in the form of preaching, (2) the fellowship through the free will sharing of our resources, (3) the breaking of the bread in the Lord's supper, and (4) the prayers. When the disciples gathered, (5) they also sang to the Lord and encouraged each other (Ephesians 5:19; Colossians 3:16). For shorthand, we called these the "five acts of worship." They were part of every Sunday morning assembly.

We restored the worship assemblies of the New Testament because we were committed to doing what God said to do and how God said to do it. We wanted to be the church of the New Testament. This meant that we did what they did and did not do what they did not do.

The important question was: *"what does God require of us?"* That was why we read the Bible. We wanted to know what to do to be saved (Acts 16:30). We wanted to know how to worship God "in spirit and in truth" (John 4:24).

We concluded that *only the Bible* authorizes what God requires and *only the New Testament* authorizes what God *now* requires. We expected the New Testament to provide a *specific, consistent, coherent,* and *complete* answer to any question about what God requires. Further, if we wanted to know what God *now* requires, only Acts and the Epistles (including Revelation) can authorize anything as a practice of the church. Everything before Acts chapter two belonged to different dispensations. Therefore, the Old

Testament and the Gospels did not speak directly to the church in terms of what God *now* required.

But how do we find authorization in Acts and the Epistles? First, we looked for *explicit commandments*. When we read that the church was commanded to do something and there were no *explicit* mitigating circumstances that rendered it local, circumstantial, or temporary, we understood that command as timeless for every congregation. *Every command in Acts and the Epistles was understood as a timeless requirement unless there was a clear reason to think otherwise.* The text commanded singing; therefore, we sang. The text commanded eating the Lord's supper, therefore, we ate.

Second, we looked for *approved (binding) examples*. Examples were *only approved* when it was practiced *as a requirement* by a congregation under the direction of an apostle. A good example may illustrate a principle, but *good examples only became approved ones when we knew the practice itself was required*. How did we know it was required? We knew it was required when we discerned that a *required command operated in the background*. For example, when Troas broke bread on the first day of the week in Acts 20:7, we knew it was a good example because Paul was there. We concluded it was an *approved example* because it fulfilled the command of Jesus to remember him.

Third, we discerned *necessary inferences*. We inferred that Acts 20:7 was an *approved example*, and we thought that inference was a necessary one. We connected the command of Jesus at the Last Supper ("do this") to the good example ("on the first day of the week they came together to break bread") and *inferred* the example specifically and intentionally fulfilled that command as part of the pattern for the church. Consequently, we *inferred* it was a binding example.

In addition, when we did what God required, we *only* did what God authorized in the way God authorized it. In other words, the Bible not only told us *what* God required but also *limited* our practices to what God authorized. This was called the "law of silence" or "the law of exclusion." *Only what God authorizes is permitted* in any worshipping assembly.

At the heart of this approach is the conviction that Acts and the Epistles contain an *exclusive detailed pattern*, a specific blueprint, for the worship and work of the church. The pattern included "the five acts of worship." The pattern was exclusive and binding. Consequently, we ought to practice what the early church practiced, and we ought to do nothing more than what the early church did.

As a result, when we considered whether and in what ways women may participate audibly or visibly in the assembly, we sought the answer in the blueprint. We found two *explicit* commands.

> *1 Corinthians 14:34–35*—"Women should be silent in the churches. For they are not permitted to speak, but should be subordinate, as the law also says. If there is anything they desire to know, let them ask their husbands at home. For it is shameful for a woman to speak in church."

> *1 Timothy 2:8, 11–12*—"I desire, then, that in every place the men should pray, lifting up holy hands without anger or argument . . . Let a woman learn in silence with full submission. I permit no woman to teach or to have authority over a man; she is to keep silent."

This seemed clear. In the assembly, men are to lead through prayer and teaching. The women are to remain silent and learn in full submission to the men. Since "the Bible gives no examples of women speaking, reading scripture, or leading prayer in a gender-mixed religious assembly," Guy wrote, all assemblies are regulated by these two prescriptions grounded in male spiritual leadership.

MY EXPERIENCE IN CHURCHES OF CHRIST

Growing up in churches of Christ, I never heard a woman's voice in the public assembly except for corporate singing and her baptismal confession. I recall no other sanctioned audible or visible participation by women. Given how we understood 1 Corinthians 14:34–35 and 1 Timothy 2:8–15, this made sense. It was, as far as I knew, the dominant and uniform practice of churches of Christ.

In the 1970s, two periodicals advocated for *full participation*. *Mission* (Kemp, Hunter, Holley) and *Integrity* (Hall, Ledbetter, Parks) regularly published supportive articles. (For more recent history and developments, see Christy.) Their fringe voices had little impact on the conservative regions I inhabited. They did, however, generate a flood of responses that reaffirmed the received practice (May).

My first personal encounters with this topic came in the context of youth devotionals. The congregation I attended and another nearby regularly shared youth activities. At one time, we gathered every other week for worship, Bible study, recreation, and fellowship. Those were good times in 1972–1974. I remember them fondly. I was even infatuated with one of the girls who attended the other congregation.

These devotionals included chain prayers. One started, the next would pray, and the next would pray until everyone had prayed around the circle. By "everyone," however, I mean all the *boys* in the circle. The girls did not vocalize their prayers.

Some raised the question of whether one of the girls might also speak during the chain prayer as long as they did not begin or end it. While our leaders did not encourage their participation, the question was discussed. This was the beginning of my own personal investment. *Is the audible and visible leadership of women in prayer, worship, or assembly permitted by Scripture?*

This question soon erupted in the major publications of churches of Christ. Articles appeared in the *Firm Foundation*

(Forehand, Shelly), the *Gospel Advocate* (J. B. Meyers, Woods), the *Spiritual Sword* (Deaver), and *The Defender* (Sattenfield). The audible participation of women in chain prayers was not only growing among youth groups but also campus ministries.

This debate shaped me in important ways. It is where I cut my teeth on the question this book addresses. At a micro-level, it unearthed significant issues. Both opponents and proponents saw this as a watershed. If teenage girls may lead in a chain prayer, how may male headship exclude women from leading prayer in other contexts? For many, it was a slippery slope. Though it seemed an insignificant question to some, it contained the seeds of future developments.

MAY GIRLS LEAD BOYS IN CHAIN PRAYERS?

From 1974 to 1977, I majored in Bible at Freed-Hardeman University under professors I admired. 1975 was the year I began to fully immerse myself in this topic.

An article by James Casey in the 1975 *Firm Foundation* ignited debate. In response to increased criticism of teenage girls participating in chain prayers, he defended the practice as a means of "spiritual growth."

Others disagreed. Forehand was "appalled to find an elder in the Lord's church who publicly endorses" the practice. Shelly wrote, "The Bible clearly prohibits such activity." Whitmire reiterated "God's plan for public worship" is male leadership. This includes any setting where men and women are worshipping together. Orbison applied this point to the home and believed male leadership excluded wives and daughters from leading their husbands and fathers in prayer.

Casey responded to his critics by publishing a small booklet with an extended defense of women leading men in prayer in small groups. Others responded with booklets of their own (Sattenfield, Hawk). Hawk challenged anyone to deny the following proposition: "The scriptures teach that it is a sin for women to pray audibly in any assembly of men and women gathered for worship."

This discussion was conducted according to the blueprint hermeneutic. People searched for explicit commands, approved examples, and necessary inferences in order to discern what God authorized. Casey suggested the general command to pray—directed at the whole church, including men and women—authorized women to lead men in prayer. This "has always been our approach to obeying *general* commands in the absence of *specifics.*" Consequently, the generic command authorizes women to lead prayer.

This works, according to the blueprint hermeneutic, *unless* there is a command, example, or necessary inference that identifies an *exclusive specific*. Opponents found *one*: "I desire, then, that in every place the men should pray, lifting up holy hands without anger or argument" (1 Timothy 2:8). This text, according to Shelly, "expressly designates males as the ones who 'pray in every place.'" For Sattenfield, "it is very clear that the context of 1 Timothy is not speaking just about the assembly." "Wherever," Shelly continued, "believers gather and engage in prayer—whether the whole church is assembled or a group of teenagers has gotten together for a devotional—the males are to be the leaders of the prayers." Moreover, "a female sins when she exercises a role which God has specifically given to the male." Whitmire argued that 1 Timothy 2:8 "speaks to the very question involved in the matter of women leading prayer *in any place* where men are present." If we disregard this explicit command, according to Forehand, then "we are at liberty to disregard any" apostolic teaching. Consequently, whether women lead prayers in small groups with men became a test case for whether one affirms the authority of apostolic teaching or not.

Wayne T. Hall, in a personal letter on May 27, 1976, highlighted the importance of the silence of Scripture. He believed "the syllogisms formulated by brethren in years gone by" regarding instrumental music in worship "have equal force" on this topic. This is particularly true because there is a *specific command* to pray. Just as there is a specific command to "sing" that excludes all items belonging to the same category (coordinates; "playing a piano" is another form of music), in the same way the specific command for men to lead prayer *excludes* women from leading prayer. Without any other commands, examples, or inferences, this specific command excludes all other options. *It specifies a particular in the blueprint.*

But Casey did not see 1 Timothy 2:8 as a *specified exclusion.* On the contrary, it is a simple statement about how and where men should pray. The supposed exclusion is actually an inference. Casey's critics moved from "I will therefore that men pray everywhere" to "I will therefore that men *lead* every *audible prayer* that is prayed in *mixed assemblies.*" To Casey, this was an *unnecessary* inference. His critics, however, did not budge.

Yet, if this specific exclusion applies to all gatherings of men and women, does it apply to family devotionals as well? Casey's critics did not shrink back. Orbison, for example, insisted "the men are to take the lead in spiritual matters and nowhere is there any example of a mother leading her family in prayer with daddy present." Furthermore, when we conduct family devotions led by women, "we teach our children that mother is not subject to father in spiritual matters." Since there was no authorization for expanding the specified exclusion, the specific command for men to pray excludes women both at home and in the assembly.

This highlights a crucial principle that was at the heart of the discussion. What is the relationship between leadership, authority, and submission? If wives are commanded to submit to their husbands, does this *imply* wives cannot lead their husbands in prayer? Does leadership imply an authority that is antithetical to submission? As Sattenfield wrote in his booklet, the basic principle comes down to "a question of subjection." If "wives are to be in subjection to their husbands in *everything* (Eph. 5:24)," Orbison wrote, since "Paul equates 'silence' with subjection in the worship service (1 Cor. 14:34), one would question her subjection when a woman 'speaks' (takes the leads) in a devotional. A woman cannot take the authority away from men. She is always to be in subjection." Consequently, whenever a woman leads a man in prayer, according to Shelly, "she is in a position of authority over the man/men present." This is a violation of a fundamental principle in God's creation order.

This raised many questions for me. I remember discussing them with friends at Freed-Hardeman. Does leading the thoughts of another in prayer assume a position of authority over them? Does all leadership entail a position of authority? When a male member leads an elder in prayer, does this mean that leader assumes a position of authority over the elder? When a wife teaches her husband a truth from the Bible has the wife assumed a position of authority over her husband? These sorts of questions would consume my last couple of years at Freed-Hardeman.

MY EARLY INVESTIGATION

Freed-Hardeman encouraged Bible majors to develop debating skills. Debates were an honored tradition. I embraced it. I joined the University's debate team, and I participated in mock debates on campus that were sponsored by the Preachers Club. My most memorable, at least to me, was in the Spring of 1976 when I affirmed this mock proposition: *The Scriptures teach that a woman has the authority to lead prayer in worship to God when men are present.*

As I reflect on that proposition now, I see how significant the issues of leadership, authority, and submission were to me. They were intertwined. Leadership entailed authority. Men have authority over women. Therefore, women are not permitted to lead men, even in prayer.

Bruce Morton, a beloved classmate, and I sent an article to Reuel Lemmons, the editor of the *Firm Foundation*, on April 18, 1976. It posed the question: "Does a woman have the right to lead a man in prayer in worship to God?" Its title was, "A Question Answered by 1 Timothy 2:12." Though the article was not published, it states the key principle at work in my thinking. As Shelly wrote in 1975, "A woman can never have a position of dominion over a man, whether in public or private."

The article offered the following syllogism.

Major Premise: A woman who leads a man in prayer is in a position of authority over a man.

Minor Premise: 1 Timothy 2:12 prohibits a woman to be in a position of authority over a man.

Conclusion: Therefore, 1 Timothy 2:12 prohibits a woman to lead a man in prayer.

1 Timothy 2:12, we argued, applied to every circumstance where men and women worship together, whether in the home, teen devotionals, Bible classes, or the public assembly. Since Paul wants men to pray "in every place" (1 Timothy 2:8), this includes every gathering whether public or private, whether the whole church or a small group. Further, because Paul expects men to lead the prayers and does not permit a woman to have authority over a man, leading prayer involves a position of authority. This position hangs almost everything on the meaning of "authority" in 1 Timothy 2:12. That is an important point to remember when we get to Part 6.

This perspective was common among churches of Christ at the time. For example, in 1973, May concluded that 1 Timothy 2:8–15 did not regulate a "woman's conduct in the assembly only."

Rather, "in every place of prayer and teaching where men and women are present, men are to lead, women to be in quietness." This principle not only applies to prayer but to teaching as well. Consequently, women are not only prohibited from preaching in the assembly, but they are also excluded from teaching a Bible class at the building or leading a small group in their home when men are present. 1 Timothy 2:12 excluded *all forms of leadership* because women must submit to men in all their relationships within the church and home.

Parks saw the implication. The "dictum that 'what the passage prohibits, it prohibits everywhere' recently led a preacher to advise a woman that she could not kneel by her husband at bedtime and pray aloud without sinning!"

I thought Parks failed to recognize the intricate relationship between leadership, authority, and submission that was rooted in God's creation order. Paul based his prohibition on this truth: "Adam was first formed, then Eve" (1 Timothy 2:13). God's creative act grounds the relationship between husband and wife. Consequently, Paul's principles of authority and submission are *especially* applicable to husbands and wives. If Paul specifies that only men should lead prayer everywhere and this is grounded in the authority of the husband over the wife, then this entails that *wives may not lead their husbands in prayer*.

WOMEN'S ROLE IN THE CHURCH

During the 1976 Spring semester, Bruce Morton and I decided to write a book. Over our last few semesters we pieced together some independent studies and research papers for assorted classes to produce a manuscript. It was published as *Woman's Role in the Church* in 1978.

Written by two single males at the ages of twenty-two and nineteen respectively, it was a bold move. We were passionate and sincerely sought to understand Scripture. Citing nearly two hundred sources, we addressed a wide range of exegetical and practical questions through the lens of God's creation order, apostolic teaching, and the meaning of authority and submission. It sought the blueprint in Acts and the Epistles for the participation of women in the assembly.

Here is the Table of Contents.

1. Creation and Subordination.
2. Liberation Theology.
3. An Interpretation of 1 Timothy 2:8–15.
4. An Interpretation of 1 Corinthians 11:2–16.
5. An Interpretation of 1 Corinthians 14:33b-36.
6. Harmonizing Paul.
7. The Limitation of Women in Worship.
8. Problem Solving.
9. Summary and Conclusions.

Appendix A: Deaconesses?
Appendix B: A Cultural Principle.

The first two chapters rooted female subordination in the creation account and addressed feminist liberation theology. The next four chapters examined 1 Timothy and 1 Corinthians. These texts warrant the silence of women when men and women are gathered to worship God, whether public or private. Chapter seven identified specific principles that limit the participation of women. Chapter eight answered twenty-seven practical questions based on those principles. Appendix A, though not dogmatic, concluded there were no female deacons in the New Testament church. Appendix B offered a principle for discerning the distinction between cultural relativity and creational normativity.

As I read back through it, I am impressed with the breadth of its investigation and its thorough argument. This was a plausible offering for churches of Christ at the time. It provided a principle for discerning how to answer complex practical questions.

The book defended the common practice of churches of Christ where women are silent (except for singing and baptismal confessions) and excluded from visible leadership in the assembly. When one attends a typical assembly of churches of Christ, women are neither seen nor heard as leaders. They are practically invisible and absolutely inaudible. Singing is permitted because it is *specifically* commanded for *everyone* (Ephesians 5:19; we sing to "one another") and, as a corporate activity, it does not involve any exercise of authority over another.

The burden of *Woman's Role in the Church* was to offer a biblical argument for excluding women from leadership when men and women gather to worship. As I summarize the book's argument, I will use its language without quoting it.

ARGUMENT FROM CREATION

Any appeal to creation is an appeal to a trans-cultural ordinance or creation law. The argument is this:

Major Premise: Creation law is part of Christ's law.
Minor Premise: Female subordination is part of creation law.
Conclusion: Therefore, female subordination is part of Christ's law.

Thus, female subordination is a trans-cultural ordinance, which is neither transitory nor relative to cultural dynamics.

Created in the image of God, Adam and Eve came from God's hand in perfect relationship with God and each other. Their humanity represents God's ideal. This obligates all human beings to mirror their relationship. Moreover, in Christ, redeemed people are new creatures, which is a restoration of the image of God. Christ's law affirms creation law and calls disciples of Jesus to comply with it. New creation renews creation law; it does not undermine it.

While the fall had a negative impact on the relationship between males and females, we argued female subordination is rooted in creation. This is evident in several ways: (1) man was created first and thus was the *primogeniture* (the rights of the firstborn) of the race; (2) woman was created *from* the man; (3) woman was created as a *helper* for man; and (4) the first man *named* the woman which assumes authority over her. Moreover, Paul rooted his subordinationist teaching in Genesis 2.

Further, we thought creation law had universal application. Creation not only forms husband/wife relationships but the general relationship of males and females in God's Edenic sanctuary, which today is the church and its assemblies. Thus, creation law applies to the home and the church.

Female subordination was purposed from the beginning. Creation law grounds male leadership and authority while also recognizing the mutuality of the male/female partnership as they share dominion over the earth. They are partners but the buck stops with the man, which is evident from the fact that God approached Adam first after their sin.

ARGUMENT FROM THE PAULINE TEXTS

1 Timothy 2:8–15, we thought, provided the fundamental principle that shapes how we answer questions about leadership. It identifies the separate roles of men and women. According to 1 Timothy 2:8, men are to lead the prayers of any group gathered to worship.

Accordingly, the exercise of authority belongs to men alone. Women should neither lead prayer nor teach when men and women are assembled for worship, prayer, or Bible study. The underlying principle is a subordination-authority antithesis which implies that a woman may not lead a man in any way that assumes a position of authority. We translated 1 Timothy 2:12 like this: "I do not permit a woman to be a teacher or in any way to have authority over a man; she is to be silent."

Its trans-cultural nature is rooted in creation law. Paul provided an explicit reason for this prohibition. Adam was formed first. Eve became a transgressor when she assumed Adam's authority to herself and led him into sin. Further, if a woman will concentrate on her domestic duties (bearing children), she will be saved from the error of exercising authority over men.

1 Corinthians 14:33b-36, we argued, silenced women in all the assemblies of Christ. In the context of 1 Corinthians 12–14, to "speak" refers to authoritative speech such as prophecy, leading praying, or teaching. Consequently, Paul prohibited women from speaking in the assembly. When assembled to worship, the principle of female subordination applies.

Further, this instruction is not limited. Paul addressed *all gifted women* but silenced their gifts in the assembly. Female prophets must remain silent in the assembly because this honors the principle of subordination. Otherwise, they would exercise authority over the males present through their speech. This would dishonor the creation order that the law demands.

1 Corinthians 11:2–16 affirmed female subordination in the context of a ranked authority from God to Christ, Christ to man, and man to woman. The male/female relationship is rooted in the creation account of Genesis 2 because the woman is created *from* the man and *for* the man. As such, the woman is the glory of man.

Man is the "head" of woman in the sense of superior rank, authority, or leader. Just as Christ is the head of the church as one who rules over the church and to whom the church is subordinate, so man is the head of the woman. Women are veiled in the assembly because the woman must honor the authority of the men present. The head-covering is a symbol of male authority.

In the 1978 *Gospel Advocate*, I explained that the use of the word "head" in the sense of superior rank did not entail female inferiority (a point also made in the book). The article, entitled "Equal but Subordinate," paralleled the relationship between God and Christ to the relationship between male and female. The Son is not inferior to the Father, and neither is the female inferior to the male. They share the same nature. The Father and Son are both divine while men and women are both created in the image of God. Nevertheless, they serve different functions. In this sense, the Son is subordinate to the Father and the woman is subordinate to the man. Just as Christ was rewarded for his willing submission to the Father, so women will find their glory in their willing submission to men.

We took a rather novel, though not unique, position on the relationship between 1 Corinthians 11 and 14. Given Paul's restrictions in 1 Timothy 2 and 1 Corinthians 14, Paul only *appeared* to permit gifted veiled women to pray and prophesy in the assembly. Paul did not *explicitly sanction* the use of these gifts in the assembly. His focus was on the physical appearance of the women. When women rose to pray and prophesy in Corinth, they did so by unveiling themselves because it was a contradiction to exercise authority through prophecy *and* wear the symbol of male authority. When Paul said women ought to wear the veil, this meant they should not exercise authority in the assembly. Wearing the veil was an implicit rejection of women praying and prophesying. In effect, Paul employed a *reductio ad absurdum*. The veil implicitly enforced silence. Paul made this explicit in 1 Corinthians 14:33b-36.

At the same time, the veil also reflected a woman's created dignity as she lived under the authority of male leadership. When she removed the veil in Greco-Roman culture, she shamed her community. Consequently, in the assembly, women were veiled and remained silent.

ARGUMENT FROM AUTHORITY AND SUBORDINATION

Woman's Role in the Church concluded that any activity where women are placed in a position of authority over men violates creation law and its principle of male headship. Further, it does not matter *where* this happens, whether the home, public assembly, youth devotionals, or small groups because a circumstance does not render positional leadership void of its authority.

While women certainly influence and form others through their wisdom and virtue, they are, by virtue of creation, excluded from any *positional authority* over a man in the home and church. Positional authority invests one with responsibility for the situation and leadership in the circumstance. The pulpit preacher, for example, holds this authority in the assembly.

Positional authority, then, is key. Wherever that applies and no matter what circumstance in the home and church, men take the lead. Using that principle, we concluded a woman may not lead any man in prayer, including her husband (whether Christian or unbeliever), in a chain prayer, or as a single leader in any assembly. We also concluded a woman may not teach any gathering of men even if paired with a man because she would still have a position of authority over the gathering itself. A woman may only teach when the circumstance does not involve any kind of positional authority like congregational singing, making a comment in a Bible class or in a small group under the authority of a male leader, a conversation between people, or the printed page. We concluded that a woman may baptize a man because there is no positional authority involved. A woman may interpret a sermon for the deaf or translate one because she serves an instrumental rather than a positional function.

Lastly, we considered whether the principle of female subordination applies in business, politics, and education. We concluded that while Scripture specifically applies female subordination to the home and church, we see examples in Scripture where women are active in judging, ruling as queens, and successful business women. Consequently, since we have *specific examples* of women exercising authority over males in the social world, *it is authorized.* But it is not authorized in the home and church because female subordination *is explicitly enjoined* there. Thus, in keeping with a blueprint hermeneutic, the specific examples of female authority in society authorize such activity and the lack of examples in the home and worshipping assembly along with the specific exclusion of women in 1 Timothy 2 enforce male authority in those circumstances. Female subordination, then, applies *only* to the home and church.

This is what I believed in 1977. Advocates for a similar position are still common among churches of Christ, including both men (F. LaGard Smith) and women (Guy).

FROM A TO Z: PRACTICAL QUESTIONS

This position generates a host of questions as particular situations arise in the home and church. I remember long nights in the dorm where my friends and I discussed these questions at length. The questions have also divided believers in many congregations among churches of Christ.

The below A to Z list of questions have troubled congregations that attempt to apply the principle of female subordination *coherently and consistently*.

Read through this list as a spiritual inventory exercise. Rowland has a more extensive list with a similar intent. How would you apply the principle of female subordination and male leadership in each of these situations? What principles come into play? What discernment is at work in making credible, coherent, and consistent distinctions?

a. Are women excluded from teaching a *baptized ten year old* male, including her own child, whether at home or in a Bible class?

b. May a woman read a Bible text in a class from her seat and *teach* the men present through commenting on it?

c. Is leading anyone in prayer—either alone, as part of group, or in a chain prayer—an exercise of authority?

d. Is serving communion, as one who stands before assembly, an exercise of authority?

e. Is the reading of Scripture in the assembly an exercise of authority over the assembly?

f. Is offering a thanksgiving in the assembly an exercise of authority over the assembly?

g. Under what circumstances is a woman permitted to exhort and teach males, if ever?

h. Is leading singing in the assembly an exercise of authority over the assembly?

i. Why does a Bible class have different rules for female conduct than the worshipping assembly in the auditorium?

j. Is the assembly the only place where women are excluded from the exercise of authority? Are they excluded from the exercise of authority in the home? Are they excluded from the exercise of authority in society?

k. Is a woman excluded from leadership in a private small group Bible study in her home, leading the singing in such a group, or reading Scripture for the group?

l. What *kind of teaching* inherently involves the exercise of authority that is prohibited in 1 Timothy 2:12?

m. Is a mother baptizing her ten year old son an exercise of authority? May she baptize her daughter but not her son?

n. May women lead and teach when there are no male Christians present but non-Christian males are present?

o. May women lead the assembly in a role where no male Christian is willing to lead (e.g., leading singing, exhorting the assembly, teaching the Bible)?

p. May a Bible teaching or sermon written by a woman be read to the assembly by a male or *vice versa*?

q. May women interpret for the deaf or translate for a male speaker in the assembly?

r. May women serve as deacons in a leadership role in the congregation?

s. Is every form of standing before the assembly in an auditorium a matter of authority?

t. May women participate in a praise team standing before the assembly (or even sitting down) when they are not *the* worship leader?

u. May women serve a congregation as paid staff? May she serve as an administrative assistant, treasurer, children's minister, youth minister, involvement minister, or benevolence minister?

v. May we sing a song written by a woman where she thereby teaches the congregation through her words?

w. May we sing songs with female leads?

x. May women count the money collected on a Sunday morning or function as a treasurer?

y. May women run the Power Point for the assembly or serve as camera operators in an assembly?

z. What kind of authority does a song or prayer leader have? Does this leader have authority over the elders while they are leading the congregation?

Were you able to identify a principle that provides discernment in answering these questions? Most employ some kind of principle rooted in male authority or "male headship," but "male headship" as an abstract principle is not sufficient. Rather, we have to move from "male headship" to its application through the lens of other principles, assumptions, and cultural perceptions. There is always a middle step between the principle of "male headship" (however that is defined) and the answer to any of these questions. Consequently, consensus is elusive.

Given the received position, sincere people have struggled to answer these questions. Congregations live with them. Though we have often answered the questions pragmatically, we have found it difficult to generate a coherent, consistent, and comprehensive principle that resolves these questions in an amicable consensus. Congregations have divided over some of them. But normally they decided on what was thought "*safe.*"

This raises a significant question for me. Should it really be this difficult? Should our understanding of women serving God be subject to such fine distinctions? Has the received understanding made this more complicated than it really is?

Questions like these planted an initial doubt in my advocacy. They rattled around in my brain for years, and they arose in the context of the congregations I served. Sometimes the questions were resolved rather innocuously but at other times with great difficulty.

But something gnawed at me more than anything else. My godly mother read *Woman's Role in the Church* in 1978. The only comment she has ever offered me over these past forty-two years was her initial response: "You sure use the word subordination a lot in that book."

I sensed the book hurt her in some way. I was oblivious as to why. I did not then have the capacity to sympathize with my mother. Over time her comment gave me pause because we did use the word subordination in more ways than the Bible did. I began to think something was terribly wrong with how I was approaching this, but it took a long time to awaken to that prospect.

PART 2

Growing Awareness

I run the way of your commandments,
for you enlarge my understanding.
Teach me, O LORD, the way of your statues,
and I will observe it to the end.
Give me understanding, that I may keep your law
and observe it with my whole heart.

Psalms 119:32–34

The Psalmist's prayer is challenging. If we're sincere, it's risky. When I pray "teach me" and "give me understanding," there is an expectation that God will "enlarge my understanding." As God widens my understanding, I am better equipped to observe God's instruction with my whole heart.

As I look back on my journey in understanding how women have served God in Scripture, I recognize such an enlargement. As my understanding has grown, I have sought to faithfully "run the way of [God's] commandments."

As my mother's comment gnawed at me, new paths of understanding opened up. My mother gave me a much needed dose of humility. History also challenged me.

HISTORICAL AWARENESS

I paid little attention to the history of women in the American Restoration Movement in the 1970s, except I recognized some nineteenth century leaders recognized deaconesses as part of the church's ancient order. Sandifer provides a long list, including Alexander Campbell, Walter Scott, James R. Howard, Tolbert Fanning, Robert Milligan, Moses Lard, B. W. Johnson, J. M. Barnes, Daniel Sommer, and E. G. Sewell. Though J. W. McGarvey, R. L. Whiteside, and others in the early twentieth century opposed the office, some continued to affirm it, such as C. R. Nichol, G. C. Brewer, J. Ridley Stroop, and J. D. Thomas. This historical lineage—as much as I was aware of it—tempered my conclusion in the appendix of *Woman's Role in the Church*. It was part of the reason for its mild ambiguity. While I believed there were no deaconesses in the New Testament church, my conclusion was "uncertain."

My first recognition, however, that churches of Christ had a *diverse* history regarding the audible participation and visible leadership of women in a worshipping assembly came from reading C. R. Nichol's 1938 *God's Woman* (see Burke). Reading it literally *shocked* me.

Nichol had unquestioned conservative credentials. His five volumes of *Sound Doctrine* (co-authored with Whiteside) were in my father's library. I read each one as a teenager. I practically memorized his Bible pocket encyclopedia. When I picked up *God's Woman* I expected a conventional perspective, but it was quite different.

He thought women as well as men were encouraged to pray audibly in 1 Timothy 2. This practice was confirmed, according to Nichol, by 1 Corinthians 11:4–5 where women audibly prayed and prophesied in the assembly when the saints gathered to eat the Lord's supper. Leading prayer in the public assembly was not restricted to men alone. 1 Corinthians 14:34–35 only silenced women who were asking questions and disrupting the assembly. Nichol thought the prohibition against teaching was a specific form of teaching where a woman "taught over a man" in the sense of exercising dominion over him. 1 Timothy 2:12 only prohibited teaching in an *inappropriate* manner. Rather than being forbidden, public teaching was a woman's privilege, though Nichol did not think it was "within the rights of a woman to preach, as did the twelve and the seventy." Nevertheless, *"there is not a prohibition found in 1 Tim. 2:12 against a woman teaching a man!"*

I could not believe my eyes. Nichol encouraged a *limited participation* of women in leadership while the churches I knew practiced *no participation*. The book unsettled me just as it had rankled others. For example, Wallace, Jr., thought the book gave "impetus to a dormant, pent-up ambition on the part of women in the church to overstep divine restrictions placed around their work." Lewis feared it encouraged women to teach and preach in public assemblies and thought Nichol conformed to "the whims and customs of some of our sisters."

I came to realize that I had stepped into a controversy among churches of Christ that had been roaring for at least fifty years prior to Nichol's book. From roughly 1888 to 1938, churches of Christ debated whether women could not only preach and exhort in the assembly but, at times, whether they could even sing. They debated whether women could teach a Bible class of men at the meetinghouse and, at times, whether women could teach anyone at all, including children, at the meetinghouse. They debated whether women could offer public speeches as educators, business people, and activists and, at times, whether women could even write for religious journals. How women might serve God in society, church, and home was more hotly disputed from 1888 to 1938 than at any other time in the history of churches of Christ until recent decades.

In the nineteenth century, it was not uncommon for women to participate in prayer and exhortation when assembled as a church (though unacceptable to Campbell and his son-in-law Pendelton, the editors of the *Millennial Harbinger*; see Massey). "Not one scripture precept can be found against women taking part in social prayer and exhortation," wrote Faurot in 1866, "that does not equally forbid her singing." He reported that he only knew of "two congregations outside of Bethany, that did not allow women to all acts of religious worship," especially exhortation. "Who shall deny her," Faurot asked, "the privilege of praising her Lord, and speaking of his goodness to her?"

In the 1860 *American Christian Review*, the conservative leader Franklin insisted that since "speaking" in 1 Corinthians 14:34–35 was equivalent to "teaching" in 1 Timothy 2:12, that is what "speaking" prohibited. Consequently, women may pray and exhort in the assembly as they "did in the primitive church." Lard insisted in 1868 that "each member in the church, whether male or female, shall pray publicly whenever called on." Further, Krutsinger of Indiana, in his weekly column in the 1887 *Gospel Advocate*, defended the audible participation of women in the worshipping assembly because women prophesied in Corinth and *all*—both men and women—were invited to prophesy in 1 Corinthians 14.

Charlotte Fanning, Tolbert's wife, led singing at the recently planted church in Franklin, Tennessee in the late 1830s as well as in chapel at Franklin College in the 1840s-1850s (Page, Scobey). She "usually accompanied and assisted" Tolbert when he held protracted meetings, according to Page, "he doing the preaching, she leading the singing." In 1873, Lipscomb wrote "in the worship . . . [e]very member ought to be called upon to read a verse, sing a hymn, pray, give thanks—ask or answer a question of Scripture teaching, [or] report a case of need . . .," though public teaching in the assembly was reserved for men alone.

These practices continued into the early twentieth century. In 1904, Wise, an eighty year old Texas father in the faith, pleaded for the continued practice of women praying: "I would go farther to hear a devoted sister pray than I would to hear a hired preacher or digressive preacher preach." He stressed that the phrase "in like manner" in 1 Timothy 2:8–10 expressed Paul's desire for the women to pray. Wise also published a pamphlet dedicated to his wife and sister. He argued "women have the same right to make their request known unto God in the public assemblage, as man; for she is part of God's family, a part of the household of faith." This is due, in part, to the "social equality" of men and women rooted in God's good creation. In 1916, given 1 Corinthians 11:4–5, McGarvey suggested "those women who have a marked ability, either for exhortation or instruction, are permitted to speak in the church." Further, as Grasham details, Lucy Warlick, the wife of the renowned conservative Texas preacher Joe S. Warlick, defended the privilege of women speaking to men in the assembly for "edification and exhortation and comfort" just as women did in Corinth. She apparently persuaded her husband on this point, and his position shifted between 1920 and 1927.

In 1876, Lipscomb did not oppose the audible participation of women. A querist reported that when "the sisters were invited to take part" in the "Lord's day meetings," some thought the women violated 1 Timothy 2:12 and 1 Corinthians 14:34–35 when they read Scripture. Lipscomb responded: "We do not believe there is anything in these Scriptures that forbids a woman reading or singing or joining in any other worship of the brethren. Singing is just as much a violation of the passages referred to as is reading." He added, "We are constrained to this belief because women did take part in the worship" in 1 Corinthians 11:4–5, though always within the "principles of modesty" and "submissive virtue." Lipscomb thought the "spirit" of Paul's teaching was to exclude women from assuming "authority in teaching" or being put "forward as preachers" in "public assemblies."

THREE CULTURAL MOVEMENTS

In the 1970s, worship assemblies among churches of Christ were uniform, and they were not like the assemblies described above. In my experience, women *never* audibly or visibly led. What was once a matter of diversity had become uniform. In my youth, I did not imagine any churches of Christ worshipping in any other way. *That uniformity, however, did not solidify until at least the late 1930s or early 1940s.*

While many in the nineteenth century practiced *limited participation* by women in the public assembly through prayer, exhortation, leading singing, and reading Scripture, by the middle of the twentieth century women did not participate in *any* audible or visible leadership role in the assembly among churches of Christ. What occasioned the move from *deaconesses and limited participation* in the assembly to *no deaconesses and no participation* in the assembly?

It was, in part, a reaction to three cultural developments. Around the turn of the twentieth century, three women's movements impacted churches of Christ: (1) the New Woman Movement, (2) the Women's Suffrage Movement, and (3) the Temperance Movement, largely led by women (Pulley). Is it possible the exclusion of women from audible and visible participation in the assembly is an expression of a *cultural church* more than a *biblical one*? Ask yourself that question again, please.

First, the New Woman Movement empowered women in society and supported careers outside the home. It was opposed by the True Womanhood Movement which, according to F. W. Smith, recognized women as the embodiment of "piety, purity, submissiveness and domesticity." That idealization excluded women from public life but honored their influence in the home. Women were designed, it was argued, for domesticity and intended to reign as queens in the home. She "may be queen, but she can never be king," Hawley wrote, because "God made man to be the leader, the ruler, and the woman to be his helpmeet." Harding, Sewell, Lipscomb, and Bell believed this principle excluded women from *leadership in society as well as the home and church.* Campbell agreed (Massey). In 1903, Harding grounded his perspective in 1 Timothy 2:12: "the same principles that prevent her from teaching in the church, prevail in the schoolroom or anywhere else; it is a question of women usurping authority over men and becoming leaders of them."

Further, Bell believed the emotional nature of a woman was tailored for home life, but she was "not fitted for public life" since "she lacks, by nature, the will power to combat successfully against the cruel, relentless business world." Consequently, a "woman is not permitted to exercise dominion over man in any calling of life," including practicing medicine, law, and politics. When a woman finds her true calling in the home, she becomes what God intended—"a companion and home-maker for man." Since managing the home is her proper vocation, public life is shameful, and "if it is a shame for a woman to be a public speaker, why is it not a shame for her to be a public writer?"

Second, the Suffrage Movement advocated a woman's right to vote. In 1919, Congress passed the nineteenth amendment. Tennessee ratified the amendment on August 18, 1920 by a single vote. That vote made it constitutional law. It was cast by Harry Burn. He had changed his vote because his mother had sent him a note. "Hurrah, vote for suffrage!" Phoebe Burn wrote, "be a good boy and help Mrs. [Carrie Chapman] Catt put the 'rat' in ratification." Mothers often have a way of moving us to do the right thing.

In contrast to Phoebe and Harry Burn, several ministers of the churches of Christ signed a petition, published in the *Nashville Banner* on August 20, 1920, opposing suffrage because it would "revolutionize our entire mode of life and will in our opinion have an evil effect not only in our homes, our churches and our families, but will affect the whole social fabric of our present generation and of generations yet unborn." Some teachers at David Lipscomb College (J. W. Grant, S. P. Pittman, and H. S. Lipscomb) and several ministers (F. B. Srygley, J. C. McQuiddy, and James E. Scobey) signed it.

In 1874, based on 1 Timothy 2:12, Porter argued women do not have the right to vote "unless, indeed, it is proposed to proceed upon what seems the absurdist of all principles; namely, subordination at home and in the Church, but independence and equality abroad." The principle of submission was universal—home, church, *and* society. Voting women violated their obligation to submit to their husbands, argued Herndon. In fact, "we regard Woman's Suffrage as containing more possibilities of evil than the saloon." Opposition to suffrage grew. The negative impact of suffrage, James A. Allen wrote in 1907, would subvert "the law of nature, and the law of God, that the influence of woman must be exercised through man." Should women be given the right to vote it would work "evil to both man and woman by lifting her out of the sphere in which she was placed by the Creator." In 1920, just days prior to Tennessee's ratification, McQuiddy published an article in both the *Gospel Advocate* and the *Nashville Banner* where he claimed that the "Bible is very much in the way of woman-suffrage leaders." They "repudiate the Bible" because the Bible, according to 1 Timothy 2:12 and Genesis 3:16, places dominion in the hands of men. Even after its ratification, McQuiddy continued his opposition because the suffragists "object to man's dominion over woman."

Third, the Temperance Movement probably had the most significant influence on congregational life. Women often took the lead in the movement, which included public speeches. Even though he recognized Mary Armor's speech "How Georgia Went

Dry" as "brilliant," James A. Allen thought, according to 1 Timothy 2:12, the Bible "condemned her for presenting them upon the platform" in a public forum. Arguably, in the South, women found their first public voice in the Temperance Movement.

These three cultural movements influenced discussions about the voices and visibility of women in the worship assembly (Bailey). While everyone was seeking to understand God's will and reading their Bibles to discover it, cultural dynamics were inescapable. Though they do not necessarily determine anyone's understanding, they do influence it. For example, the exchanges between Silena Moore Holman, of Fayetteville, Tennessee, and Lipscomb in 1888 illustrate the impact these movements had upon churches of Christ.

Holman was an elder's wife who was also the President of the Women's Christian Temperance Union in Tennessee. She also supported women's suffrage and many other aspects of the New Woman Movement (Leonard Allen). In many ways, she epitomized the cultural shift these movements represented.

When in March 1888, Hunsaker asked whether anyone should object to a woman reading Scripture during a Bible class based on 1 Corinthians 14:34 and 1 Timothy 2:12, Lipscomb replied this was an inappropriate application. He thought women could and should teach men in modest ways at home or in Bible classes at the meetinghouse. Though Lipscomb recognized "there are difficulties in drawing" the line "between the permissible and prohibited," he thought it prudent to distinguish between what is *public* (before the congregation) and what is *private* (Bible classes, teaching at home, and other modest spaces). "If the language [of 1 Timothy 2 and 1 Corinthians 14] is pressed *literally* on all occasions when brethren meet for worship," Lipscomb observed, "a woman cannot sing or open her mouth or do anything else where brethren and sisters meet" (emphasis mine).

Holman responded to Hunsaker with an article entitled "A Peculiar People" in which she claimed churches of Christ were a bit "peculiar." It was peculiar that anyone would object to a woman "taking part in the reading of the Scriptures, teach and ask questions in the Sunday-school!" Apparently, she mused, "brothers and sisters know that passage from Paul, 'Let your women keep silence in the churches,' better than any other passage in the whole Bible." She objected that 1 Corinthians 14:34–35, "detached from *the balance of the Bible*," would mean "that a woman should neither sing nor pray nor preach, nor open her mouth on any subject while at church, or to teach in Sunday-school or ask questions in the Bible class" (emphasis mine). Though "in the morn of the resurrection a woman was counted worthy to bear to the disciples the glad tidings of a risen Lord," Holman continued, "in the nineteenth century she is counted by some brother unworthy to tell the same tidings to the little children in the Sunday-school."

While Lipscomb was uncertain about how *literally* to apply these commands, Holman thought they were more situational because of the *balance of the Bible*.

In response to several critics, she continued her advocacy with "Let Your Women Keep Silence." She took aim at the distinction between *public and private*. "Suppose a dozen men and women were in my parlor and I talked to them of the gospel and exhorted them to obey it? Exactly how many would have to be added to the number to make my talk and exhortation public instead of a private one?" This was a pertinent question since most congregations in the New Testament conducted their worship assemblies in homes. For Holman, the example of Philip's daughters and the women in Corinth was sufficient reason to invite women to participate in the assembly because prophecy edified assemblies. Whatever the meaning of 1 Corinthians 14:34–35 (and Holman confessed she did not know "exactly" what Paul meant any more than Lipscomb wondered how literally to press the question), it does not silence women in every respect. Otherwise, would it not be "a violation of this injunction for women to sing in the Church?"

The discussion within the *Gospel Advocate* between Holman and her critics went on for years until her death in 1915. Lipscomb published her articles, including her perspectives on the New Woman Movement. He did not shrink back from giving her a voice in the *Gospel Advocate*, even though he opposed many of her perspectives.

The effect of these cultural movements and discussions in the *Gospel Advocate* silenced women in the assemblies of the churches of Christ. F. W. Smith, who promoted the True Womanhood Movement, illustrates this. As churches of Christ were ebbing toward a uniform practice, he offered this summary in 1929:

> I conclude, therefore, not dogmatically, but to be on the safe side, that since the word of God does not *clearly* and *explicitly* inform us that it would be Scriptural for a woman to lead the prayer in the assembly of the saints, it would be best to conform to the custom in this respect of the 'loyal' churches.

Safe and *loyal*, but *not dogmatic*. *Safe* because there is no specific and explicit blueprint authorization. *Loyal* because northern churches are headed into apostasy due to their adoption of instrumental music in the assembly. But he could not be *dogmatic* about this particular question. Nevertheless, half the church was silenced in the assembly by the end of the 1930s because the blueprint hermeneutic could not find a specific authorization in Acts and the Epistles.

This perspective became entrenched across the vast majority of churches of Christ and shaped them for the next one hundred years. Two public examples in 2020 illustrate this.

The mayor of Wylie, Texas, also the respected minister of a local congregation, claimed 1 Timothy 2:11–12 and 1 Corinthians

14:34–35 meant a woman should not lead prayer to open city council meetings. "I believe a lady can be president of the United States, I believe a lady can be CEO of a company, the superintendent of a school district," Hogue said, but "when it comes to [picking] somebody to lead the invocation at a city council meeting, because of those two sets of verses, I'm going to choose a male."

Savannah Nelson, a devout teenage disciple of Jesus in Alabama, wrote in the *Christian Chronicle* that she led her female classmates in prayer but declined to lead prayer for her swim team because males were present. She understood "everywhere" in 1 Timothy 2:8 to mean that wherever "there's a guy present, he should be the one in spiritual authority." Though she recognized how "ultra-conservative" this view was, she would "rather be safe than walk the line."

PUBLIC VS. PRIVATE

The contrast between my own experience of assemblies in churches of Christ and this history is profound. For example, in my experience, women were never permitted to teach a Bible class of men or lead a small group of men and women. Lipscomb and Harding, however, encouraged women to teach classes that included men at the church building and in their homes. They did not think it improper for a woman to lead prayer in those circumstances. I wondered how we moved from a past *full participation* in Bible classes to a present *limited participation* (e.g., women can neither teach nor lead the class in prayer though they can read Scripture and make comments). It began to dawn on me that our present practices were not even the *normal* practices in the late nineteenth century. What we practiced as the biblical norm was actually a shift away from some of the giants in our heritage (Lipscomb, Harding, Nichol).

Lipscomb, among others, identified a principle for discerning when it was appropriate for a woman to pray, teach, or speak and when it was inappropriate. Given the exclusion of women from any role in the public life of society, this was also the principle for life in the church. As Bell wrote, women "must pray and teach, but not publicly."

This principle meant that wherever Scripture described a teaching function on the part of women, it was regarded as private rather than public because 1 Corinthians 14:34–35 excluded a public venue. Thus, Priscilla taught Apollos along with Aquilla *privately*. Phillip's daughters prophesied *privately*. Corinthian women prayed and prophesied in some place other than the public assembly (or they were exceptions because they were inspired). "Women announced the resurrection to the eleven" and the Samaritan woman "proclaimed" Jesus "as the Christ to the people of her city," but not in a public assembly. "The fact that," Harding continued, "women in the apostolic age prophesied (spoke by inspiration) makes it clear to my mind that women who know God's Word now should teach it," but this "by no means necessarily implies that she taught in the public meetings of the church."

The discerning principle is not whether a woman may teach or not teach, pray or not pray. Rather, it is the *sphere* in which she teaches or prays. Context determines the nature of the leadership involved. "[T]heir spheres are different," Carr wrote. Her sphere is the home rather than the "great assembly." Since God created man as "the leader, the ruler," Harding wrote, when a woman "assumes the leadership" through prayer or teaching in the public sphere as she "directs and controls" the "thoughts" of others, she then "takes a place for which she was not made." That sphere belongs to men. Women were given "the humbler, better place and more difficult work" in the home, according to Hawley. "Her place," Poe wrote, "is at home to guide the house [and] rear the children." This principle is rooted in creation and illustrated in Genesis 3. Eve, according to Harding in 1902, "wrecked things when she took the leadership in Eden."

I Tim. 2:8-15   Eve sinned 1st

The home, however, is a place where women may teach. She may teach her own husband—"even though he be a very great man"—and gatherings of men as well as children and other women, according to Harding. When, for example, Priscilla studied Scripture with Apollos, "no leadership was assumed," but rather "there was a social home-circle talk about the things of the kingdom of God." Succinctly, according to Bell, a woman "can teach anybody anywhere except in cases where publicity is connected with it."

But may women "teach" a Bible class composed of both men and women on the first day of the week at the church building? Bell, Lipscomb, and Harding believed that women may read Scripture, answer questions, ask questions, and even *teach* men in a Bible class on Sunday at the church building when to do *any of these* in the public assembly at the church building would be sinful. In 1910, Lipscomb wrote: "At the Sunday school the woman does not usurp the place of a man in teaching all present. Only a few who wish to be taught" attend.

Another reason this distinction was important was the rise of the non-Sunday school movement in the first two decades of the twentieth century. Typically, these congregations thought Sunday schools or separate Bible classes were unscriptural because there is no *specific authorization* in Acts and the Epistles for dividing the assembly into classes. Some argued that 1 Timothy 2:12 prohibited women teachers, *period* (Wyatt, Highland Preacher). When women taught others (whether women, children, or men) in a Sunday school, they disobeyed the Lord. For example, the Nashville Bull Run church of Christ advertised their congregation in this way (*Tennessean*, October 6, 1945): "We have no Sunday school or women teachers." This was debated throughout the 1920s and into the 1950s (Warlick, Deaver).

Lipscomb responded to Wyatt with a simple principle. Bible classes are *private*, but the worshipping assembly is *public*. "Public preaching and teaching is what is condemned," Lipscomb noted. "[T]here is nothing in Paul's language that prohibits a woman in a private manner teaching children or others." Lipscomb believed women may teach men in Bible classes because they were private, modest events. In Bible classes, women may read Scripture and teach, according to Lipscomb in 1886, but "when assembled for worship on the first day of the week," women may *not* "read a portion of Scripture and offer comments (or thoughts) thereon." The rationale, according to Harding, was that 1 Timothy 2:8–15 specifically designated male prayer leaders and prohibited the exercise of authority over men in the *public assembly* or in any other *public sphere*, whether church or society.

This distinction between public assembly and private Bible classes was problematic to me because the churches where I served never permitted women to teach a Bible class of men at the church building or in a small group at home. Hawk provides many examples that illustrate how this principle was used throughout the twentieth century among churches of Christ to encourage women to teach men privately but forbade them to teach men publicly. By the mid-twentieth century, the Bible class became a public event rather than a private one nor did women lead small groups of men in their homes any longer. For Lipscomb, private spaces empowered women to lead as long as they maintained a modest demeanor while the principle I learned and articulated in *Woman's Role in the Church* was that women may only act in ways that submit to men. In other words, whether public or private, women may not lead or teach men when circumstances entailed an *exercise of authority* over them.

A WOMAN'S PRIVILEGE

Many northern non-instrumental churches of Christ, represented by the *American Christian Review*, *Christian Leader*, and *Octographic Review*, advocated *limited participation* in the worship assembly in contrast to the *no participation* stance of the *Gospel Advocate*. These northern papers encouraged female leadership in the worship assembly through reading Scripture, prayer, leading singing, and exhortation. In 1897, for example, Atkins offered "a Scriptural call for women to resume Christian activity in the church, praying, speaking, exhorting, singing, teaching, as in the apostolic age in Corinth."

Though friendly, the 1904 union of the *Christian Leader* and Harding's *The Way* highlighted several differences. Harding found himself in hot water with some readers when he staked out his position on women as co-editor of the new *Christian Leader & the Way*. Brown cautioned that "before we force upon the churches our narrow, ignorant interpretations of the Bible, we ought to go back and study the question again." Harmon tersely rebuked some writers: "Don't forbid these women, as you have been doing." W. Foster wrote that "it is not counted immodest here, in these times, for a woman to speak or pray, even in the churches" and since "we find where they prophesied" in the New Testament, "why not now?"

The leading conservative paper in the North, the *American Christian Review*, shared this perspective. For example, in 1867, Franklin thought it was an "extreme" position to forbid "women to open their lips in any worshipping assembly." He encouraged their singing, exhorting, and praying in the assembly.

Daniel Sommer, a conservative Indiana leader among churches of Christ at the turn of the twentieth century, affirmed certain privileges for women in his article entitled "Woman's Religious Duties and Privileges in Public." "Extremes beget extremes," Sommer began. The extreme of female preachers among a few Christian Churches had begat the extreme of completely silencing women in the assembly among some churches of Christ. The latter had become, he claimed, a hobby for some. He suggested another path which had been the practice of churches in his experience. "Any reasoning which will prevent women from praying in public," he concluded, "will prevent her from communing and singing." It was a woman's privilege to "*publicly read* in audible tones a portion of Scripture" in the assembly as long as she did not comment, apply, or enforce "its meaning" since she would thereby become a "*public teacher*;" which I Timothy 2:12 prohibited. However, "it is a woman's privilege to teach a class in a meeting house." Further, since exhortation (offering a word of encouragement or testimony) and teaching are different, he argued, "if a sister in good standing wishes to arise in a congregation and offer an exhortation it is her privilege to do so." A woman's privilege, then, includes audible prayer, public reading of Scripture, and public exhortation in the assembly, as well as teaching both men and women in a Bible class at the church building.

Among the congregations associated with Sommer, the phrase "rights, privileges and duties" was a mantra that impressed others with the sanctity of women's voices in the assembly. These "privileges," according to Glover, were "singing, praying, exhorting and teaching one another, giving thanks, breaking bread, and laying by in store as the Lord has prospered" on the first day of the week, and "no local legislation" should "interfere with these duties in the Lord." Frazee stressed that the "rights, privileges, and duties pertaining to the worship" belong to all and everyone has the "same rights and privileges to participate as far as their ability will permit." While this does not include teaching that takes the "oversight of the Church," it does include "speaking unto men to edification, and exhortation, and comfort" like the female prophets in Corinth. Most thought I Corinthians 14:34–35 only applied to disorderly and disruptive women. This segment of churches of Christ did not understand I Corinthians 14:34–35 as a timeless prescription that totally silenced all speech by women in the worshipping assembly.

While many of us have thought the instructions in the Bible regarding women were clear, the above history illustrates how complicated and uncertain our historic understanding and application of these texts has been. The blueprint is not as clear as we have sometimes assumed.

CULTURAL AWARENESS

The convergence of Suffrage, Temperance, and New Woman movements alarmed churches of Christ in the South. Lipscomb, for example, thought they subverted the natural order of creation where men were leaders and women were submissive helpmeets. 1 Timothy 2:8–15 was foundational for the exclusion of female leadership in the public worship assembly *and* public roles in society.

The True Womanhood Movement, which honored domesticity and opposed public careers for women in society, shaped the perspective of the *Gospel Advocate* as intensely as any Feminist cultural agenda shaped discussions in the late twentieth century. This movement deeply influenced how southern churches of Christ read 1 Timothy 2:8–15. Due to this text, they excluded women from public roles in both church and society.

Of course, all interpreters—both past and present—are *profoundly* impacted by their cultural context. History reminds us that *our spiritual ancestors were as culturally situated as we are.* Everyone reads the Bible in their own cultural location through their own cultural lenses. This ought to humble us and encourage us to listen to diverse voices and viewpoints in the past as well as the present.

The *Gospel Advocate* ultimately won the day among churches of Christ. It did, however, moderate its views on women in society so that one heard little opposition to female doctors, lawyers, and CEOs by the end of the twentieth century. In essence, the *Gospel Advocate*, among other papers and institutions, silenced the voices of women and excluded female leadership from the public assemblies of churches of Christ by the 1940s while accepting a wider role for women in society. The openness that characterized the northern congregations died the death of marginalization as southern churches of Christ overwhelmed them in number, influence, and institutional power (e.g., colleges and papers). Sommer's position, though largely forgotten, was unwittingly renewed in some quarters in the late twentieth century as some churches of Christ began to invite women to participate in *limited* ways.

When Nichol published his book in 1938, he recognized what had been lost. Walking back through that history raised a caution flag for me. While no *bona fide* Bible major graduate of Freed-Hardeman University would ever exalt a human teacher above divine Scripture or find normative authority in any human tradition, our ancestors in the faith instruct us, provide a horizon of self-understanding, and humble us. They studied the Bible, too. When we listen to them, we recognize *there was no uniform exclusion of women from leadership in the public assembly in the history of churches of Christ until at least the late 1930s.*

Listening to our ancestors, I began to realize in the late 1980s that women had not always been silent in the assemblies of churches of Christ as they were in my own experience. This gave me pause. Had we misread something? Had we not listened well? Did we succumb to the cultural impact of the True Womanhood Movement when we opposed suffrage, female leadership in the Temperance Movement, and public careers for women? *Did culture shape us more than Scripture?* In the 1980s, I began to listen to those questions as this history became clearer to me. It was troubling because *it shattered my illusion of uniformity*; the past was not as homogeneous as my own experience assumed.

HERMENEUTICAL AWARENESS

Reading the views of my spiritual ancestors revealed how they employed different interpretative strategies in applying Paul's instructions to their own settings. That history illuminated how cultural assumptions shape the reading of the biblical text. This, among other things noted in *Searching for the Pattern*, led to my own emergent hermeneutical sensitivity.

Everyone is culturally situated, including Lipscomb, Holman, Sommer, myself, and every reader of the Bible. Everyone reads the Bible in their own cultural context; it is inescapable. Moreover, *the biblical text is also culturally situated.*

Perhaps that sounds strange, but it is easily recognized. The Bible was written in multiple human languages (Hebrew, Aramaic, Greek) in different cultures (Ancient Near East, Greco-Roman) by different people in different geographical regions over hundreds of years. The Bible comes to us through the particularity of human language in settings shaped by ancient customs and practices. From arranged marriages to washing feet, from wearing tassels to greeting with a holy kiss, and from anointing with oil to burial practices, the Bible reflects the varied cultural circumstances in which it was written.

This is not a negative. In fact, it speaks volumes about God's intent to communicate with us. God spoke in the language of the Hebrews and addressed Greco-Romans in the context of their cultural habits so that they might understand God's communication. God did not speak in the language of angels but in human ones. God did not address humanity with a text dropped from the sky but one *generated through the processes of human culture under the guidance of the Holy Spirit.* The God who became human is also the God who communicated with humanity *through* human culture.

Consequently, if we are to read the biblical text well, *we must read it as God has given it to us.* Given its cultural situatedness, it makes sense that we would pay attention to the cultural context in which it was written in order to better understand it. The original text is addressed to its original audience in their setting and in their language. *The Bible was not written to us, though it was written for us.* It was written as a guide *for* all God's people throughout history, but it was written *to* its original readers in their cultural situation.

This means that *every* text in Scripture is *occasional* in nature. It was written to an ancient people in a particular setting to accomplish a specific thing or to address a specific problem. In other words, *nothing in the Bible is written as a timeless, contextless proposition.* Every statement in Scripture has an ancient context that shapes its form and gives it meaning. If we reproduce the practices of Scripture solely because they are in Scripture without any discernment or interpretation, then we will reproduce its ancient culture. Such reproduction would mean we greet each other with kisses, women wear veils, and we wash each other's feet.

This does not mean Scripture is wholly relative and provides no sure guidance or norm for contemporary faith and practice. As we recognize the cultural situatedness and occasional nature of the biblical text, God invites us to discern the theology at work in the text's address to its original setting. When we discern that theology, we apply it rather than reproduce the text. *Searching for the Pattern* discusses this hermeneutical process.

Scripture's situatedness does not mean that we have no sure footing or security in the story of God. That story, which pervades the whole of Scripture, is repeated, summarized, and articulated in various ways and in different circumstances across various cultures and times. That story not only lies on the surface of the biblical text, it is the source from which all the biblical books arose as they were written within the stream of God's redemptive history.

We hear the story of God in Scripture. The creator God liberated a people from slavery and invited them to participate in God's mission. This people gave birth to the Messiah who was sent from God to liberate humanity from its slavery to sin and death by the Spirit. The Messiah renews the people of God for mission and invites them to disciple all nations in the hope of new creation. That story pervades the Bible; it is the drama of Scripture.

Every proposition in Scripture is situated in and arises out of that story. Further, if every proposition in Scripture has a culturally situated context, then *there are no contextless, timeless statements in Scripture.* Every proposition in Scripture must be read through the lens of the culture in which it originated, just as its original language must be translated. Every sentence in Scripture is connected to its context *and* the situation to which it responds. In this sense, every text in Scripture is occasional and relative to the circumstance it addresses. *At the same time, however, every text in Scripture assumes a theological story that gave rise to it.* Enculturated, occasional biblical texts give voice to a theological story that gives identity to the people of God and calls them to participate in God's mission.

As I began to think about this, I instinctively pushed back. Is not "love your neighbor" a *timeless* command? It is, to be sure, *true across the whole story of God* as it calls us to love our neighbors whenever and wherever we encounter neighbors. But it is not timeless in the sense that it is contextless or lacks a particular situatedness. "Love" needs definition, and it is defined by the story of God's love in the Exodus and ultimately in Jesus the Messiah. "Neighbor" needs definition. *"Love your neighbor" needs context, definition, interpretation, and application.* The Parable of the Good Samaritan illustrates this when the lawyer asked, "who is my neighbor?" (Luke 10:29).

Herein lies the hermeneutical crux. *If there are no specified, timeless prescriptions in the biblical text, how do we discern a norm grounded in the story that lies behind a situated application?*

AN ILLUSTRATION

In 1 Timothy 2:9–10, Paul wrote:

> I also want women to dress modestly, with decency and propriety, not with braided hair or gold or pearls or expensive clothes, but with good deeds, appropriate for women who profess to worship God.

Some, including a few Pentecostal traditions, read Paul's command as a *timeless* prescription. They forbid women to braid their hair, wear gold or pearls, or dress in expensive clothes. If we were to plaster this sentence on a billboard, put it on a large bumper sticker, or state it as the major premise in a syllogism, it would give the *clear impression* that Paul *absolutely* prohibits these accessories.

Paul's statement, however, has a context. It addresses women living in Ephesus during the first century. Braided hair, pearls, gold, and expensive clothes have a *cultural* meaning in that setting. Moreover, the text addresses women living in a community disturbed by false teachers, agitated about marriage and widowhood, and troubled by the spread of myths. How are braided hair, gold, pearls, and expensive clothes understood in that *particular context*? Further, is this a dress code for the public assembly or day to day life in the Ephesian culture?

Whatever we might say, Paul's command is not contextless; *it is culturally situated.* Therefore, it is not timeless. But it is not thereby rendered useless or irrelevant. On the contrary, Paul's command arises out of his application of the gospel to the context in which the Ephesians lived (Thompson). The gospel story, heard in a particular cultural setting, yields a particular application.

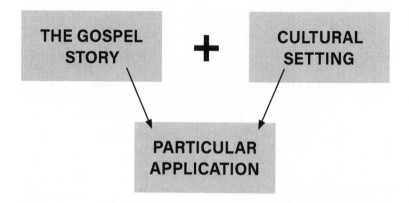

Whatever the specific context of Paul's instruction, when that context was combined with the gospel, it yielded a prohibition against braided hair, pearls, gold, and expensive clothes. In a different context, that same gospel might yield a totally different application (e.g., braided hair in sub-Saharan Africa). *The gospel story may yield different applications in different contexts.*

Given that Paul's directive arises from his application of the gospel story in a particular context, the theological point is discerned by understanding the biblical text in its context. Once we discern the theological point, then we apply it to our own contemporary situation, which involves understanding our own context.

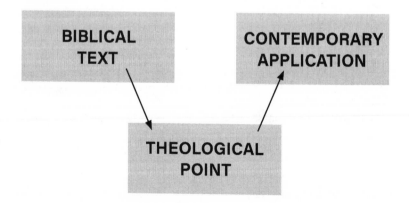

The contemporary application, then, depends on discerning the theological point from reading the story-formed biblical text in its literary, occasional, and cultural context.

To some degree, the specific context of 1 Timothy 2:9–10 is elusive. Some think this is about seduction and/or prostitution; others think it relates to signs of wealth, status, and power; and still others believe it describes the dress of Artemis devotees. Even though we are uncertain about its precise cultural meaning, their dress, conduct, and ungodliness is part of a general disturbance in Ephesus. Consequently, women are encouraged to pursue good works instead of pursuing the agenda these accessories promote.

What is the theological point? The theological point is a call to *godliness and good works* in contrast to using clothing and accessories in a way *that subverts godliness*. Without devoting much attention to exploring the theological point applied, the principles of humility and service as the proper evidence of one's godliness are rooted in the mystery of godliness (1 Timothy 3:16). This is the goal of all believers: to train ourselves in godliness (1 Timothy 4:7–8), pursue it (1 Timothy 6:11), and practice it (1 Timothy 5:4). Every teaching and practice must promote godliness (1 Timothy 5:3–6). "Good works" is a general reference to ministry, including generosity and shared resources (1 Timothy 6:18). Whether the prohibition of accessories applies to seduction, wealth and power, Artemis devotees, or something else, *the call to ministry through godliness is a pervasive theme in Scripture itself.* More specifically, the mystery of godliness (1 Timothy 3:16) is the ground of our own piety, and the good works of Jesus are the ministry into which we are called.

What, then, is a contemporary application? Briefly, it calls us to dress modestly and live humbly in ways that embody the gospel no matter the cultural setting. Moderation is a mark of godliness as believers live in their distinct cultures.

The text is not a timeless prohibition against wearing gold or else we should stop wearing wedding bands. Nor does it provide a timeless prohibition against braided hair. Whatever braided hair meant in Ephesus, in many contemporary cultures it is consistent with humility and modesty. In other words, how Paul applied this theological principle in Ephesus yielded a different directive than when we apply the same principle to our culture. *While the principle remains the same, the application may vary in different cultural contexts.*

This is why context matters. The literary context matters—how does the whole letter of 1 Timothy help us understand 1 Timothy 2:9–10? The situational context matters—what issues or questions occasioned the letter? The cultural context matters—what customs shaped how Paul applied the gospel story?

Consequently, we cannot merely select a proposition in Scripture, lift the words from its setting, and place them in a syllogism in order to discern what God desires. When we lift a proposition from its context and place it in a syllogism, the syllogism gives it a *new context.* That new context may yield a meaning inconsistent with the biblical text in its original context. Instead of discerning the theological point of the gospel story, the syllogism draws a conclusion from abstracted, contextless, and seemingly timeless propositions.

1 Timothy 2:9-10	1 Timothy 2:12
Paul prohibits wearing gold.	Paul prohibits women to teach men.
Whatever Paul teaches is timeless.	Whatever Paul teaches is timeless
Therefore, wearing gold is forbidden.	Therefore, women are forbidden to teach men.

That is why I was so adamant about my syllogistic constructs in the 1970s. To me, *my conclusions were timeless truths.* But they were actually abstractions based on assigning a new context to biblical statements removed from their own context.

BLUEPRINT OR THEOLOGICAL HERMENEUTICS?

As we approach the biblical text, it is important to ask a hermeneutical question. Recalling the language of *Searching for the Pattern,* do we approach Scripture seeking a specific and exclusive *blueprint* for how to conduct a worshipping assembly or do we seek the *theological* point that is at work in these texts? The former identifies a command and directly enjoins it upon a contemporary assembly as part of the timeless blueprint for the public assembly discovered in Acts and the Epistles. The latter recognizes that the hermeneutical process has a middle step that discerns the story-formed theological point that gave rise to the text.

For example, the expectation to greet one another with a kiss (Romans 16:16; 1 Corinthians 16:20; 2 Corinthians 13:12; 1 Thessalonians 5:26; 1 Peter 5:14) may seem rather innocuous, but it is an *explicit command* (five times). Yet, most recognize the command does not enjoin a direct practice but expresses a theological principle. Typically, we have applied the principle by recognizing different cultural contexts. Rather than kissing, in the United States we shake hands. A command, then, does not necessarily entail a direct, one-to-one correspondence. *We do not reproduce the command but apply the principle.*

However, 1 Corinthians 14:34–35 and 1 Timothy 2:12 are often employed as *direct and obvious blueprint prescriptions* for worshipping assemblies. They are, in the lingo of churches of Christ at the turn of the twentieth century, *positive* instructions. This language identifies a particular practice in the blueprint (Fuqua). These texts are specific injunctions for a faithful assembly. According to

Sewell in 1897, "nothing in the Bible is more positively forbidden" than public speaking by women (in both society and church). Public speech by women, whether teaching, exhorting, praying, or reading, violates the positive prohibition.

This seemed clear to Lipscomb in 1888. He concluded that 1 Corinthians 14:34–35, "given as it is," was "an absolute and universal rule. We can find nothing in the context or occasion that would modify it by temporary or local surroundings." If there are no mitigating circumstances, we receive the instruction as universal and timeless. This is the blueprint hermeneutic at work. Every command is *absolutely* normative *unless* there is something *explicitly* circumstantial about it.

How do we know what is circumstantial about "Greet one another with a holy kiss"? Perhaps our own cultural location reveals how culturally limited a "holy kiss" is. Jesus left us an example to wash feet. Perhaps our own cultural practice reveals how culturally limited washing feet is. One of the factors at play in our discernment about whether something belongs in the blueprint or not is *our own sense of cultural awareness* and the distance between our culture and the ancient one. If something seems incongruent with our own cultural practices (for example, we no longer wash feet as a communal activity), we tend to more easily discern the situated character of the command. We still embrace the principle even though we do not replicate the practice.

Lipscomb was aware of this. Consequently, he wrote, "The reason given [for silence] is one of universal application," but it must not "conflict with the clear examples and teachings of the apostles in other places." Consequently, the nature of the theological principle at work and "the balance of the Bible" (as Holman put it) must come into view as well. As a result, though 1 Corinthians 14:34–35 explicitly silences women in the public assembly, 1 Timothy 2:12 imposes no other limit, according to Lipscomb, except "women assuming the position of public teacher or preacher, of assuming authority in the management of church affairs, of conducting the worship of the church." Consequently, Lipscomb believed women could lead men in small groups and teach Bible classes at the meetinghouse on Sunday. In other words, Lipscomb has a *limited application* of 1 Corinthians 14:34–35; *it only applied to public assemblies of the church.* At the same time, he also cautioned in 1888 that one cannot press this language "literally on all occasions when brethren meet for worship." Moreover, a woman "may engage in those acts of service in the church assembly that she can do in a modest way, neither taking the lead, assuming authority or attracting public attention to itself." This, Lipscomb wrote in 1876, is the "spirit of the passage."

While women may not speak or lead ("conduct") the assembly, according to Lipscomb in 1876, there is room for public acts of service on the part of women in the assembly as long as she acts in "modest" ways and does not attract "public attention" to herself. *The cultural investment here is high.* What does "modest" mean? In what sense is "attracting public attention" immodest? What does that look like? This seems burdened with its own cultural assumptions, practices, and expectations rather than something drawn explicitly or theologically from the biblical text.

The True Womanhood Movement lies in the background here. For example, when Lipscomb responded to Holman, he located her blindness to the clarity of the prescribed silence in 1 Corinthians 14:34–35 within her *emotional* nature: "Our sister struck it when she spoke of her 'emotional nature, her intensely loving heart,'" he wrote. "These blind her to facts, shut out reason and lead her headlong where her emotions prompt her and so unfit her for leadership." His rationale is more attuned to True Womanhood than *explicit* biblical theology. But if her emotional nature is so delimiting, why does Lipscomb encourage women to teach men privately and in Bible classes at the meetinghouse?

Nevertheless, the universal application of the command in 1 Corinthians 14:34–35 needs justification. Lipscomb finds it in (1) the lack of mitigating circumstances that might localize the text, (2) the principle in which the injunction is grounded, and (3) its coherence with the rest of the Bible. In other words, it is not simply that 1 Corinthians 14:34–35 says X, therefore we do X. Rather, 1 Corinthians 14:34–35 says X, and we *discern* in what way X is applicable to us through the *occasion* of the injunction, the *principle* that lies behind it, and its *coherence* with the rest of Scripture. Re-read that last sentence; it is an important one.

Stated that way, Lipscomb moves toward something more *like* a theological hermeneutic than a blueprint one, except that Lipscomb still seeks *specific authorization* for how the church conducts its public assembly on Sunday.

Given the discussions among churches of Christ from 1888 to 1938, it seems 1 Corinthians 14:34–35 and 1 Timothy 2:12 are not as obvious and clear as we have sometimes thought. Texts must be interpreted and applied. Lipscomb, in March 1888, before he began his discussion with Holman, confessed "it is a difficult question to determine *exactly* the limit of the law forbidding women to teach or to usurp authority publicly" (emphasis mine). The questions at the end of Part 1 illustrate how "difficult" that is.

Both Holman and Lipscomb wondered about the exact meaning and application of 1 Corinthians 14:34–35. They weren't the first. They won't be the last.

PART 3

My Move to Limited Participation

Your hands have made and fashioned me,
give me understanding
that I may learn your commandments.

Psalms 119:73

As far as my memory serves me, the first time I heard a woman audibly speak in a public assembly was in 1983 at an African American congregation in Alabama. At some point in the service, the minister asked if anyone wanted to confess sin, bear witness, or ask for prayers. Several women stood up from where they sat and responded with their testimonies, confessions, and requests. I was twenty-five years old when I first heard a woman's voice in the assembly other than singing or their baptismal confession. I was shocked. I did not know what to make of it. I said nothing, but it bothered me. (For African American practices, see Birt and Hairston.)

In 1989, *Image* requested I submit an article on 1 Corinthians 14:34–35. I entitled it: "Worship in 1 Corinthians 14:26–40: The Injunction of Silence." I repeated the argument in *Woman's Role in the Church.* 1 Corinthians 14:34–35 prohibited authoritative speech, including prophesying and tongue-speaking. What is forbidden, then, is not any kind of speech but the exercise of spiritual gifts and leadership through tongues, teaching, or prophecy. Though Paul refers to female prophets in 1 Corinthians 11:4–5, I argued he does not approve them but waits to silence them when he corrects them in 14:34–35. This silence is grounded in the principle of submission evident in Genesis 2 ("the law"), which means women may not exercise authority over men in the assembly.

After the article's publication, I was invited to present the material at a lectureship and prepare a manuscript for its book. Honestly, I was uneasy with my *Image* article. I wrote what I believed, but I did not admit my doubts. I resolved to reexamine my thinking, update my research, and see where the evidence led me.

That process changed my mind. The lectureship manuscript affirmed the audible participation of women in prophetic speech and prayer in the public assembly. My view shifted from the *total exclusion* of the voices of women and leadership to a *limited inclusion*. While I excluded women from a preaching role (due to my understanding of 1 Timothy 2:12 at the time), I came to believe, like Franklin, Sommer, and Nichol, that women have the privilege of audible participation in the reading of Scripture, prayer, and exhortation in the public assembly. *The reason for my shift in thinking was **textual** in character rather than ideological, theological, or experiential.* In other words, I changed my mind because I believed it was dictated by the *biblical text*.

Understandably, the lectureship rescinded my invitation and did not include my manuscript. I have no resentments about that. It was best for me as well.

That December I presented the paper at a regional meeting of the Institute for Biblical Research in Jackson, Mississippi. Though I never published it, it is accessible on my blog in its original 1990 form.

What changed my mind?

SILENCED SPEECH

1 Corinthians 14:34–35 is important because it enjoins, in some sense, silence in the assembly and grounds that silence in the principle of submission, which the law requires.

Difficulties

The discussion of 1 Corinthians 14:34–35 throughout the history of churches of Christ has raised many questions about its meaning and application. Before engaging the details, it is helpful to name some of its difficulties. How we resolve them shapes how we understand and apply the text.

1. Since there are no punctuation marks in ancient Koine Greek, it is uncertain whether 14:33b ("as in all the assemblies of the saints") goes with what proceeds (14:33a) or with what follows (14:34)? What difference does it make?
2. What is the occasion of this instruction? Does it apply to every assembly of the church or *only* assemblies where the "whole church" is gathered? If every assembly, does this apply to believers gathered in a home, Bible class, or small group? If only when the "whole church" is gathered, what constitutes such an assembly? If it is the same assembly as in 1 Corinthians 11:17–34, does it envision only assemblies where the Lord's supper is administered?
3. Who are "the women" in 14:34–35—every woman in the assembly, all the wives, the wives of the prophets, or some other specific group of women?
4. To what does "speaking" refer? Is it any kind of speech including singing, all speech except singing, any kind of authoritative speech (prophesying or judging other

prophets), or any disorderly speech that disrupts the assembly? How does one decide what speech is silenced?

5. To what does "the law" refer? Is this the Torah in general or a more particular text like Genesis 2 or 3, or another text? Does it refer to practices in Jewish or Roman culture? Does it refer to the "law" of order and decency that is appropriate for a worshipping assembly?

6. To whom or what are the women to submit? To their husbands? To all the men in the assembly? To the customs of the whole assembly? To a principle of decency and order? To Roman or Jewish custom?

7. Why does 14:35 specify wives? If only wives, what relationship do the never married, divorced, and widowed in the congregation sustain to Paul's concern?

Difficulty #1 raises the question whether "as in all the churches of the saints" (14:33b) belongs with "God is not a God of disorder but of peace" (14:33a) or with "the women should be silent in the churches" (14:34a). Most older translations and some modern ones connect it with the former (Wycliffe, Tyndale, Geneva Bible, Bishop's Bible, KJV, ERV, NASB, NLT, NIV [2011]) while several modern translations connect it with the latter (ESV, ASV, NRSV, CEB, HCBS). The former makes more sense to me because patristic, contextual, and text-critical evidence suggest it, but no one can be certain.

Nevertheless, whichever is the case, it is immaterial because, whether Paul prohibits authoritative or disorderly speech, both are prohibited in all assemblies *given analogous circumstances.*

Four Approaches

There are four basic approaches to 1 Corinthians 14:34–35. The first two are seldom seen among churches of Christ. The second two are more frequent options.

One suggests 14:34–35 is an addition to the original text (Fee, Payne, Bartlett). At some point, early in manuscript transmission when the text was copied by hand, a scribe moved a comment from the margin into the text itself. While the text appears in all extant manuscripts, some locate verses 34–35 after verse 40. Though this is a *possible* explanation because the evidence cannot *absolutely* rule it out, it is not a mainstream position. Most affirm the text's authenticity (Witherington, Niccum).

The second approach, which has greater probability, claims verses 34–35 are a quotation from Paul's Corinthian opponents who objected to women praying and prophesying in the assembly (Bilezekian, MacGregor, Allison, Peppiatt). They may have believed it was shameful for women to speak in the assembly due to Jewish or Roman sensibilities (Ruden). The law, Paul's opponents may have argued, silenced women because they should submit to their husbands in the assembly, which is proper decorum for Jewish women.

This deserves serious consideration. It gives full weight to women praying and prophesying in 1 Corinthians 11:4–5; it makes sense in the context of the disorder that Paul addresses; Paul does encourage "all" to prophesy in 14:31; the introduction of the women is abrupt and may indicate an opposing response that wants to silence female prophets (who were included in the "all"); a Greek particle in 14:36 that responds to the quotation may be translated "Nonsense;" and Paul does quote his opponents in 1 Corinthians several times (e.g., 6:12 7:1). But, unlike the others, this would be a long quotation and does not bear the same characteristics of other quotations in Corinthians (Payne). Nevertheless, I don't think we can totally exclude this possibility. Any judgments about the applicability of these verses to contemporary assemblies is *dubious* until this option is *definitively* eliminated. I don't think it has been.

The third approach understands the prohibition as absolute (Woods, Fuqua). It enjoins *total silence*. This includes singing (James). Typically, in this view, the assembly in chapter fourteen is undertsood as different from the one where the Lord's supper is celebrated in 11:17–34. However, few take this third approach because chapter fourteen, similar to 11:18, is an assembly of the "whole church" (14:23) such that there is no distinction between the assembly of 11:17–34 and chapter fourteen.

The fourth approach *qualifies the prohibition* in some way but differs over how. On the one hand, some argue Paul prohibits any form of *authoritative* speech. Some think it excludes praying and prophesying (House, Ferguson, Lightfoot). Others think it excludes women from judging the prophets (Grudem, Carson, Hurley). On the other hand, many believe Paul is addressing *disorderly* speech (Oster, Keener). Some believe he is silencing the wives of the prophets who are disrupting the assembly by interrupting prophetic speech (Ellis, Witherington, Hommes, Burke, Osburn). Others believe Paul is silencing the disorderly chatter of women mimicking the practices of some Greco-Roman cults that much of Roman culture found objectionable (Kroeger). This fourth approach is where, historically, most of the discussion among churches of Christ lies. I will focus my attention here.

Who are the Women and What are They Doing?

This prohibited speech is *qualified* in some way. For example, it does not prohibit singing or baptismal confessions. Is there any indication in the text as to *how* it is qualified? *One characterization is explicit.* "If they want to learn something, they should ask their own husbands at home." Some women were asking questions because they wanted to learn. Moreover, they did not simply ask a few questions but peppered the speakers with questions. The present infinitive form of the Greek verb (*lalein*) suggests a continuous speaking. Apparently, they were persistently asking questions. Moreover, the Greek term for "ask" has an intensifier (eperōtatōsan) which indicates it is a rather insistent sort of asking, like Pharisees asking Jesus questions (Matthew 12:10; 16:1; 17:10; 22:23). This is the only time Paul himself uses this word outside of a biblical quotation. "Asking," at the very least, is the speech Paul prohibits.

Further, Paul explicitly identifies the women as wives. They have "their own" husbands. Married women were constantly asking questions in the assembly in ways that interrupted or disrespected whoever was speaking, perhaps even their own husbands. Paul wants these wives to hold their questions until they get home. When wives incessantly interrupt a speaker with questions, it is a disgrace because it disrespects their husbands and/or the order of the assembly.

Should 14:35 ("ask their own husbands") qualify 14:34 ("the women")? 14:35 identifies the women about whom Paul is speaking and what they are doing. In fact, some manuscripts read "your women" (KJV; Tyndale says, "your wives") in 14:34, which represents a way of understanding this text in Christian history. Most manuscripts read "the women." Paul is likely addressing *the wives* who are asking questions. The women of 14:34 are the same ones who have "husbands" in 14:35. Consequently, the address of 14:34 probably means "your wives" (wives of the prophets?), though it may simply refer to "wives" (Guin). These wives are inappropriately asking questions when those questions could wait until they got home.

Further, women are to submit *themselves*. Paul does not say to whom or what they should submit. Some surmise, based on 14:35, that the wives are to show respect for their husbands. A submissive demeanor means that wives should not disrespect their husbands in the assembly, as the law demands. *The text does not say that the law demands silence.* Rather, the law expects *submission*. If this is submission to husbands, it does not necessarily imply some kind of authority or rank (Padgett). It may reflect a *mutual submission* akin to what Paul describes in Ephesians 5:21 or the *mutual authority* husbands and wives share in 1 Corinthians 7:4. Paul expects wives to *respect* their husbands in the assembly (if that is to what "submission" refers).

Nevertheless, when Paul refers to "the law," no one is certain what Hebrew text Paul intends. Is he alluding to a general principle in the Hebrew Bible or something specific? *Nowhere does the Torah explicitly command wives to submit to their husbands.* Interestingly, Holladay suggests it alludes to Miriam who, along with Aaron, disrupted Moses's leadership in Numbers 12.

However, Thiselton believes it is submission to the principle of order (versus disorder) articulated in the creation story of Genesis 1–2. This sort of submission was also expected of the prophets in 1 Corinthians 14:32. They were to exercise control over their gift and yield to others when appropriate. They were to submit themselves *just like* the women. The women, in context, are expected to practice the *same* submission that the prophets did. The women should *submit to the principle of order and decency* in the assembly (14:40). Submission, in this context, is not about marriage but about order in contrast to chaos (Osburn). I think this is the best way to understand submission in this context: the wives and the prophets are both expected to submit to the order of the assembly.

But no one is certain. Whatever we say, submission to husbands does not preclude praying and prophesying because women honored their heads (husbands?) even as they prayed and prophesied in 1 Corinthians 11:4–5. Praying and prophesying in an assembly is not *necessarily* insubordinate or disrespectful because women may do such while honoring their heads.

At this point, my best understanding goes something like this: "The wives [of the prophets?] should silence themselves and stop interrupting their husbands with questions out of respect [submission] for order within the assembly. If they want to learn something, instead of asking while their husbands (or others) are speaking, they should ask at home because when a woman speaks in this way in the assembly, she disgraces herself before the assembly. Wives are not permitted to speak in such a disorderly and disrespectful manner."

Is Authoritative Speech Prohibited?

Typically, authoritative speech refers to an authority one has over the audience through teaching the assembly or judging prophetic speech (14:29).

If Paul means authoritative speech, this raises a few questions. Why does he specifically name wives as the speakers he silences in 14:35? How does "asking" their husbands at home address the situation he is silencing? "Asking" is the only type of speech *explicitly* identified. Paul limits their "asking" rather than their judging, prophesying, or praying.

If silencing authoritative speech is Paul's intent and it excludes praying and prophesying, why does it not exclude singing? Paul parallels praying and singing in 14:15. Singing is a speaking function in light of the activities of 14:26. Just as one might speak in a tongue or speak as a prophet, singers speak as well. Just as one might have a "teaching" to share with the assembly, others have a "hymn." In short, *if a woman's teaching is excluded by 14:34–35*, it seems these passages *would also exclude her from singing*, given that singing is one of the gifts some exercised in that assembly (14:26).

Moreover, "authoritative speech" is ambiguous. Does this include making announcements or giving a report from the mission field? Does it include a confession of sin in the assembly or a testimony from a woman who has suffered abuse? What exactly does authoritative speech include and not include? How does one decide? Is it only preaching? The gray area here is wide. Consequently, it is uncertain what the text specifically forbids.

If we specify the authoritative speech as the act of judging the prophets, 14:29 is quite removed from verse 34. *It is a different topic about a different group in a different paragraph.* Further, to equate "speaking" in 14:34 with judging in 14:29 constricts the meaning of "speak" with a word alien to 14:34–35. If judging is what Paul intended, why did he not simply use the word "judge" here as he did in 14:29 instead of the verb "ask"?

Further, to read "speak" as the exclusion of *authoritative speech* introduces an alien thought to chapter fourteen. From where does the language of *authority* come in this context? Though many assume "submission" always entails authority or rank, it may only refer to mutual deference and respect (Padgett). Moreover, the submission may refer to the principle of order rather than authority in this context (as is the case with the prophets in 14:32). Further, the *authority* Paul names in 1 Corinthians 7:4 is *mutual.* Prophetic speech or praying are nowhere identified as authoritative speech in the sense that the speaker holds some kind of authority over the assembly. *The word authority never characterizes any speech in these contexts.* More particularly, prophesying and praying are specifically identified as a kind of speech in which women participated while honoring their heads (1 Corinthians 11:5).

The idea of *authoritative teaching*, it seems to me, is introduced from an assumed meaning of 1 Timothy 2:12 and inserted into a reading of 1 Corinthians 14. Because some believe that women should not teach men in an authoritative manner, it is subtly assumed that authoritative speech is excluded here. I once thought about it that way. Consequently, this redirects the question to 1 Timothy 2:12, which I will address in Part 6.

Disorderly Speech?

If we read 1 Corinthians 14:34–35 in its own *specific* context *as well as* in the light of 1 Corinthians 11:2–16 (which does come first in the letter), it only forbids *disorderly speech.*

Paul's teaching in chapter fourteen *includes* women. Some texts, for example, obviously include women such as "pursue love" (14:1). Do others as well? In the following verses I have italicized plural verbs and nouns. The plurals include *both* men and women, and "brothers" (14:6, 20, 26, 39) includes both just as it does in all other texts in 1 Corinthians (1:10, 26; 2:3; 3:1; 4:6; 5:11; 6:5, 8; 7:24, 29; 10:1; 12:1; 15:1, 31, 58; 16:20; see Stelding).

14: 1— *Pursue* love and *strive* for spiritual gifts, and especially that *you may prophesy.*

14:5— Now I would like *all of you* to speak in tongues, but even more to *prophesy.*

14:6— *Brothers*, if I come speaking to *you* . . .

14:12— Since *you* are eager for spiritual gifts, *strive* to excel in them for building up the church.

14:20— *Brothers, do not be* children in your thinking.

14:23— If, therefore, the whole church comes together and *all speak* in tongues. . .

14:24— But if *all prophesy*. . .

14:26— What shall be done then, my *brothers*?

14:26— When *you come together*, each one has a hymn, a lesson, a revelation, a tongue, or an interpretation.

14:31— For *you can all prophesy* one by one, so that *all may learn* and *all be encouraged.*

14:39— So, my *brothers, be eager* to prophesy, and *do not forbid* speaking in tongues.

Perhaps some read these plural verbs and nouns as exclusively male, but is that consistent with *all the plurals*? Others may read them as both male and female, but in the end Paul excludes women from exercising these gifts in the assembly. But is the "each one" of 14:26 *only men*? Are the "brothers" of 14:6, 26, 32, and 39 *only men*? Does the "*all*" in 14:31 include *only men*? *All* are invited to prophesy so *all* may learn and *all* be encouraged. Which "*all*" excludes women? When Paul tells the church to "be eager to prophesy" in 14:39, does this address *only men* when we know there were female prophets in the church at Corinth? Does Paul encourage *all* to prophesy in 14:31 and then 14:39 only to deny women the privilege of prophesying in 14:34–35 when Paul has already recognized female prophets in 11:5? More naturally, Paul invites *both men and women* to participate in the edification of the assembly (14:26) but silences the *disorderly* behaviors of *both men and women* in 14:27–35.

Paul *limited* the number of speakers by silencing their disorderly conduct. He *silenced uninterpreted tongue speech* because it was disorderly (14:27–28), but this did not totally silence them in the assembly. He then *silenced prophets when another prophet received a revelation* (14:29–32), but this did not totally silence them in the assembly. Finally, *he silenced wives who persistently interrupted their husbands* (14:34–35), but this did not totally silence them in the assembly. Paul insists that everything be "done decently and in order" (14:40) because "God is not the God of confusion but peace, as in all the assemblies of the saints" (14:33). Paul is silencing disorderly speech by tongue speakers, prophets, and wives. He calls for order in all the assemblies of the saints. In every assembly where tongue speakers, prophets, or wives are disorderly, they should control (submit) themselves and be silent.

Just as there was a proper decorum for women *and* men who prayed and prophesied in 1 Corinthians 11:4–5 (women must be covered, men uncovered), there was a proper decorum for tongue speakers, prophets, and wives in chapter fourteen. Each group is silenced under *particular circumstances*. However, Paul neither totally silences tongue speakers nor prophets. Why, then, do we suppose Paul totally silences wives in every respect? Tongue speakers and prophets are only silenced in relation to their disruptive behavior. This is also true of wives. It is a *conditional silence* rather than an absolute one.

- *If* there is no one to interpret, *let them* be silent in the assembly (14:28).
- *If* a revelation is made to another, *let them* [the ones speaking] be silent (14:30).
- *If* there is anything they desire to know, *let them* ask their husbands at home and be silent. (14:35).

The silence is conditioned upon the circumstances. It is not absolute silence for any participants.

Persons	Occasion	Imperative	Adjustment
Tongue Speakers	No interpreter	Be silent (v. 28)	two or three speakers only
Prophets	Another receives a revelation	Be silent (v. 30)	two or three speakers only
Wives	Disrespectful or Disorderly Speech	Be silent (v. 34)	ask at home

Chapter fourteen invites *everyone* to participate. Everyone should pursue love and seek a spiritual gift. Everyone should use their gift in the assembly for the edification of the body of Christ. When the whole church comes together, *"each one"* (men and women) should bring a song, a teaching, or some edifying speech before the assembly. *Everyone is invited to share their gift in an orderly and edifying manner.*

FEMALE PROPHETS IN CORINTH

While reading 1 Corinthians 14:26–40 as a prohibition against disorderly speech makes sense, my shift from *no participation* to *limited participation* also came from studying 1 Corinthians 11 where women prayed and prophesied in an assembly.

Difficulties

1 Corinthians 11:2–16 is filled with problems. It reflects an intricate relationship between culture, theology, and church practices in the first century. There are significant uncertainties. Here are eleven.

1. What is the meaning of "head"? Sometimes it is literal, sometimes metaphorical. Is it a metaphor for authority or rank, or a metaphor for source or origin?
2. What covers the literal head? Is it the woman's hair or an artificial covering?
3. What is the occasion of this text? Does this gathering include men as well as women? Is it an assembly of the whole church or is it something else? Is it the same assembly as 1 Corinthians 11:17–34 where the Lord's supper is eaten?
4. Does headship apply to every assembly of the church or only to some assemblies? Does it apply to Bible classes, small groups, and home devotionals?
5. What is the nature of praying and prophesying? Is it silent or audible? Is it simultaneous or one at a time? What kind of leadership, if any, do they entail?
6. What is the balance between 11:7–9 and 11:11–12? How do the two sections interpret each other?
7. What is the meaning of "because of the angels" in 11:10?
8. What is the meaning of "authority" in 11:10? Does it have a passive ("a sign of authority") or active ("has authority") meaning?

9. What is the meaning of "churches of God" in 11:16? How does this characterize the nature of this gathering and its practices?

10. What are the "traditions" Paul assumes in 11:2 and 11:17?

11. Is Paul quoting opponents in some parts of 11:2–16?

It is possible that the answer to question eleven is "Yes." There are credible arguments to suggest that some lines are quotations from Paul's interlocutors in Corinth. This perspective has not found much advocacy among churches of Christ, but it is growing in credibility among scholars (Peppiatt, Padgett). I am not convinced but neither is it preposterous.

Another ambiguity (#2 above) is the nature of the covering on a woman's head. Interpreters are divided. Payne believes it is the woman's hair. Loose hair reflects sexual freedom or availability, but hair put up on the head is modest and proper. Consequently, Paul wants women to put their hair up and honor their husbands. Most, however, believe it is an artificial covering similar to a veil. While some interpreters understand the covering as a sign of the husband's authority, many believe it was a symbol of modesty and chastity for married women (Winter, Westfall). It was also a mark of religious piety for both men and women (Oster). Either way, whether loose hair or unveiled heads, the exposure of the hair signaled sexual availability, impropriety, and/or impiety. There is little evidence in the Greco-Roman world that the veil symbolized a husband's authority. For a married woman to rise unveiled in a mixed assembly would, at the very least, dishonor her husband because it conveyed a sexual message. The covering ensures the dignity of both married and unmarried women in the assembly and protects them from cultural disgrace and sexual aggression (Westfall).

While understanding Paul's argument about the covering is important, it does not bear directly on my focus. Whether women put up their hair or wore veils, *woman prayed or prophesied when attired in culturally appropriate ways.* Since my purpose is to understand the activities of women in the assembly in 1 Corinthians 11:2–16, the following questions are more significant: (1) what does it mean for women to pray and prophesy; (2) what is the setting of their praying and prophesying; (3) what is the nature of headship, and (4) where does a woman get her authority to pray and prophesy?

What is Praying and Prophesying?

Whatever it means for women to pray and prophesy, *it means the same as it does for men. Both* are praying and prophesying in 1 Corinthians 11:4–5. In 1 Corinthians 14:13–15, prayer is linked with speaking in tongues and paralleled with singing. In 1 Corinthians 14:3–5, when people speak in interpreted tongues, they edify the assembly, and those who prophesy edify the assembly.

1 Cor 11	Prayer in 1 Cor 14	Prophecy in 1 Cor 14
Any man who prays or prophecies . . . (11:4).	Interpreted tongue speaking edifies the assembly (14:5).	Those who prophesy speak to the assembly for their edification, exhortation, and consolation (14:3).
Any woman who prays or prophesies . . . (11:5).	If I pray in a tongue . . . (14:14).	Those who prophesy edify the assembly (14:4).
Is it proper for a woman to pray to God with her head unveiled? (11:13).	I will pray with the spirit, but I will pray with the mind also (14:15).	All prophesy one by one so that all may learn and all be exhorted (14:31).

There is no apparent difference between praying and prophesying in chapters eleven and fourteen. *They are both audible, visible, and edifying.*

Some suggest the women who prayed and prophesied in Corinth were only those who exercised charismatic or inspired speech. If God moves a woman to prophesy, then we listen. Otherwise, some argue, she must remain silent. But if God moves a woman to prophesy, then God is the source of her gift. If God affirms the exercise of her gift in the presence of men, then there is nothing insubordinate about a woman prophesying in the presence of men (Mark Black). God does not inspire women to do something inherently insubordinate or that violates God's intent in creation. Consequently, the fact that God inspires women to prophesy in the presence of men entails that other forms of leadership (prayer, exhortation, singing, etc.) do not *necessarily* violate the principle of headship either.

Some minimize the gift of prophecy as something more like subjective testimony (Grudem), but this gift is ranked *ahead* of evangelists, teachers, and elders in Ephesians 4:11. Further, Paul explicitly lists "first apostles, second prophets, and third teachers" (1 Corinthians 12:28). Prophets speak the word of God in ways that transcend evangelists, teachers, and elders. God gifts prophets with encouraging words, and God gifts all races, classes, and genders as prophets. *God gifted women as prophets*, both in the Hebrew Bible (Part 5) and in the Messianic age (Acts 21:9).

Some minimize this example because, it is argued, the gift of prophecy has ceased. Whether it has or not, God gifted women as prophets. *God does not gift women and sanction the use of those gifts in ways that inherently violate God's own intent in creation.* If women prophesied (even if they no longer do) with God's sanction and gifting, they can also preach because *prophesying was more substantive than teaching or preaching.*

When men and women prayed and prophesied in the Corinthian setting, it was *audible, visible, and edifying.* Both functions reflect the worship traditions of Israel. For example, her singers and musicians "prophesied with the lyre in thanksgiving

and praise to the Lord" (1 Chronicles 25:1). Prophecy sometimes came in musical form. Sometimes it came as sermons.
Prophesying is a form of preaching as the parallel in Amos 7:16
assumes. *Prophets spoke the word of God to the people of God.* At
Corinth, as in Israel, this included women.

What is the Setting of this Praying and Prophesying?

Two major answers are offered. On the one hand, some suggest
this gathering is something *different* from the assembly in chapter
fourteen and/or 1 Corinthians 11:17–34. Some limit it to women
only (McGuiggan) while others believe it is an assembly distinct
from the gathering of the whole church (Ferguson). Others think
women prophesied in public spaces in the city (like some cults
did) but not in the assembly (Morton). Still others think this
assembly is where the church observed the Lord's supper as a
closed, private meeting while chapter fourteen is an open, public
meeting where it would have been shameful for women to speak
in Roman culture (Prohl, Almlie). The range of options should
give us pause. Has misreading 1 Corinthians 14:34–35 created the
necessity to find a distinction where there is none?

On the other hand, the majority of interpreters believe 11:2–
16 and chapter fourteen (and 11:17–34) are the *same assembly*.
The primary interest in distinguishing between assemblies is the
seeming contradiction between women prophesying in 11:4–5 and
the silencing of women in 14:34–35. If I am correct about chapter
fourteen, *there is no contradiction.* Paul opposes *disorderly* practices in *both* chapters fourteen and eleven. The disorder in chapter
eleven is the uncovered head.

The nature of the assembly is an important question. By distinguishing between two different assemblies, some suggest Paul
permits women to pray and prophesy in private, special, or partial
assemblies but prohibits them when the "whole church" (14:23)

is gathered. Many contemporary interpreters within churches of Christ have adopted this approach. I have heard it often.

Other than a particular interpretation of 14:34–35, the *primary argument for distinguishing* the occasion of 11:2–16 and the assembly of the "whole church" in 14:23 is a perceived contrast between 11:2–16 and 11:17–34. Whatever the occasion of 11:2–16 is, the Lord's supper is a moment when people "come together as a church" (assembly; 11:18). According to this view, the church gathers as an assembly when it observes the Lord's supper in 11:17–34, but the occasion in 11:2–16 is not, so the argument goes, identified as a gathering of the church (assembly). While women may pray and prophesy in the latter gathering, they cannot in the assembly when the whole church is gathered for the Lord's supper. In other words, according to the argument, there is an *implicit* difference between the assemblies. One involves the whole church gathered to eat the Lord's supper, but the other does not. As a result, there are *different rules* for women in two *distinct gatherings*.

I don't think this distinction is justified. There is, in fact, no *explicit* distinction between assemblies within 1 Corinthians 11–14.

First, the application of this perspective creates some significant problems. The distinction between assemblies for which there are different rules is confusing. What other rules are different? Where are those rules explicitly identified? Is it only about the voices and leadership of women? If women are silenced due to submission and authority in 14:34–35 (as is typically argued), does not this submission apply to other assemblies as well—whether public, private, or outside of the assembly? Is the assembly of the whole church around the Lord's table *the only place* where submission entails silence?

In terms of our contemporary settings, does 14:34–35 only apply to Sunday assemblies where *the whole church* is gathered for the Lord's supper? If this is the definition of an assembly, then Wednesday evenings, small groups, Bible classes, retreats, lectureships, University classrooms, and *every other gathering* of Christians are open to the voices and leadership of women because 11:2–16 describes a space where women pray and prophesy. But this is neither what is typically argued nor the historic practice of churches of Christ. Women are not silenced *only* in assemblies where the Lord's supper is observed. Typically, women cannot teach, facilitate, or lead small groups in their own home when men are present much less teach a Bible class at the church building when men are present, preach in a Gospel Meeting on Monday night, or serve as the keynote speaker at a lectureship on a Tuesday night. Moreover, *are there assemblies when the church is not the church*? Whenever the people of God gather in the name of Jesus to pray, according to Matthew 18:20, they are the assembled church (Hicks, Melton & Valentine). When disciples gather to pray, they are the church (an assembly; Matthew 18:17, "tell it to the church"), whether it is a small group at home, a Bible class at the church building, a prayer group in a park, or gathered to eat the Lord's supper together on Sunday morning.

At this point, recall Holman's question. She asked, how many does it take to have an assembly so that a private event becomes a public one? When does an "assembly" become an "assembly of the whole church"? When we come together to pray, we are church whenever, wherever, and no matter how many come together. Whenever people gather to pray as disciples of Jesus, they are an assembly of the saints.

Second, the textual argument assumes, based on the *seeming* contrast of 11:2–16 and 11:17–34, that because 11:17–18 explicitly states that Corinth gathered as a church (assembly), they did not gather as a church (assembly) in 11:2–16 because it is not *explicitly* stated they gathered as a church (assembly; though look at 11:16). Does the presence of the word church in 11:17–34 *imply* that Corinth had *not* come together as a church in 11:2–16? I don't think so. At the very least, it is not a *necessary* inference. If

14:34–35 did not exist, it is unlikely any would propose differentiated assemblies in chapter eleven. On the contrary, (1) the necessity of head coverings is due to the presence of men gathered with women and (2) the communal activities of praying and prophesying are the same as the activities in the assembly of the "whole church" in chapter fourteen.

There is another way to account for Paul's language in chapter eleven. Perhaps he calls explicit attention to the gathering as church (assembly) in the context of the Lord's supper because the assembly was *divided*. Instead of eating the Lord's supper, they were eating *their own suppers* because the rich excluded the poor from the full table and did not wait for them. Rather, everyone who participates in the supper should discern the *body* than only a piece of it. In other words, there is a good reason why Paul uses the word church in the context of the Lord's Supper. This implies nothing about why he did not use it in the earlier section (even though he actually did in 11:16). *The seeming contrast is due to Paul's emphasis on the communal nature of the supper rather than a distinction between assemblies.*

Third, whatever Paul means by "custom," 11:16 affirms that "if anyone is disposed to be contentious—we have no such custom, nor do the churches [assemblies] of God." What Paul describes in 11:2–16 connects, in some way, to a common practice of *the assemblies of God*. Paul is describing what happens *in the assemblies*. This is the exact phrase, though singular, that Paul uses in 11:22, "the church [assembly] of God" (the plural in 14:33, "the churches [assemblies] of the saints"). Thus, both 11:16 and 11:22 address a situation regarding the assembly of God. In the former Paul commends them, but in the latter he does not (11:2, 17). Both are *assemblies*. Paul makes no *explicit* distinction between them. The words church (assembly) in 11:16 and church (assembly) in 11:17–18 serve as a hinge. Both texts describe what the Corinthians did in their assembly.

Fourth, in 11:2 Paul praises them for keeping the "traditions" and then in 11:17 & 23 critiques them because they did not keep a particular tradition well. Is the tradition of 11:2 something that applies only to private assemblies (Ferguson) or to public events outside the assembly (Morton)? Do not "the traditions" also apply to *all assemblies*, including where the Lord's supper is observed? The use of the term "tradition" in 11:2 and 11:17 & 23 connects the two sections together under a single topic—they are practicing or failing to practice the traditions that are part of their assemblies. After discussing why Christians should avoid pagan worship (10:14–11:1), Paul turns his attention to the assembly and its traditions (11:2–14:40). The parallel structures of 11:2–16 and 11:17–34 indicate that they are talking about the same assembly (Osburn). There is no break in thought or context. Indeed, the similar phraseology of "praise over traditions" kept or not kept links the two together.

Fifth, while I think 11:2–16 and 11:17–34 describe activities in the same assembly, it is also true that the principles of 11:2–16 would apply to *any assembly where men and women are gathered* to praise God and edify one another. If man is the "head of woman," *should not that apply in every assembly*? If the principle applies in every assembly, why are women permitted to pray and prophesy in some assemblies where both men and women are present but not in the assembly of chapter fourteen or where the Lord's supper is observed? *What is the principle that distinguishes the function of headship from one assembly to the other*? Doesn't the principle of headship apply to 11:17–34 as well as 11:2–16? Why are women silent in one but not the other? Nevertheless, if headship entails the silence of women *only* for Sundays when gathered for the Lord's supper as in 1 Corinthians 11:17–34, all other spaces, times, and assemblies are open to the voices and leadership of women unlike the recent practice of churches of Christ. In other words, to affirm two distinct sorts of assemblies entails women are *only* required to be silent when the "whole church" is gathered for the Lord's supper (the assembly of 11:17–34 and 14:23). Essentially, that is an *inferred* rule rather than an *explicit* pattern. This raises the interminable question about what rules apply to what assemblies when we seek to discern how one assembly differs from another. But, it seems to me, an assembly gathered in the name of Jesus to pray is an assembly, *no matter where or how many are gathered* (Matthew 18:19–20). An assembly is an assembly.

Headship

What is the nature of the headship relationship between men and women? One of the more thorny problems in chapter eleven is the meaning of "head" (*kephalē*). Generally, there are two perspectives. Some assign it the metaphorical meaning of ruler, authority, or rank (Grudem) while others suggest it is a metaphor for source or origin (Cervin). While Westfall adeptly explains the meaning of *kephalē* as source that excludes any sense of hierarchical authority and Pierce helpfully contextualizes *kephalē* in the context of divine order and relationality rather than authority, it is unnecessary for *my present purpose* to argue for a particular metaphorical meaning. Consequently, I will use the word "head" as a literal translation that has a disputed metaphorical meaning in 1 Corinthians 11.

In some sense, Paul affirms male headship. This does not necessarily imply any inferiority because Christ, whose head is God, is not inferior to God. The one through whom God created the world (1 Corinthians 8:6) is the same one who shared *equality* with God before the world was created (Philippians 2:6). Whatever the meaning of *kephalē*, there is no implied ontological subordination between God and Christ. Both share the same divine nature. In the same way, there is no ontological subordination between men and women either as both are created in the image of God.

Men do not, in the context of 1 Corinthians, exercise gifts that are forbidden to women because of this headship. *Both* men *and* women pray and prophesy. The *only difference* is that men exercise their gifts with uncovered heads and women with covered heads. That distinction relates, in some way, to cultural propriety *rather than something ontologically inherent to headship*, which is why congregations today no longer insist on a head covering. In the Corinthian culture, a woman covers her head because it honors her husband or as a matter of sexual propriety. She ought to honor her husband because she is from the man and complements the man. [More on 1 Corinthians 11:8–9 in Part 5.] In her, the fullness of male delight and purpose find their fulfillment, which is also evident in Genesis 2 where her creation is the apex of creation (Reid). This does not diminish the woman. She is also created in the image and glory of God as is clear from Colossians 3:10 where *all believers* are *renewed* in the image of their creator.

Further, whatever Paul means by his application of headship in 11:7–9 is immediately *balanced* with mutuality in 11:11–12. "Nevertheless" in 11:11 is not a denial of 11:7–9 (though it could be read that way as if Paul is quoting opponents) but a fuller vision of the male-female relationship. If someone wants to take male headship too far or attach a meaning incongruent with God's good creation, Paul reminds them that though the woman came *from man*, now all men come *through women*, and everyone *comes from God*. This makes even more sense if "head" means source in that just as man was the source of woman in the beginning, now women are the source of men through childbirth. This testifies to their *mutual reciprocity* "in the Lord" rather than any rank. Moreover, all headship is rooted in God as the source of all things, and every human lives before God rather than ranked beneath other human beings.

This is the critical point: *headship, whatever it means, does not deny women the privilege of participation and leadership*. Women audibly edified the assembly through praying and prophesying. Even if we define headship as some kind of authority, praying and prophesying do not subvert it; *not all leadership is a function of headship or belongs only to headship.* Leadership, including praying and prophesying in the assembly, does not assume headship authority (*if* that is the metaphorical meaning of "head"). Indeed, women prayed and prophesied in the Corinthian assembly while, *at the same time,* they honored their heads (husbands). Praying and prophesying is *not* an act of insubordination. Rather, if done with propriety (whatever the covering means), a woman honors her head even as she edifies the assembly. Women may prophesy in an assembly as long as they do so in a culturally appropriate manner (presumably uncovered women sent inappropriate sexual messages). *Consequently, male headship, whatever that means, does not silence women in the assembly.*

I have essentially stated that last sentence twice. It is an important point for those who advocate *limited participation,* as I did throughout the 1990s and into the early 2000s (see my handout for a Madisonville, Kentucky, conference; also Archer). On the one hand, according to the *limited participation* perspective, male headship invests men with responsibility and accountability for spiritual leadership. On the other hand, that same headship, in this perspective, empowers women to use their gifts rather than obstructing them. *Headship does not entail that all leadership functions in the assembly belong to men.*

While headship, in the *limited participation* view, is not typically about power and control but about responsibility and empowerment, according to Paul, w*omen do not receive their authority or right to participate from men.* Rather, women have that right by virtue of God's gifting. *They have their own authority.* Their participation does not depend on male authorization or male counterparts.

Authority

Where does a woman receive her *authority* to pray and prophesy? The answer to that question was significant for me in 1990. *Her authority comes from God*, not a man or husband.

1 Corinthians 11:10 says, "For this reason a woman ought to have a symbol of authority on her head, because of the angels" (NRSV), or "a woman ought to have authority over her own head because of the angels" (NIV, 2011).

This is a difficult text for at least two reasons. First, the reference to angels is unclear. It probably refers to the presence of angels in a worshipping assembly. Since the church participates in the heavenly realms as the saints join the angelic chorus gathered around the throne, a covered head somehow respects the angels.

Second, what does Paul mean by the term "authority" in 11:10? The verse parallels 11:7, a man "ought not to have his [physical] head covered." Using the same language, 11:10 *literally* says, "the woman ought to have authority over/upon [physical] head." Men should uncover their heads while praying and prophesying, but women should cover their heads while praying and prophesying. Yet, Paul uses the word for "cover" when he refers to men, but "authority" when he refers to women.

The exact phrase is "has authority" (*exousian echein*). Many interpret this in a passive sense. While wearing the covering, she wears the *sign of her husband's authority*. She "has authority" in the sense that she honors the authority of her husband (or men in the assembly) through the covering. If we read it this way, Paul authorizes women to pray and prophesy as long as they have a *sign of authority* on their head. Therefore, according to this understanding, she has the privilege of praying and prophesying *because* she properly respects male headship.

But, *literally*, the Greek text is *not* passive ("sign of authority"). The word "sign" is not in the Greek text. The verb is active in voice; the woman *possesses or has authority* on or over *her own* head.

Authority (*exousia*) is not used in reference to male/female relationships elsewhere in 1 Corinthians except for *mutual authority* (1 Corinthians 7:4). It is not the husband's authority that gives a woman the privilege of exercising her gifts, but the authority *that belongs to her* through appropriate cultural propriety and divine gifting. When covered, she has authority over her own head. It is an *authority from God*; it is not male authority.

Wherever Paul uses this phrase in 1 Corinthians, it refers to the right of people to exercise their *privilege*. For example, "Don't we *have the right* to food and drink? Don't we *have the right* to take a believing wife along with us?.. Or is it only Barnabas and I who *have no right* to refrain from working for a living?" (9:4–6). Used three times in 9:4–6, it refers to the right of the apostle to exercise his options. In the same way, *the same phrase* in 11:10 means covered women *have the right* to pray and prophesy in the assembly (Hooker, Liefeld, Bartlett). She *has authority* on her own (physical) head. Just as Paul had a *right* to food and drink, covered women have a *right* to pray and prophesy.

Consequently, any interpretation which ignores the right of women to pray and prophesy in 11:2–16 is misguided. Some suggest Paul does not sanction the praying and prophesying by women in chapter eleven but waits to silence them in chapter fourteen analogous to how Paul handles the eating of meats in chapters eight and ten (Pendleton, Ferguson, Fewkes). Others have argued that the covering denies women the right to pray and prophesy because submission entails silence and the covering is a sign of submission (Weeks). But *Paul does not deny women the privilege of praying and prophesying but authorizes it.* Paul does not simply leave his view unstated in chapter eleven. Rather, *he approves the praying and prophesying of the women* in 11:10. A woman has authority to pray and prophesy in the assembly of the saints when she does so with cultural propriety. She has her own authority to pray and prophesy.

When men use their "headship" to deny women the right to pray and prophesy, manage them with their own presumed authority, or demand a woman have the "covering" of *male* authority, they subvert the authority God has given women through *God's own gifting of women*. That is a precarious place to stand.

Yes, I know, I have yet to address the meaning of 1 Timothy 2:12. That will come in Part 6.

THE CORINTHIAN SITUATION

In 1 Corinthians 11–14, Paul addressed disturbances connected with the assembly. There were multiple concerns, which indicates how chaotic the assembly in Corinth was. There were problems with

- how they handled customs typical of the assemblies of God (11:16).
- how they practiced traditions handed down to them (11:2, 17).
- the divisive way in which they ate the Lord's supper (11:18).
- jealousy between people with different gifts (12–13).
- competition between tongue-speakers and prophets (14:1–25).
- disorder in how people used their gifts in the assembly (14:26–40).

To those problems Paul applies the themes of *love, mutuality, and order*. Both men and women prayed and prophesied in the assembly. Both men and women sat at the Lord's table. *All*, both men and women, were baptized in the Spirit (1 Corinthians 12:13). The unity of the body transcended Jew and Gentile, enslaved and free, and men and women. Though Paul does not specify male and female in 12:13, he had already included male and female in that giftedness in chapter eleven. Both were gifted. There are no gender distinctions regarding gifts in chapter twelve. Both men and women were called to pursue love with faith and hope. Both men and women were encouraged to desire spiritual gifts and seek to prophesy as well as pray in interpreted tongues. Everyone, both men and women, brought their gift to the assembly in order to glorify God and edify the people of God. *All* were encouraged to prophesy. The assembly was designed to reflect the peace of God and proceed without confusion or disorder for the sake of edification and witness to unbelievers. Paul corrected Corinth's disorderliness.

- It was disorderly for men to pray covered and women to prophesy uncovered.
- It was disorderly for the rich to eat the Supper without the poor.
- It was disorderly to exalt gifts over mutual love for one another.
- It was disorderly to make the assembly a competition over gifts.
- It was disorderly for tongue speakers to speak without an interpreter.
- It was disorderly for prophets to speak when another received a revelation.
- It was disorderly for wives to interrupt their husbands with questions.

At the same time, "*each one*," Paul wrote, may bring their gift to the assembly for the glory of God and the edification of the body. Paul authorized the orderly use of gifts by both men and women, both Jew and Gentile, and both enslaved and free in the assemblies of God's saints.

Pentecost and the inauguration of new creation made that possible.

PART 4

My Move to Full Participation

I am your servant,
give me understanding
that I may know your testimonies!
Psalm 119:125

Walking through the Corinthian texts is difficult. In 1990, those texts challenged me to acknowledge that women prayed and prophesied in the assemblies of God at Corinth. *Women participated audibly and visibly in the assemblies while, at the same time, honoring their heads.* This led me to conclude, as others had among nineteenth century and early twentieth century churches of Christ, that women are authorized to lead in *limited* ways in the assembly. Advocates of *limited participation*, however, have different boundaries for women. For some, it only excludes women from preaching. For others, it excludes women from leading worship or presiding at the table. Limited participation is expressed differently. Though most agree preaching is excluded, there is no consensus on where the boundaries lie beyond that.

I embraced *limited participation* in the 1990s. While some may regard that as a slippery slope, by reading the text more closely sometimes we do "slide" into more healthy practices as we begin to recognize the problems with our previous positions. In my early experience among churches of Christ, women *never participated* in audible or visible ways in the leadership of the assembly. Given my shift in understanding, in the late 1990s Gary Ealy and I, along with a core group, planted a new congregation in Memphis where women might participate in more expansive, though limited, ways. In the early 2000s, the congregation where I worshipped in Nashville expanded the participation of women in the assembly but with limitations on preaching and leading worship.

At the same time, I was increasingly disturbed both by how the remaining boundaries created incongruities and how different rationales were offered. I often heard that men gave women permission or invested authority in them to lead prayer or read Scripture. However, that is not what Paul said in 1 Corinthians 11:10. Rather, *women have their own authority to pray and prophesy*.

Further, the limitation typically included preaching. But prophesying in the Scripture is no mere experiential testimony. *It is a word from God*. Prophesying, which is ahead of teaching in 1 Corinthians 12:28 and Ephesians 4:11, is more like preaching than an experiential witness. Prophets *edify*, *encourage*, and *exhort* (1 Corinthians 14:3, 31). It is important to remember a "word of exhortation" not only describes a synagogue homily (Acts 13:15) but the whole book of Hebrews itself (13:22). Exhortation is how Timothy, as an evangelist, served the Ephesian church in the context of the reading of Scripture and teaching (1 Timothy 4:13). It was something more than a testimony or simply reading Scripture. Moreover, the church was founded on the teaching of the apostles *and* prophets (Ephesians 2:20; 3:5). Prophesying is categorized along with knowledge, teaching, and revelation (1 Corinthians 14:6). Prophesying, as a word from God, instructs, edifies, and exhorts the assembly of God. Since female prophets

prophesied in the Corinthian assembly and prophesying is analogous to preaching, why are women limited from preaching in
the assembly?

The presence of prophets turned my attention to Pentecost
because prophecy was integrally connected to the pouring out of
the Spirit. I remember wondering if there was more to Pentecost
than the inauguration of the Jesus community (as important as
that is). When I began linking the gifts of the Spirit with the
initiation of new creation and the outpouring of the Spirit, this
became another marker on my journey. Pentecost, in conjunction
with a deeper appreciation of the meaning and presence of new
creation, moved me to embrace the *full participation* of women
in a worshipping assembly. Still, however, 1 Timothy 2:12 loomed
large, and I had no intention of ignoring or abusing that word
from God (see Part 6).

At the same time, Pentecost and new creation, in the light of
the whole story of God in Scripture, grounded my move from
limited participation to *full participation*.

A caveat. If I had read what follows in 1980, I would have
been frustrated by its analogies. I understand that. I ask, however,
for patience as I attempt to draw out the profound meaning of
Pentecost as not only the birthday of the church but the inauguration of new creation through the resurrection, ascension, and
enthronement of Jesus the Messiah. In what ways did Pentecost
change how God gifted the people of God?

THE POURING OUT OF THE SPIRIT

On Pentecost, God poured the Spirit on the disciples of Jesus,
both men and women. "They were all together," according to
Acts 2:1. *All* one hundred and twenty men and women of Acts
1:15 were gathered together. The disciples reaped the harvest of
the resurrection and enthronement of the Messiah. Though the
ruling powers killed the Messiah, God raised him from the dead

and seated him at God's right hand. In this way, *God restored Israel through the reign of Jesus whom God declared both Messiah and Lord.*

Centuries earlier, in the midst of a corporate lament, the prophet Joel (2:28) hoped for the restoration of Israel.

> I will pour out my spirit on all flesh,
>> your sons and daughters shall prophesy,
>> your old men shall dream dreams,
>>> your young men shall see visions.
> Even on male and female slaves,
>> in those days I will pour out my spirit.

On Pentecost, after the Spirit had descended on the disciples, Peter announced, "This is that!" (Acts 2:16–17.)

The significance of this moment is difficult to overestimate. Whatever we say is less than its full meaning. It is a surprising work of God that explodes all expectations, anticipations, and conventions. What Joel envisions is the veritable shaking of the cosmos. The universe has reversed course or, perhaps better, been put back on course—the trajectory arising out of God's creative intent in Genesis 1–2.

During Israel's journey through the wilderness from Sinai to Canaan, God took "some of the spirit that was on [Moses] and put it on the seventy elders; and when the spirit rested upon them, they prophesied" (Numbers 11:25). Some saw this as a threat to Moses. Even Joshua wanted Moses to silence them. Moses's response anticipated Joel's words: "Would that all the Lord's people were prophets, and that the Lord would put his spirit on them." A comparison of Numbers 11 with Joel 2 reveals how the future out-pouring of the Spirit expands the categories.

Numbers 11:24-25	Joel 2:28-29
Seventy	All
Prophesy	Prophesy
Men	Men and Women
Old (Elders)	Old and Young
Free (Recently Liberated)	Free and Enslaved

On Pentecost, God poured the Spirit upon *all* Israel. On that day, everyone who committed to Jesus as Lord, repented of their sins, and was immersed in water for the forgiveness of sins received the gift of the Holy Spirit (Acts 2:38).

But Joel's words say more than this. Not only does Peter declare that all Israel now receives God's Spirit, he also—even without his own full understanding—announces the seismic change that began that day.

God now includes *all flesh* within the people of God. Joel foresaw a moment when God would pour out the Spirit on the Gentiles. God promised Abraham that his seed would bless all nations, and that promise includes the Holy Spirit. As Paul wrote in Galatians 3:14, "in Christ Jesus the blessing of Abraham" came "to the Gentiles, so that we might receive the promise of the Spirit through faith." That God pours out the Spirit on all flesh means that God includes all, no matter what their ethnicity.

This was difficult for Peter to see. It is still difficult for us. Centuries of racism in the church testify to this. There was a time when some believed black people had no human soul and indigenous peoples were but savages. During the Jim Crow era black Christians were told to worship in separate congregations. I have seen white Christians walk out of an assembly the first time an African American led singing. It has taken over nineteen hundred years for Christian people to recognize, even if not yet fully, racism.

When Peter said "This is that," he said something is different. The Gentiles are now included. *They are not powerless, ungifted outsiders to God's covenant community.*

God also makes no distinction between enslaved and free in the pouring out of the Spirit. From the beginnings of human culture, slavery has been part of its economic and political systems. The social fabric of both the Ancient Near East and the Greco-Roman world was a top-down system topped by kings with the enslaved at the bottom. Since slavery was at the heart of the imperial system, the infant church was powerless to rid the empire of its evil.

The pouring out of the Spirit, however, is the gospel seed that destroys slavery. Enslaved people receive the Spirit of God. They are empowered to minister in the Spirit just like any free person. In this, we see how the presence of the Spirit subverts cultural norms and rails against the empire. Because the enslaved are Spirit-filled and Spirit-gifted human beings, the hierarchical world of the empire was challenged in the church. The Spirit teaches the church that slavery is evil. No human being may steal another human being, own another human being, or exploit another's labor for their own selfish interests. When God poured out the Spirit on the enslaved, the movement toward the abolition of slavery was embedded in the church's theological vision of God's goal for all humanity even though racial slavery only ended in the United States a little over one hundred and fifty years ago. Unfortunately, it took over eighteen hundred years for most Christians to recognize the evil of slavery in both its economic and racial forms.

When Peter said "This is that," he said something is different. Enslaved people are now free in the Spirit. *They are not powerless, ungifted people in the covenant community.*

There is a third group in Joel's words. God makes no distinction between male and female in the pouring out of the Spirit. The oppression of women has pervaded history. We don't have to look far in the ancient world to see how men abused, used, and marginalized women. With few exceptions, they had little to no power.

At the same time, the pouring out of the Spirit destroys this marginalization. God gifts women with the Spirit, and, by the Spirit, women, like men, prophesy. They dream dreams and see visions. God communicates with women in the same way God communicates with men. No distinction is made.

There were, of course, female prophets in Israel (see Part 5). They anticipate the fuller pouring out of the Spirit that Joel envisions and is actualized on Pentecost. There are no barriers. Women are gifted just like men. God intends to liberate women from exploitation and cultural conventions. Unfortunately, the church, as with racism and slavery, has often perpetuated barriers of various kinds.

Many among churches of Christ used 1 Timothy 2:12 to oppose women's suffrage. Many have denied women any kind of public voice or visible presence in both church and society. Some have used biblical texts to silence women from audibly praying in the presence of their husbands or daughters teaching in the presence of their fathers (see the story about my daughter in Part 6). When God poured out the Spirit on women, it spelled the end of their exclusion even though women only gained the right to vote in the United States a hundred years ago. It took almost nineteen hundred years for Christian people to recognize how they had limited not only women's opportunities and careers but also their voices and visibility in a worshipping assembly.

When Peter said "This is that," he also said something is different. Women are now free. *They are not powerless, second-tier assistants in God's covenant community.*

Peter says, "This is that!" All people, whether Jew or Gentile, free or enslaved, or male or female, are now gifted by the Spirit.

Over the centuries, the church has had to tease out the meaning of Pentecost and embrace its full application. Pentecost, as the fulfillment of Joel 2:28, liberates ethnicities, the enslaved, and women. It destroys all distinctions in giftedness based on race, economics, and gender.

The church has had to learn that God includes all races and nations, though many Christians throughout history have oppressed and subjugated various nations and races. The church has had to learn that God intends to free all enslaved peoples, though many Christians throughout history have enslaved people, traded in their buying and selling, and defended slavery as a good. The church has had to learn that God empowers women to prophesy, though many Christians throughout history have silenced women in their assemblies.

Pentecost affirms the dignity, gifts, and Spirit-filled lives of all nations and races. God has poured out the Spirit on all flesh. Pentecost affirms the dignity, gifts, and Spirit-filled lives of all believers and liberates people from every form of slavery. God has poured out the Spirit on the enslaved as well as the free. Pentecost affirms the dignity, gifts, and Spirit-filled lives of women. God has poured out the Spirit on both male and female.

Paul echoed Joel 2:28–29.

Joel 2:28-29	Galatians 3:26-28
All Flesh	Jew/Greek
Sons/Daughters	Male/Female
Free/Enslaved	Free/Enslaved

Galatians 3:28–29 declares the meaning of Pentecost.

> There is no longer Jew or Greek, there is no longer slave
> or free, there is no longer male and female; for all of
> you are one in Christ Jesus. And if you belong to Christ,
> then you are Abraham's offspring, heirs according to
> the promise.

A NEW CREATION

As soon as I raise the specter of Galatians 3:28, two polarizing perspectives dance about in my head. While many think Galatians 3:28 is wholly about salvation and has nothing to do with leadership gifts (Cottrell), others insist its primary import is the liberation of people groups for full ministry in the body of Christ, the "Magna Carta of Humanity" (Jewett).

Paul is describing inheritance. Galatians employs the terminology six times (3:18; 3:29; 4:1, 7, 30; 5:21). The inheritance comes through God's promise to Abraham. Those who are children of God by faith in the Messiah are heirs of that promise. This includes the present experience of the Holy Spirit who fills our hearts and by whom we cry, "Abba" (Galatians 3:14; 4:6–7).

The inheritance comes to all believers who have put on Christ in baptism. This is a reversal in redemptive history. Gentiles did not share in the inheritance of Abraham, only his descendants; enslaved people did not inherit, only children; and daughters only inherited when there were no sons. Something is different now. Now Gentiles, the enslaved, and daughters inherit along with free Jewish males. That is the meaning of Pentecost because the "promise" is for the Gentile, the enslaved, and women just as it is for free Jewish men (Acts 2:33, 39).

The connection between Pentecost and Galatians, which is the fulfillment of the Abrahamic promise in the experience of the Spirit, is an important one. The conjunction of the promised Spirit, creation language ("male and female" from Genesis 1:27), and new creation (Galatians 6:15) is significant. The confluence of these three ideas tell a larger story about what inheritance means and its fuller significance. Inheritance includes the movement from creation to new creation through the promised Spirit (Cutler).

The Abrahamic promise is ultimately fulfilled when his descendants inherit the cosmos (Romans 4:13), the new heaven and new earth (Revelation 21:1, 7). New creation, which Paul named in Galatians 6:15–16, is another way of describing this. "New creation," Paul wrote, "is everything." Moreover, Paul called this the "rule" by which believers walk.

Rule is the word *canoni*, which refers to a measuring stick or ruler. The canon to which Paul refers is not a written document but the act of God in Jesus through the Spirit who creates anew (see *Searching for the Pattern*). This is what matters; circumcision and uncircumcision do not (Galatians 6:14–16). Whether you are Abraham's physical descendant or not, whether you are circumcised or not, no longer decides who inherits.

But *what* do we inherit? What is the meaning and significance of this inheritance for the church, its salvation, and its giftedness?

God has inaugurated new creation through the resurrection and enthronement of Jesus the Messiah. God has initiated new creation in us by sending the Spirit into our hearts as a down payment, a "pledge of our inheritance toward redemption as God's own people" (Ephesians 1:14). Through the Spirit, we already share in our inheritance as new creatures in Christ. The gift of the Spirit is the first fruits of our inheritance even as we await our full adoption as children of God through the redemption of the body (Romans 8:16–17, 23). The indwelling Spirit promises a *future* inheritance, and, by the Spirit, we *already* experience this inheritance.

The link between new creation and the Holy Spirit underscores how important it is to think about the *fuller meaning of salvation.* Salvation is not simply about *justification* by faith or entrance into the church though it includes both. It is also about (1) *sanctification* as we grow into the likeness of Christ and (2) *glorification* when God will fully redeem the creation in the new heaven and new earth. Galatians 3:28 is about salvation, and salvation is *new creation.* When we read Galatians 3:28 and only think in terms of entrance into Christ, justification, or conversion, we narrow the import of the role of the Spirit and the promise of new creation that *lies at the heart* of Paul's argument.

The language of Galatians 3:28 is drawn from the creation account (Genesis 1:27). Paul uses "male *and* female" rather than "man or woman." This is not typical for Paul who only uses "female" elsewhere in Romans 1:26–27. He draws the language directly from Genesis. Paul echoes the original vision of creation where "male *and* female" form an explicit partnership and share responsibility for the creation. This creation language is driven by the hope of new creation in the "present evil age" (Galatians 1:4).

This appeal to creation is important because what Paul describes "in Christ" is part of the "new creation" (Galatians 6:16). This new world renews the partnership of the original creation when God created "them" in the divine image, "blessed them," and told "them" to co-create and co-shepherd God's good creation. In other words, the partnership envisioned in Genesis 1:26–28 is renewed in the new creation (Stelding).

New creation not only renews creation but *redeems all that is broken* within it and reconciles humanity with God, the creation, and itself. New creation means *not only* that inheritance is not dependent upon ethnicity, economics, or gender but that the *experience of that inheritance in the present is without those same boundaries.* The gifts of the Spirit are not bounded by those categories. God poured out the Spirit on all peoples. *The Spirit gifts all,* whether enslaved or free, male or female, or Jew or Gentile, as Pentecost teaches us.

The common inheritance of the people of God includes the gifts of the Holy Spirit. There are no ethnic criteria for the gifts of the Spirit. There are no economic criteria for the gifts of the Spirit. And there are no gendered criteria for the gifts of the Spirit. Just as the *fruit* of the Spirit knows no ethnic, economic, or gender boundaries neither do the *gifts* of the Spirit. Both men and women are formed into the likeness of Christ, drink of the same Spirit, and are gifted by the same Spirit (1 Corinthians 12:4–7, 12–13). Women prophesy as well as men (1 Corinthians 11:4–5; cf. Acts 21:9).

There is more going on in Galatians 3:28 than entrance into the community of faith, our initial union with Christ, or a subversion of circumcision as an identity marker (though it includes all of the above). Rather, it describes the *reality of the inheritance itself which is already present but not yet fully realized.* We are one in Christ. That unity—rooted in a shared Spirit through a shared baptism into Christ—includes our communal inheritance. We are all heirs, and, even now, we all share that inheritance through the Spirit. In this way, new creation functions as a hermeneutic, a way of seeing the world and understanding the story of God. It sees the world through the work of the Spirit who actualizes new creation in the present.

Consequently, the categories of Jew/Gentile, enslaved/free, and male/female are now understood through the lens of new creation rather than through the lens of the present evil age. Thus, Paul is not *only* describing justification for believers in Christ, but the reality of the new creation itself where the community of faith lives by a *new rule* or canon.

While exploring the full implications of Galatians 3:28 in the light of a new creation hermeneutic is beyond the scope of my purpose, (1) the promised Spirit is given to all; (2) the Spirit gifts all; and (3) whether one is male or female is no barrier to the exercise of those gifts within the new creation. *Gifts are part of the inheritance itself.* This includes the leadership gifts found in

Ephesians 4:11 and Romans 12:6–9 (Byrd). Gifted, women are invited to participate in the ministry of the new creation as God renews the original partnership of *male and female as part of God's good creation.*

Why would heirs of the Abrahamic promise ever think that God has *gender boundaries* for giftedness and the exercise of those gifts in the power of the Spirit? I remember how I once answered that question: 1 Timothy 2:12. Part 6 will address that text, but *no other text explicitly* identifies a gender boundary in the exercise of the Spirit's gifts.

But before we open up that can of worms, it is important, as Holman said, to put into play the "balance of the Bible" and read it in the light of God's intent for creation and its renewal.

PART 5

From Creation to New Creation: The Balance of the Bible

My mouth will tell of your righteous acts,
of your deeds of salvation all day long,
though their number is past my knowledge.
I will come praising the mighty deeds of the Lord God,
I will praise your righteousness, yours alone.

Psalm 71:15–16

God created heaven and earth with humanity as God's representative within the creation, *chose* a people from among the nations as a light to the nations, *sent* the Messiah into the world for the sake of the world, *sent* the Spirit to renew a people to participate in the mission of God, and will *renew* heaven and earth. Scripture proclaims God's mighty deeds and righteous acts.

Multiple storylines flesh out that grand drama. One is the vocation of women. I once regarded much of that storyline as inadmissible for a blueprint reading of Acts and Epistles because the texts do not specifically relate to Christian assemblies. Because the blueprint hermeneutic seeks *specific texts* for *specific authorization* for worshipping *assemblies* in Acts and the Epistles, much of the story of women in the Bible became irrelevant. If there are no specific authorizations, then it is forbidden because we can *only* practice what is authorized in Acts and the Epistles. Essentially, the blueprint hermeneutic is limited to Acts and the Epistles and minimizes the gifts of women in, what Holman called, "the balance of the Bible."

A theological hermeneutic, however, attends to the *plot* of God's story regarding men and women. It explores the theology that shapes how men and women honor each other, serve God together, carry out their shared mission, and utilize the gifts distributed among them as signs of God's gracious work. The theological hermeneutic recognizes how the gifts of women throughout Scripture echo God's intent in creation and serve as signposts for new creation itself.

My narration is not so much a comprehensive argument for something as it is a perspective for hearing the story of women in the Bible anew. The biblical drama provides a framework for applying a theological hermeneutic to the assemblies of God.

CREATION

The pinnacle of creation on the sixth day is humankind (*adam*), who is both male and female. Genesis 1:27 reads:

So God created humankind in his image,
in the image of God he created [humankind],
male and female he created them.

Humankind (*adam*) is the image of God. Humanity is both male and female. Humanity (*adam*) is incomplete without either. Together, they constitute *adam*. Their diversity as male and female contributes to the divine mission. Without that diversity, God is not fully represented within the creation.

Men and women have a *shared identity*. Both are created in the image of God. This shared identity entails a mutual respect and honor for each other. There is nothing within their nature that differentiates their dignity or intrinsic worth.

Women and men also have a *shared vocation*. Genesis 1:28 reads:

God blessed them, and God said to them,
> "Be fruitful and multiply, and fill the earth and
> subdue it;
>> and have dominion over the fish of the sea and
>> over the birds of the air and
>>> over every living thing that moves upon
>>> the earth."

Both male and female are blessed, and *both* are summoned to be God's junior partners. God shares divine dominion with human beings and invites both male and female to participate in God's mission. Their vocation involves not only populating the earth with other human beings but also filling it with God's glory through a people who represent God in the creation, subdue the chaos remaining in the creation, and shepherd the creation as co-rulers with God. This is the human vocation.

Both share responsibility for the human vocation. Neither can fully accomplish the task without the other. *This does not mean that everyone must marry.* It means human community is only *fully human* when both women and men share the mission that arises out of their shared identity.

Creation of Woman

Genesis 2 describes the origin of men and women. Alone, *adam* is ill-equipped to execute the human vocation. *Adam* needs an *'ezer*. Genesis 2:18 reads:

> Then the Lord God said, "It is not good that the man (*adam*) should be alone; I will make a helper ('*ezer*) as his partner."

When woman was formed from *adam*, humanity was differentiated as male and female. They are different but share the same essence. Their diversity makes a shared vocation possible as partners. Neither is sufficient alone. Whether people experience this partnership as married couples or as singles in community, life together is necessary to fully pursue the human vocation.

'*Ezer* refers to a powerful helper or rescuer who can partner with another to complete a task—a co-worker rather than an underling. God is often called humanity's '*ezer* (Deuteronomy 33:7; Psalms 54:4; 70:5; 146:5). Further, '*ezer* is modified by "corresponding to him" (the literal meaning). This identifies the '*ezer* as one who stands alongside of *adam* rather than beneath or above. She is a companion, a human *ally* (Byrd) or a *powerful ally* (Bartlett). Though our English idiom ("helper") often connotes a secondary person or a subordinate, this is not the import of the Hebrew term. The woman is a *full and empowered partner* in the human community.

The woman is created "from man" (1 Corinthians 11:8). Man is the source of the woman, just as God is the source of both men and women. As the woman was created from (*ek*) man, so also both men and women come from (*ek*) God. Though the woman came *from* man, now men come *through* women. In other words, whatever "from man" means, it is *balanced* with "through woman." In this way, "in the Lord woman is not independent of man or man independent of woman" (1 Corinthians 11:11–12). Without each other, there is no full representation of God's image. Without each other, they cannot accomplish the human vocation.

The woman is also created "for the sake of the man" (1 Corinthians 11:9). This does not mean the woman is a subordinate.

Rather, she is the one whose creation fully equips humanity. Through the creation of woman, male and female are mutually equipped to participate in the divine mission together and execute their shared task. Whether chronological order has any significance for that task, I will consider when we examine 1 Timothy 2:13 in Part 6. There is, however, no hint of any rank or authority in Genesis 2 unless we read Genesis 2 through the lens of a *particular interpretation* of Paul's words (Marrs).

Male and female are interconnected—a mutual relationship. In marriage, they execute their shared task together. Single females or males execute their shared task through community. Each, whether married or single, contributes to the whole, and the whole is deficient without the other. Neither finds their value independent of the other but in relation to the other in marriage or in community.

Just as Genesis 1 reached its pinnacle in the creation of humanity on the sixth day, Genesis 2 arrives at its apex in the creation of the woman (Reid). The man discovers a shared humanity in her. This is not only a *shared* flesh ("bone of my bone, flesh of my flesh" in Genesis 2:23) but a *union* of flesh ("one flesh" in Genesis 2:24), an intimacy of both heart and body. The text emphasizes both differentiation and unity; males and females are different but *one in flesh, vocation, and identity*. There is no rank in this relationship. Authority is never mentioned in Genesis 1–2 except the dominion *they share* over the creation. In fact, according to 1 Corinthians 7:2–5, husbands and wives have *mutual authority* over each other's bodies.

Echoing Genesis 2, Paul says the woman is the "glory of man" (1 Corinthians 11:7). Some suggest "glory" means "reflection" or mirror such that the woman reflects the image of the man because she was created in the image of God just as he was. Others think this means women are a lower rank than men. Some even think Paul denies their creation in the image of God. However, it does not *necessarily* imply such. Just as Adam fathered Seth in "his image," Seth nevertheless bore, at the same time, the image and glory of God (Genesis 5:1–3). In a similar way, because the woman is sourced from the man, the woman is also the glory and image of God just as every male born in the image of Adam is *also* the glory of God. *She is not less*; she shares human identity with man.

She is not less; *she is actually more*. As the glory of man, she brings something to humanity that men cannot bring (Westfall). Women bring glory to men and God through their participation in the mission of God just as men bring glory to God and glory to women through their participation in the mission of God. In other words, women are not less than men—*men cannot fully participate in the mission of God* without women, whether in marriage or in shared community. In this sense, woman is the glory of man because woman was created from man and for man in order to bring humanity to its full complementarity, which is necessary for the pursuit of the human vocation. Neither is independent of the other in the Lord, and all men come through women. And both come from God (1 Corinthians 11:11–12).

She is the glory of man because, partnered with her, man is able to fully participate in God's mission, whether as single persons in community or as married couples. *She is the culmination of creation, which is man's glory* (and God's glory as well). It was a glorious moment where the man discovered an *ally corresponding to himself*—one who will serve in the trenches of God's mission with him and share life with him as a missional partner. Genesis 2 moves from human incompleteness (solitary *adam*) to human completeness (man and woman as human community). The creation of the woman brings humanity to its completeness. This is man's glory—to discover in the woman the fullness of humanity. Together, man and woman are the glory and image of God even as each one is *personally* the glory and image of God.

Nowhere in the story of Genesis or the Hebrew Bible is the man ever called the "head" of the woman. Authority is not a word used to describe the relationship between men and women in Genesis 1–2. The relationship is one of source, which is balanced in the history of humanity by the fact that women are the source of men because men come into the world through women. That, it seems to me, is the meaning of headship in 1 Corinthians 11:2–16. *It is not about authority but relationality.* The first woman came from man, but now all men come through women, and both come from God. There is balance and mutuality. Headship does not entail authority or rank but relationship (Westfall).

East of Eden

Genesis 3 provides the reason the man and woman were expelled from the garden of Eden. They both ate the forbidden fruit. Whether the woman's role in this has any bearing on how men and women carry out their shared vocation I will consider in Part 6. For the moment, I will focus on the consequences of this expulsion.

The characters in this narrative are introduced in successive order: first the serpent, then the woman, and finally the man (Genesis 3:1–7). When God confronts them, the order is reversed: first the man, then the woman, lastly the serpent (Genesis 3:8–14). The serpent is the hinge that moves back through the series: serpent, woman, and man (Genesis 3:15–19).

(1) Serpent
   (2) Woman
      (3) Man
      (3) Man
   (2) Woman
(1) Serpent
   (2) Woman
      (3) Man

This literary device brings symmetry to the account that culminates in the consequences for each in the world east of Eden. Though some suggest God recognized male authority when God addressed Adam first, *no authority relationship is explicit in the text*. To *infer* such is unnecessary and depends upon importing ideas from elsewhere. Moreover, God did not ask Adam about Eve but only about himself. God addressed Eve on an equal basis with Adam and did not speak to Eve about Adam. God accentuated their *shared and equal responsibility*. There is no hint that one was *more* responsible than the other. The serpent addressed *both* the man and the woman (plural verbs in Genesis 3:1–5), *both* were present (the man was "with" the woman; Genesis 3:6), *both* the woman and the man ate the fruit, *both* are responsible, and God addressed *both* the man and the woman individually.

God addressed the serpent first and cursed it by demoting the animal among God's creatures and putting enmity between the serpent and humanity. The result, due to the introduction of moral chaos, is the mutual harm animals and humans will do to each other.

Then God addressed the woman. God multiplied the anxiety of birthing children as she would now live east of Eden. Another result, due to the introduction of moral chaos, is some kind of struggle between women and men.

Finally, God addressed the man. God cursed the ground which created an anxious struggle for food in place of Eden's gracious provision. Another result, due to the introduction of moral chaos, is toil and death.

The crucial text is Genesis 3:16b, whose meaning is highly disputed. Traditionally, many have seen it as the *beginning of divinely prescribed* male leadership (Sewell, Fuqua). Others, paralleling it with Genesis 4:7, suggest it refers to the *woman's desire for control* and man's oppressive response, which is an abuse of God's intent for male leadership (Foh, Grudem). In this view, the "battle of the sexes" began here and *distorted* God's design for men to exercise a benevolent authority over women. Others believe, again in light of the parallel with Genesis 4:7, this is the *beginning of male authority itself as a negative consequence* of the introduction of moral chaos (Payne, Bartlett).

While Genesis 4:7 is instructive, there is another option. The woman "turns" toward Adam for sexual fulfillment and conceiving children as part of their vocation. This is supported by ancient translations, patristic writers, and some contemporary scholars. In other words, women will "turn" toward their husbands in some way (sexually, devoutly, or submissively) and men will rule them. If we put this in a sexual context, it fits well with the first two lines of Genesis 3:16. Given life east of Eden, the anxiety and toil of women are increased in birthing children. Carol Meyers translates it this way:

> I will make great your toil and many your pregnancies;
> with hardship shall you have children;
> your turning is to your man/husband,
> and he shall rule/control you [sexually].

If we think of this turning or desiring as sexual, then the male mastery or control is about sex (Reid). Due to moral chaos, the man rules the woman sexually. We see the evidence of this power in objectification, pornography, rape, sexual harassment, and domestic violence. Due to moral chaos, when the woman turns to or desires the man sexually in order to participate in the human vocation, the sexual struggle between men and women erupts and distorts the Edenic intent.

The Hebrew term for "desire" or "turning," except for Genesis 4:7, only occurs elsewhere in Song of Songs 7:10. The Song of Songs offers an Edenic picture of the relationship between a husband and wife. This reverses distorted male rule by giving the woman in the Solomonic drama *full mutuality*. In this renewal of

Eden, the woman says, "his *desire* is for me." Indeed, she takes the lead in the sexual relationship; she speaks, invites, and "seizes" him (3:4; 8:1–2). Thus, the Song of Songs transforms the power relationship in Genesis 3:16b into a relational mutuality that restores the divine intent of Eden. Whatever the meaning of Genesis 3:16b in its context, the poet in the Song of Songs envisions the restoration of the Edenic sexual harmony. As such, *the Song of Songs is a reversal of Genesis 3:16b* (Barton).

What existed before the introduction of moral chaos was not a form of ruling but the mutuality of human sexuality (which is what exists in Christ as well, 1 Corinthians 7:4). Genesis 3:16b is the corruption of sexuality (which is assumed in the "one flesh" language of Genesis 2) rather than the corruption of a prior relationship of authority or rank (which is never mentioned in Genesis 1–2). In other words, the human vocation, due to the introduction of moral chaos, generates an anxious sexual struggle between men and women as they pursue their shared vocation.

Immediately after these pronouncements, "the man named his wife Eve" (Genesis 3:20). The man did *not* "name" his wife in Genesis 2 but recognized *their mutuality* that makes "one flesh" possible: *ish* (man) and *ishah* (woman) or "bone of my bone and flesh of my flesh." With the introduction of moral chaos, the man *names* the woman. This is an exercise of authority over her analogous to his exercise of dominion over the animals. But this exercise of authority over the woman comes in the context of a *disordered* world. Nevertheless, it honors the woman as the "mother of all living," which is the point of the next move in the Genesis narrative. Even as the man begins to exercise a domineering authority, God does not abandon the woman.

In Genesis 4:1, Eve appears east of Eden as one who is already subverting the "man will rule over the woman" script of Genesis 3:16b (Nugent). Just as Adam named her, *she names a man.* The woman has her own authority to name her son, whom the text calls a "man" (*ish*).

Eve produced (*qanah*) a man (*ish*) with God's help. Cain (*qayin*) is the noun form of *qanah*, and Cain is called an *ish* rather than a child, a human, or a boy. Eve gave birth to a *man*, and *named the man*. Just as Adam named the woman "Eve," in a moment of reversal Eve names a man (*ish*) whom she has brought into the world with God's help. This is God's grace to Eve. It is her pushback against male domination. Women are empowered to participate in the mission of God as part of the human vocation. Their participation, however, is not limited to childbearing. Still, childbearing is the way the whole world will one day be redeemed as God will send the Son to be born through Mary in order to redeem the world (Galatians 4:4).

THE PEOPLE OF ISRAEL

The story of women in Israel confronts us with some troubling realities. Women lived within an Ancient Near Eastern culture dominated by men. This shows up in the Hebrew Bible in various ways, including the violent abuse of women (Judges 19–20). At the same time, Carol Meyers suggests there is a trajectory within the Hebrew Bible that frees women from that domination in ways that empower and protect them. Further, she argues "patriarchy" is not the best model for understanding ancient Israel and describes Israelite culture as more patrilineal (inheritance comes through the male line) and heterarchical (different and overlapping spheres of power) than patriarchal. However, it is beyond my scope to address the numerous questions about the status of women in Israel. Instead, I will focus on a few aspects that connect to my purpose.

I often minimized, dismissed, or neglected the story of women in Israel because that story was irrelevant to the church's blueprint. I overlooked, however, how the theology of creation is still applicable to Israel. Does God ever empower women with gifts and authorize women to act in ways that violate the divine intent in creation? If not, then nothing women do in Israel that God authorizes violates whatever God intended in creation. Therefore, let us pay attention to how women served God in Israel by which the church may learn about its own life through Israel's example precisely because the church participates in the *renewal of creation* and continues the story of Israel itself.

As a beginning, here is an important fact. *No text in the Hebrew Bible silences women in its assemblies.*

Miriam (Exodus 15:20–21; Numbers 12:1–15; Micah 6:1–8)

The first prophet named in the Torah is Abraham (Genesis 20:7). The second is Aaron (Exodus 7:1). *The third is Miriam* (Exodus 15:20). The fourth is Moses (Deuteronomy 18:15). That is an impressive list. She also makes another notable list, "I sent before you," God says, "Moses, Aaron, and Miriam" (Micah 6:4).

The Exodus was led by Moses, Aaron, and Miriam. This sibling trio was commissioned to lead the people of God ("I sent"), and God gifted them for this mission. *All three were prophets.* All three were *apostles* to the people (the Septuagint uses a form of *exapostellō,* "I send out").

While Moses occupied a more elevated position than everyone else because he was "entrusted with all [God's] house" and spoke "face to face" with God, Aaron and Miriam were prophets to whom God spoke in dreams and visions (Numbers 12:7–9). Both Aaron and Miriam were spokespersons for God and served as Moses's co-workers in leading Israel. When Miriam and Aaron questioned Moses's marriage, God distinguished between how God spoke to Moses ("face to face") and how God spoke to his siblings (dreams and visions). God affirmed Aaron and Miriam as authentic prophets who heard and spoke the word of the Lord but punished Miriam for questioning Moses. She had made the accusation (literally, "*she* spoke against Moses," 12:1); her punishment was not because she was a woman but because she spoke against Moses. She was no more punished for being a woman than Korah was punished for being a man (Numbers 16). Rather, they both spoke against Moses.

Her leadership is highlighted in Exodus 15:20–21. Once Israel crossed the sea, Miriam took her tambourine and, with other women, played and danced before the Lord. Miriam, Exodus 15:21 says, "sang to them" (literally, "answered them"). She responded to the song just sung in Exodus 15:1–19.

Our English translations do not typically specify to whom "them" refers. Most people, in my experience, assume it refers to the women. The Hebrew text is clear: "them" is *masculine*. Miriam sang to the men (probably the whole congregation of men and women). Moreover, the imperative (command), "Sing to the Lord," is also *masculine* plural. She invites, commands, and leads the men. In other words, Miriam led Israel's first communal worship after its exodus. She led the whole assembly of Israel and *commanded* the men to sing. It was the "whole congregation" of Israel that journeyed through the wilderness (Exodus 16:1; cf. 12:6, 47). This was God's church (assembly) in the wilderness (Acts 7:38). A *worshipping assembly* celebrated their liberation from Egyptian slavery, and Miriam led it. "Under the law of Moses," Lipscomb wrote in 1907, "Miriam sung and improvised and led in the song. (Ex. 15:20.)," and "the same rule governs [in 1 Corinthians 14:34] as in 'the law' (of Moses)." To extrapolate from Lipscomb's point, if Miriam led men in singing and if the same "law" governs the assembly in 1 Corinthians 14:34, then for women to lead singing is no violation of 1 Corinthians 14:34.

After their exodus from Egypt, a female prophet led Israel in the worship.

Deborah (Judges 4–5)

The *next named prophet* in the Hebrew Bible is Deborah. Two of the first five prophets in the Bible are women.

Deborah is also the second judge named in the book of Judges. She is the *only* named person in Judges recognized as *both a prophet and a judge*. Only Samuel in 1 Samuel would have that same distinction.

Judges were official leaders. The book of Joshua identifies Israel's leadership as elders, officers, and judges (Joshua 8:33; 23:2; 24:1). Moreover, judges between the conquest and the monarchy are *God's representatives* among the people. "God raised up judges, who delivered" Israel from various oppressors. God sent these judges as spokespersons (Judges 2:16–18). Moreover, "judges and officials" were appointed throughout Israel in all its towns, and they *exercised authority* through their judgments (Deuteronomy 16:18–20). Their authority is *paralleled with the authority of priests* (Deuteronomy 17:12).

Consequently, when Deborah performs the official task of judging, God raised her up to *serve in a place of authority* over Israel. Her function is analogous to Samuel who was also a prophet that judged disputes (1 Samuel 3:20–4:1) in the same region as Deborah (1 Samuel 7:15–17). Samuel followed in the footsteps of Deborah.

Significantly, the text pictures Deborah as one who *exercises authority* in her context *analogous* to Moses (Davis).

Action	Moses	Deborah
Judge	Exodus 18:13	Judges 4:4
People came to them	Exodus 18:13	Judges 4:5
Proclaimed word of the Lord	Exodus 7:16	Judges 4:6
Prophets	Deuteronomy 18:5	Judges 4:4
Pronounced blessings	Exodus 39:43	Judges 5:24
Pronounced curses	Deuteronomy 27:15	Judges 5:23
Both had military generals	Joshua	Barak
Both instructed Israel about how to defeat her enemies	Exodus 14:14	Judges 4:6
Lord caused enemies in chariots to panic and flee	Exodus 14:24	Judges 4:15
God's victory told in prose	Exodus 14	Judges 4
God's victory told in poetry	Exodus 15	Judges 5
Led Israel in victory songs	Exodus 15:1	Judges 5:1

This comparison affirms Deborah's sanctioned authority. She was an honored prophet. She spoke, and her words came true. Her song, celebrating the victory, takes up the whole of chapter five.

Some minimize her authority. A few think she only judged and prophesied in private. But the "palm of Deborah" is a public place where she "judged" Israel; they came to her "for judgment." This is a public forum analogous to Samuel. Some observe that she is not mentioned in Hebrews 11 even though Barak is, but neither are Miriam or Rachel mentioned while Rahab and Sarah are. It is impossible to draw any sure inference about the omission of Deborah. In any case, it does not detract from Deborah's significance any more than it detracts from Miriam or the many male leaders also absent.

Others think she was a substitute for weak men who refused to lead. Why is Barak commended in Hebrews 11 if he was so weak that God had to choose a woman? He is in the roll call of faith because he *obeyed Deborah*. God raised up Deborah, like *all judges*, to deliver Israel. Even *if* male weakness *occasioned* her ministry (which I don't think is the case), God invested a woman with the *authority* (1) to judge, (2) speak as a prophet who *represents God*, and (3) *co-lead* a military action. *She exercised both religious and political authority.* She "summoned" Barak to her presence and gave him a command from the Lord. God spoke *authoritatively* through her. Barak submitted to Deborah's word as God's representative and followed her instructions.

Whatever we might say about the circumstances, even though nothing in the text indicates this was an anomaly (Miriam was a prophet-leader), it is not a violation of God's intent in creation for a woman to *exercise authority* over men as a judge and prophet. "Since God himself raised up Deborah as a judge, and that which God chooses to do cannot be *intrinsically wrong*," Davis argues, "it cannot be intrinsically wrong for a woman to exercise authority over a man." Directly called by God, her ministry is affirmed. Her ministry did not subvert God's good creation order or else God would not have called her.

A woman exercised authority over men in Israel as judge and prophet.

Huldah (2 Chronicles 34:19–28)

When Judah began repairs on the temple around 630 B.C. and they discovered a book (Deuteronomy?) in its ruins, King Josiah charged his officials and Hilkiah the high priest to inquire of the Lord and seek intercession. To pray on behalf of the people is one of the functions of a prophet (Jeremiah 7:16; 11:14; 14:1; 42:1–6). Josiah sought both guidance and prayers. Significantly, *he sent them to Huldah rather than Jeremiah.*

Unlike other prophets in Chronicles, Huldah receives the longest introduction. She is the wife of Shallum, keeper of the wardrobe, who probably kept the priestly garments (cf. Leviticus 8:7–9). Huldah may have been a temple prophet connected with its service. Consequently, Josiah asked her about the authenticity and significance of the book recently discovered in the temple repairs.

A woman, *independent of her husband*, delivered God's word to the king of Judah through God's high priest. Her message, which bears the authority of God ("thus says the Lord"), was two-fold (2 Chronicles 34:24–28): God announced (1) the coming disaster on the temple and subsequent deportation and (2) a word of mercy for Josiah whose eyes would not see the disaster. Moreover, she affirmed the veracity of the text about which they asked. In effect, *Huldah confirmed the discovered book was Scripture*. She authorized the use of this book as Scripture for Josiah and his high priest.

Huldah spoke with authority and her message was typical for Israel's writing prophets. Huldah, like Jeremiah, spoke a word of judgment and hope.

A female prophet spoke the words of God to Judah's highest religious and political authorities, the high priest and the king of Judah.

Heralds

Psalm 68 celebrates the movement of Israel from Egypt (v. 7) to Sinai (v. 8) and then to Canaan (vv. 9–14) whereupon God ascends the throne on Mount Zion in Jerusalem (vv. 15–18). Paul uses Psalm 68 to describe the ascension and enthronement of Jesus in Ephesians 4:8. Jesus rose from the grave, ascended to the throne, and *gave gifts* to the church through the pouring out of the Holy Spirit.

Psalm 68:25 places women in the liturgical procession of singers and musicians to the temple. Like Miriam, young women play tambourines as part of the procession. They *visibly* participated in Israel's public worship in the assembled congregation.

Psalm 68:11 reads: "The Lord gives the command; great is the company of those who bore the tidings" (KJV). In the Septuagint "bore the tidings" is the same word as in the New Testament for "preaching the gospel" (*euangelizomenoi*). They proclaimed good news as evangelists.

Significantly, in Hebrew, the word is *feminine*. Psalm 68 envisions a *great company of women* who declare the good news (ASV, ESV, NRSV, NIV). In the light of Paul's application of Psalm 68 to the ascension of Christ, we hear an echo of the gifting of women to preach the gospel when God poured out the Spirit and gifted the church with a variety of functions. This included prophets and evangelists (*euangelistas*; preachers of the gospel) in Ephesians 4:11. Indeed, both men and women preached the gospel (*euangelizomenoi*) when persecution scattered them (Acts 8:1–4).

Women preach the gospel.

Levitical Singers

When Nehemiah finished building the wall, he appointed gatekeepers to watch over the city and Levitical singers to serve in the temple (Nehemiah 7:1). Most of these singers were descendants of Asaph (among other families; 1 Chronicles 25), who was one of the leading musicians and a prophet from the time of David (1 Chronicles 16:7; 2 Chronicles 29:30) as well as the author of several Psalms (50, 73). The Levitical singers led the worship of Israel (2 Chronicles 5:12; 35:15).

Nehemiah's singers included "male and female" (Nehemiah 7:67; cf. 2 Samuel 19:35; Ezra 2:65; 2 Chronicles 35:25). Women were part of the Levitical choir that led the temple worship. Women are not singled out in 1 Chronicles 25 due to the emphasis on the patrilineal and genealogical character of the report. This does not, however, exclude women as we see from Chronicles,

Ezra, and Nehemiah as well as the procession in Psalm 68. We might remember also the original prophet singer and worship leader, Miriam. In fact, Heman's three daughters are singers as well (1 Chronicles 25:5–6, note "all" includes the daughters).

It is also important to recognize the prophetic function of singers in the Levitical choir. Singing was a form of prophesying (1 Chronicles 25:1).

Women served on Israel's Levitical praise team.

Sages in Israel

Several unnamed women in Israel were sages or wise women—one from Tekoa and another from Beth-maacah (2 Samuel 14:1–20; 20:14–22). These women are mentioned because their words impacted history in momentous ways. Male leaders listened to their advice. Given the occasional nature of these texts, female sages probably populated the villages of Israel beyond what is known in the Hebrew Bible.

Also, wisdom is personified as a woman in Israel's literature. Proverbs 8 is the classic expression. She speaks to men so that they might gain knowledge and understanding (8:4, 9–10). In fact, she publicly heralds (*kerussō* in Greek) or preaches wisdom from the mountain peaks (8:1). Her "voice" is heard. The metaphor of a woman heralding or speaking knowledge to the community makes little sense if that never happened in the life of Israel. In addition, the woman of valor in Proverbs 31, who was engaged in public life as well as home life, is herself the personification of wisdom. This reflects the significant role female sages had in Israel's communal life.

Women served their communities, including men, as wise sages.

Queen Esther

While there were other queens in the history of Israel, Esther stands out because a whole book tells her courageous story as the queen of Persia. It explains the origins of the Feast of Purim. That feast is an *addition* to the Torah. Esther *authorized* it. Esther *added* to the Torah.

Esther "gave full written authority" to inaugurate the feast and provided its regulations (Esther 9:29–31). In Hebrew, "gave" is both *singular and feminine*. Though Mordecai was associated with the action, Esther was responsible. "The command of Esther," the Bible says, "fixed these practices of Purim" (Esther 9:32).

Esther exercised both political and religious authority over Israel.

Priests

Women are prophets, worship leaders, singers, musicians, judges, sages, and queens in the story of Israel but not priests.

In one sense, everyone in Israel was a priest as part of the "priestly kingdom and holy nation" (Exodus 19:6). However, only males from the tribe of Levi who descended from Aaron were qualified for the *sacrificial* priesthood, and there were further qualifications pertaining to marriage, age, physical health, and ceremonial cleanliness. *Most* Jewish males were *excluded* from the priesthood.

Though women were not priests in Israel, they did participate in its religious life. Women were active in support roles such as weaving garments, preparation of meals, and maintenance of cultic areas (P. Bird). Women were attendants at the tabernacle (Exodus 38:8; 1 Samuel 2:22). As noted previously, women participated in the liturgy through music and dance. Moreover, individual women initiated sacrifices, prayers, and vows (1 Samuel 1:10–16; 2:1–10, 24–28) in addition to performing rituals required for cleanliness (Leviticus 12:18–8; 13:29–39; 15:19–29). In effect, *women were neither unseen nor unheard in Israel's religious contexts.*

The priestly situation changed, however, in the Messianic age. Just as the Spirit was poured out on the Gentiles, the enslaved, and women at Pentecost, so the move *from the Levitical priesthood to the priesthood of Melchizedek* enlarges the scope of priesthood. All female believers are priests (1 Peter 2:9; Revelation 1:6; 5:10). In the light of Pentecost, the Spirit empowers women for priestly service. They, too, like males, offer spiritual sacrifices to God (Hebrews 13:16; 1 Peter 2:5).

Though the rationale is unstated, the sanctity of blood probably excluded women from the priesthood due to the menstrual cycle. This also precluded regular participation in the Levitical system. Moreover, the exclusion of women from the priesthood was common practice in the Ancient Near East (P. Bird). *Nevertheless, it is nowhere stated women are excluded because of male authority over women.* More than likely, it was due to the function of purity codes and blood rituals. Similar to how eunuchs were excluded from temple service but are now fully included in the Messianic kingdom (Isaiah 56:4; Acts 8:26–40), women are now included in the priesthood though they were excluded from priesthood in the Mosaic covenant. Whatever the rationale (and every rationale is an inference), *the order of Melchizedek replaced the Levitical order* (Hebrews 5, 7). This involves a different set of considerations and qualifications.

Though excluded from the Levitical priesthood (along with *most* males, including eunuchs), the presence of female prophets in Israel means women assumed *authoritative speaking functions* within the religious life of Israel. The daughters of Sarah through faith in Jesus the Messiah, however, are *no longer* excluded from priesthood in the Messianic era.

Summary
- Women are *never silenced* in the assemblies of Israel.
- Miriam, a female prophet, *led Israel in worship.*
- Deborah *exercised authority* over men in Israel as judge and prophet.

- Huldah *exercised prophetic authority* over the king and high priest of Judah.
- Women *preached* the gospel.
- Women served on Israel's *praise team*.
- Women served as *wise sages* in the villages of Israel.
- Wisdom, personified as a woman, heralds her message and *teaches men*.
- Esther *exercised both political and religious authority* over Israel.

If God blessed women to serve in these ways and God does not violate God's own intent in creation, then the exercise of political and religious authority over men is not inherently wrong or contrary to God's design in creation. Let that point sink in for a moment.

THE MINISTRY OF JESUS

In the Gospel of Luke, the ministry of Jesus is defined by Isaiah 61:1–2 (quoted in Luke 4:18–19).

> The Spirit of the Lord is upon me,
>> because he has anointed me
>>> to bring good news to the poor.
> He has sent me to proclaim release to the captives,
>> and recovery of sight to the blind,
>>> to let the oppressed go free,
>>>> to proclaim the year of the Lord's favor.

Jesus ministered to the oppressed. The Gospel of Luke emphasizes the inclusion of the poor, tax collectors, Gentiles, sinners, Samaritans, and women. It highlights the presence and participation of women in the ministry of Jesus more than any other Gospel. That interest extends into Acts, Luke's second volume.

While it is legitimate to see Luke's emphasis on women as sharing in the missional meaning of the ministry of Jesus to release the oppressed (Witherington), Allen Black suggests a larger backdrop. Given how Isaiah 40–66 provides the theological frame for Luke's understanding of salvation and the renewal of Israel, Isaiah's identification of "sons" and "daughters" speaks to the full inclusion of women (Isaiah 43:6–7; 49:22; 60:4). In the quotation of Joel 2 at Pentecost and throughout Acts, Luke highlights the inclusion of both "men and women" (Acts 2:18; 5:14; 8:3; 8:12; 22:4). *Everyone* who calls upon the Lord shall be saved, and everyone who participates in the renewal of Israel is gifted with the Holy Spirit for the sake of mission (Acts 2:38; 5:32).

When we place the ministry of Jesus in the context of Israel's renewal, which culminates in new creation, we see the significance of women in the ministry of Jesus. His practices often pushed beyond the boundaries of first century Judaism and Greco-Roman culture. As Jesus broke those barriers, he bore witness to the prospect of new creation that broke into the world through his ministry and the outpouring of the Spirit in Acts 2. For brevity, I will highlight only four aspects of Jesus's ministry in Luke.

The Birth of the Messiah

Second century Christians recognized how the birth of the Messiah through Mary reversed the chaos that came through Eve. Since the world was plunged into moral chaos through a woman's initial act, Irenaeus reasoned, it was also rebirthed through another woman's initial obedience. God favored Mary among all women (Luke 1:28, 42) as the new Eve. Through her, God inaugurated a redemptive path for the renewal of Israel. Respect and honor, as Elizabeth proclaimed, belong to the "mother of my Lord" (Luke 1:43), and generations upon generations have called her "blessed" (Luke 1:48).

Moreover, Mary is the model of an *obedient disciple*. As the new Eve, who will become the mother of all who live through the Messiah just as Eve is the "mother of all living," Mary receives the Messiah in her womb and hears the messianic word of promise and liberation. She obeys. "Here I am," Mary responded, "I am the servant of the Lord, let it be with me according to your word" (Luke 1:38).

Encountering Elizabeth, Mary burst out in a song that serves as an anthem for her son's Messianic mission. This song of reversal plays out in the ministry of Jesus. Speaking of the future as if it has already happened, she prophesied (Luke 1:52–54):

> [God] has brought down the powerful from their thrones,
>> and lifted up the lowly;
> he has filled the hungry with good things,
>> and sent the rich away empty.
> He has helped his servant Israel,
>> in remembrance of his mercy.

Mary's song subverts the self-interests of the rich and powerful for the sake of the poor and powerless. This is God's redemptive work that rescues the people of God from their oppressive enemies (Luke 1:71). Through Mary, God raised up a "mighty savior" who will sit on the throne of David and fulfill the promise God made to Abraham (Luke 1:55, 69).

When Mary and Joseph took their baby to the temple, they encountered the prophet Anna. Earlier Simeon, "guided by the Spirit," praised God for the gift of seeing the one who would be a light to the Gentiles (Luke 2:25–32). Unlike Simeon, *Luke specifically identifies Anna as a prophet*. This elderly widow had dedicated herself to "fasting and prayer night and day" in the temple for decades. Recognizing the Messiah, she "began to praise God and to speak about the child to all who were looking for the redemption of Jerusalem" (Luke 2:36–38). As a temple prophet, she spoke (the same verb as in 1 Corinthians 14:34) to everyone, including men ("all" is *masculine*), who sought God's redemptive grace. She spoke in holy, *public* spaces to men where Israel gathered for worship, teaching, and prayer. This female prophet celebrated the arrival of the Messiah by proclaiming the hope of the gospel. *Anna preached the gospel* as she spoke about Jesus to the people.

But, some might ask, why did God incarnate as a male? Is this an expression of male authority over women?

Perhaps we don't know why God incarnated as a male. We are never told explicitly. Nevertheless, given that God decided to become human, God had to become a *particular* human being. Consequently, God must dwell in the flesh in a particular geographical location, at a particular time in history, and as a particular ethnicity and gender. We might imagine many reasons why God came as a male from cultural accommodation to his role in Israel as the Davidic king. But the point is not that God in the flesh represents only male Jews descended from David who live in Palestine in the first century but that God in the flesh represents *all humans*. The incarnate Christ is the image of God, and everyone—Jew or Gentile, male or female, enslaved or free—is called to conform to the image of the Messiah. The Christological goal—conformation to the image of Christ—includes both men and women. The particularity of the incarnation, necessary for authentic existence as a human being, does not limit its significance for all human beings. Because God incarnated as a male does not mean women are less than men, or that men have a greater value or responsibility than women.

Whatever reasons we might assign to God's incarnation as a male, they do not imply that only males are gifted for leadership any more than God's incarnation as a Jew implies that only Jews are gifted for leadership.

Disciples of Jesus (Luke 8:1–3, 10:38–42)

Luke 8:1–3 summarizes the ministry of Jesus who "proclaim[s] and bring[s] the good news of the kingdom of God." In a succinct but poignant manner, the Greek text literally says, "the twelve with him and women." Clearly, the twelve were a distinct group who were invested with a *unique* function in the renewal of Israel, but to add "women" indicates the importance of this entourage, which included Mary Magdalene, Joanna (the wife of Herod's steward), Susanna, and "many others." This was an unusual but significant practice: unmarried and married women attached to a group of non-relative males. It was a discipleship group engaged in ministry. The women are patrons who provided for the ministry of Jesus out of their own resources. The women *served* Jesus and his apostles. The verb (from *diakoneō*) is a cognate for the noun deacon. The women functioned as *the Messiah's diaconate.*

Strikingly, for first century Jewish culture, Martha welcomed Jesus to her home when usually one is welcomed by a male host (Luke 10:38–42). Also extraordinary is the description of Mary as a disciple who "sat at the Lord's feet and listened" to his teaching. Jesus transcended a social barrier by calling women as his disciples and accepting the invitation of a female host.

The story emphasizes women, the tasks of ministry (*diakonein* in 10:40), and the supreme value of discipleship. Sometimes women are assigned tasks like serving tables (as if their primary role is homemaking and cooking) rather than recognizing their full status as disciples who are invited to learn at the feet of the Messiah. Mary was commended for her interest in learning. Jesus did not oppose Martha; her choice was good and useful. But he blessed Mary's choice as a better one. Unfortunately, the church seems to encourage women to serve in the role of Martha while Mary's choice is seldom valued.

At Table with Jesus (Luke 22:24–30)

The Messianic mission is embodied at the table of the Lord. At the Last Supper, Jesus proclaimed his mission through his own self-giving. "This is my body," Jesus said, "which is given for you," and this blood is "poured out for you" (Luke 22:19–20). Jesus served by giving himself for our sakes.

At that same table, the disciples argued about greatness. They debated their relative positions in the kingdom of God. They pursued status instead of self-giving service. In response, Jesus contrasted his reign with the kingdoms of the nations. While their kings seek control, power, and authority (*exousiazontes*) as they dominate and rule (*kurieuousin*, lord over) their subjects, those who sit on thrones in the kingdom of God are not so oriented. They do not seek control, power, and authority; they imitate the servanthood of Jesus.

Servanthood is the heart of God. God served humanity in redemption, particularly through the incarnation, life, ministry, and death of Jesus. The incarnate Son served his disciples at the table ("I am among you as one who serves" [*diakonōn*]). This service is no mere blip on the screen. Rather, Jesus will serve humanity at the table in the new heaven and new earth. "Blessed are those slaves whom the master finds alert when he comes," Jesus said, "truly I tell you, he will fasten his belt and have them sit down to eat, and he will come and serve (*diakonēsei*) them" (Luke 12:37).

God conferred on Jesus a kingdom, and Jesus governs this kingdom through service. In the same way, Jesus conferred a kingdom on his disciples. However, their rule was not about control or power. Rather, they were to lead through self-giving service like Jesus did.

The table of Jesus is not about power and control. It is not about clerical authority. It is not about prerogatives and status. It is not about hierarchy. It is about mutual service and ministry. The table is where we serve each other. The table embodies the mutual love and respect we have for each other as we sit at the table with the host who served and continues to serves us.

Unfortunately, the table—like leadership in the worship assembly—has become the place for hierarchical positioning. In some traditions, only clergy may serve the table. In others, only men may serve the table. But disciples sit at the table as servants, not authoritarians, hierarchicalists, or males. *We sit at the table to serve each other rather than exercise authority over each other.* When we use the table to promote hierarchical values, we undermine the oneness of the people of God. All disciples are called to imitate Jesus by serving the table. *To deny an authentic disciple the opportunity to serve the table is to deny them the opportunity to imitate Jesus.* When women are excluded from serving the table of the Lord, it becomes a symbol of hierarchy that denies their status as servants in the kingdom of God.

Jesus offers a new way of thinking about power structures and hierarchical relationships. His own life subverts those structures so that no one exercises authority over another at the table in the kingdom of God. When people seek control and power, it subverts the reign of the Messiah who humbled himself as a servant among the people. The gospel of Jesus commends servant leadership. Sadly, control and power are more often at play among the people of God than self-giving service.

Resurrection Witnesses (Luke 24:1–12)

While the apostles scattered, the women gathered.

The women who had followed Jesus from Galilee gathered at *both the cross and the burial* (Luke 23:55). They were the last ones at the cross and the first at the tomb, which they found empty (Luke 24:1). Like Mary in the opening of Luke's Gospel, angelic messengers appear to women as the Gospel closes. As with Mary, the angels have a message. Whereas the word to Mary was about the future, the message delivered in the empty tomb was about new creation. At the cross, they saw the death of an innocent man, but at the empty tomb they realized his victory. The one who served humanity through his death is now vindicated by God through resurrection.

Women were the first to hear about it, experience it, and tell the "brothers" about it (Matthew 28:10; John 20:17). They are the first to see the risen Lord. They are the first disciples commissioned with the good news of the gospel, which is something all the Gospels record (Matthew 28:7, John 20:17–18, Luke 24:9; Mark 16:7). Mary Magdalene headed this delegation, and Joanna, Mary the mother of James, and "the other women with them" (Luke 24:11) accompanied her. These women served Jesus in Galilee and travelled with Jesus to Jerusalem. As the Gospel of Mark specifies, "they followed him." They were disciples of Jesus (Mark 15:41).

Two disciples ate with Jesus in Emmaus (Luke 24:13–35). We know the name of one, Cleopas. His wife's name was Mary (Clopas in John 19:25). Likely, Cleopas and Mary were walking home when they encountered Jesus and invited him to the table where Jesus revealed himself in the breaking of the bread. Probably, the first disciples to break bread with Jesus after his resurrection were a man and a woman.

Women were with Jesus from the cradle to the grave, from the cross to the empty tomb. A woman birthed him; a female prophet announced him; women followed him, supported him, and served him; women were present at his death and watched over his burial; and women were the first to see him after the resurrection; and women were the first to announce the gospel.

Male Apostles

Why did Jesus choose only male apostles? Women were included in the community of disciples, but they are not, like most other male disciples, appointed to the circle of the Twelve.

The number twelve symbolizes Israel's twelve patriarchs, the twelve sons of Jacob. The appointment of twelve male apostles established continuity between Israel and the ministry of Jesus. But does it mean more than that? Does it say something about male leadership for the church? That is never *explicitly* stated.

The twelve apostles were *free Jewish men* who had been with Jesus since his baptism. The apostleship of the Twelve was limited to those categories. The Twelve was an inherently limited number. Consequently, it says *nothing* about the nature and extent of gifted leadership within renewed Israel. Rather, it speaks to the continuity between Israel and the church reflected in the twelve patriarchs and the twelve apostles. If we regard the maleness of the apostolate as excluding women from leadership in the church, then we should also regard its Jewishness as excluding Gentiles from leadership in the church. No Gentile ever belonged to the Twelve.

The maleness of the apostolate does not undermine the wide range of gifts to both men and women. While the Twelve retained a unique honor in the Christian community, after Pentecost the gifting of the Spirit also extended to the enslaved as well as free, Gentile as well as Jew, and women as well as men. Leadership was no more limited to men than it was limited to Galilean Jews. The pouring out of the Spirit in Acts 2, in fulfillment of Joel's prophecy, enlarged the community of gifted leadership from *free Jewish me*n to *enslaved Gentile women*. While the Twelve remained a unique group, gifted leadership included more than them, including people called "apostles" who were not part of the Twelve (including Paul, James, Barnabas, and, as we will see, a woman named Junia).

EARLY CHURCH

For brevity, I will focus on Paul's letter to the saints in Rome. It has a lengthy section (Romans 12–15) that calls both men and women to embody the gospel. Also, Romans 16 contains the highest concentration of names and functions in the New Testament within at least three house churches in Rome.

House churches are a different contextual environment than contemporary church buildings (Banks; Finger). Congregations typically met in homes, which usually accommodated about fifty people. In that domestic setting, there is no stage, long hall, or audience. Rather, there is more likely a community gathered around a table or scattered across a room sitting on a floor. It is an intimate home gathering.

In that setting, "leadership" is an ambiguous term. On the one hand, as each one had a hymn, a prayer, or a teaching, they would lead in the sense that others would listen and be edified by the one who sang, prayed, or taught. On the other hand, leadership had no formal character by virtue of the setting. Informality and intimacy eroded barriers of perceived authority and formal structures that are so often created by contemporary worship spaces and architecture.

Rather than authority, what emerged in house church settings was giftedness. Giftedness is less likely to go unnoticed in a house church than in a large assembly where we look at the backs of each other's heads. Indeed, giftedness is where Paul begins in Romans when he turns his attention to how to live in community.

Gifts to the Body of Christ

As Paul turns from explaining the gospel in Romans 1–11 to how to embody it communally in Romans 12–15, he appeals to believers to present themselves to God as living sacrifices (Romans 12:1–2). This is addressed to all believers, both male and female, enslaved and free, Jew and Gentile, and rich and poor.

The church is "one body" with "many members." Since these members do not have the "same function," Paul recognizes a diversity of gifts. Romans 12:6–8 names them.

We have gifts (*charismata*) that differ according to the grace given to us:

- Prophecy, in proportion to faith
- Ministry (*diakonian*), in ministering (*diakonian*)
- Teacher (*didaskōn*), in teaching (*didaskalia*)
- Exhorter (*parakalō*), in exhortation (*paraklēsei*)
- Giver, in generosity
- Leader (*proistamenos*), in diligence
- Compassionate, in cheerfulness

These diverse gifts serve the unity of the body as well as its multiple functions. The gifts are given according to God's grace. Gender does not appear in Romans 12–15 as a distinguishing characteristic among the gifts.

The list is not exhaustive but illustrative. The gifts of Ephesians 4:11 and 1 Corinthians 12:28 include some of these but not all and *vice versa*. There is no exhaustive list of gifts in Paul's letters because each list is occasional and selective. Some gifts are absent from every list like music, art, cooking, and engineering.

It is important to notice how unrestricted these gifts are. There is no reason to think some of these gifts belong to Jews but others to Gentiles, or some belong to the enslaved but others to free people, or some to the rich but others to the poor. In the same way, given the context, there is no reason to think some belong to men but others to women, or that some gifts only belong to men. There are no explicit distinctions in the text *except the measure of grace* God has given.

Indeed, we know women exercised *these gifts*. For example, Philip's daughters *prophesied* (Acts 21:9). Priscilla with Aquilla *taught* Apollos (Acts 18:26). Tabitha had the gift of *generosity* (Acts 9:36). Phoebe was both a *diakonos* (servant or deacon) and a *prostatis* (leader, Romans 16:1–2). Mutual exhortation, encouragement, and edification are expected within the community of faith without distinction between male and female (1 Thessalonians 5:11, 14; Hebrews 3:13; 10:25). *No delimitation is evident.*

The *only* reason for introducing *any limitation* that excludes women from these gifts (including evangelist and teacher) is how 1 Timothy 2:12 is understood and applied. For some 1 Timothy 2:12 only applies to the assembly of the saints rather than to Bible classes or small groups, while for others it applies to any setting where there is a gathering of men and women for prayer, praise, or worship. This results in some practices like the following.

- We affirm the gift of teaching or prophecy for women but women cannot exercise that gift either publicly (or privately for some) when men are present. Consequently, as I applied it, women cannot lead a small group or teach a Bible class at the building when men are present.
- We affirm the gift of ministry, but women cannot exercise that gift over men. Consequently, as I applied it, women cannot have charge of a ministry in the church where they have authority over men, including nursery staffing and scheduling.
- We affirm the gift of exhortation, but women cannot exercise that gift when men are present. Consequently, as I applied it, women cannot encourage a group of men *as a speaker* in the assembly, small group, or Bible class.
- We affirm the gift of administration or leadership, but women cannot exercise this gift over men. Consequently, as I applied it, women cannot be treasurers for the community or vote in the business meetings of the congregation.

This only makes sense if one imports a particular understanding of 1 Timothy 2:12 into Romans 12. It thereby becomes the *lone text* which cuts a swath across the ministry of the church whereby women are excluded from or restricted in the use of the grace God has given them unlike any other differentiation in the community such as rich and poor, enslaved and free, and Jew and Gentile.

While 1 Corinthians 14:34–35, as typically applied, only regulates the public assembly, 1 Timothy 2:12 is used to regulate the use of gifts across all the ministries of the church. In this way, 1 Timothy 2:12 became a key mandate in the blueprint of the New Testament church. By the 1940s, it became a *required and essential mark of the true church* among churches of Christ. Thus, churches who invited women to participate in teaching, in forms of ministry over men, and in leadership over men, including serving the table in the assembly, were disloyal because they violated 1 Timothy 2:12—a blueprint detail.

That principle or *any such distinction*, however, is *missing in Romans*. Instead of authority and subordination, Paul emphasizes *mutuality*. This is evident when we pay attention to the "one another" (*allēlous*) statements in Romans 12–16.

- Romans 12:5   we are members *one of another*
- Romans 12:10   love *one another*
- Romans 12:10   outdo *one another* in showing honor
- Romans 12:16   live in harmony with *one another*
- Romans 13:8   love *one another*
- Romans 14:13   let us no longer pass judgment on *one another*
- Romans 14:19   let us pursue what makes for peace and *mutual* upbuilding
- Romans 15:5   live in harmony with *one another*
- Romans 15:7   welcome *one another*
- Romans 15:14   instruct *one another*
- Romans 16:16   greet *one another* with a holy kiss

I can hear my old self say, "Yes, of course, we want to live out these 'one another' exhortations. We should apply all of them in our congregations and to both male and female but with *one exception.*" 1 Timothy 2:12, then, limits the ways we practice these "one another" commands. But do the "one another" texts apply *everywhere but* in the assembly? Do they apply *everywhere except* when women are gathered with men to pray?

However, even though all women are commanded to be silent when the whole church gathers (as some read 1 Corinthians 14:34–35), the justification for women singing in the assembly is the *whole church* is commanded to sing to "one another" (Ephesians 5:19). That "one another" constitutes an exception to silence. Is not the whole church commanded to "instruct one another"? *Why is not "instruct one another" also an exception to the rule of silence in the assembly?* Why are not Ephesians 5:19 and Romans 15:14 *equally* applicable to the assembly?

Again, 1 Timothy 2:12 is imported to distinguish between gifts in a way that Paul does not do in Romans 12–16. In fact, Romans undercuts this application of 1 Timothy 2:12 if we give *full weight* to the language of both Romans 12 *and* 16.

A Cross Section of the Body of Christ.

Romans 16 is a window into the activities and ministry of the body of Christ in Rome around 58 A.D. Hutson identifies twenty-nine people; ten are women. Hutson also notes fourteen descriptors that characterize these believers, including six specific functions. Of those functions, women serve in six of them while men only serve in three. Hutson's chart summarizes the data.

Individuals in Rome (Romans 16:1–16)

Description	Men	Women
1. Deacon		Phoebe (16:1)
2. Patron		Phoebe (16:1)
3. Coworker	Aquila (16:3) Urbanus (16:9)	Prisca (16:3)
4. Host of a house church	Aquila (16:5) Aristobulus (16:10)? Narcissus (16:11)?	Prisca (16:5)
5. Laborer		Maria (16:6) Tryphaena (16:12) Tryphosa (16:12) Persis (16:12)
6. Apostle	Andronicus (16:7)	Junia (16:7)
7. Sister		Phoebe (16:2)
8. Kinsman/- woman	Andronicus (16:7) Herodion (16:11)	Junia (16:7)
9. Fellow-prisoner	Andronicus (16:7)	Junia (16:7)
10. Beloved	Epainetus (16:5) Ampliatus (16:8) Stachys (16:9)	Persis (16:12)
11. Approved	Apelles (16:10)	
12. Elect	Rufus(16:13)	
13. Members of a house-church (no descriptor)	Asyncritus (16:14) Phlegon (16:14) Hermes (16:14) Patrobas (16:14) Hermas (16:14)	Rufus' mother (16:13)
14. Members of another house- church (no descriptor)	Philologus (16:15) Nerea (16:15) Olympas (16:15)	Julia (16:15) Nerea's sister (16:15)

The diversity of functions and the number of people is impressive. Some of these ministries are carried out by women in other Pauline letters. For example, Nympha and Chloe hosts house churches in Laodicea and Corinth respectively (Colossians 4:15;

1 Corinthians 1:11), and Euodia and Syntyche were Paul's fellow-workers in Philippi (Philippians 4:2–3). For brevity, I will focus on three women in Romans 16.

Phoebe

Paul commends Phoebe. The significance of this is often underestimated. Typically, debate swirls around what it means to call her a *diakonon* (deacon or servant). But this overlooks something quite noteworthy. Why does Paul commend Phoebe *in this letter*?

Acquaintance with the Greco-Roman practice of letter writing and delivery is illuminating. For example, Paul did not physically write the words on the page. Tertius was "the writer of this letter" (Romans 16:22). In the same way, letters were sent by couriers. That Paul commended Phoebe suggests she was the courier. Couriers represented the author and often read the letter to the community addressed (e.g., Judas and Silas in Acts 15:30). Moreover, since they knew the mind of the author, they answered any questions the recipients might have. Phoebe served as Paul's representative to the Roman house churches. She probably visited the various house churches to read the letter and answer questions. In other words Phoebe—a woman—was probably the first to read the letter of Romans to a congregation and explain its meaning (McKnight, M. Bird). Let that sink in for a moment.

Phoebe was a gifted person. The phrase *"deacon of the church"* appears *only* here in the New Testament. If Paul wanted us to think of something more general like "servant," more non-specific language was available. Moreover, this does not refer to the church in general but to the specific congregation *at Cenchreae*. If this had been said of Philip rather than Phoebe, few would doubt this identified a *deacon* rather than a generic servant. Most likely, Phoebe was a member of a class of gifted persons which Paul characterized as the leadership of a congregation in Philippians 1:1, "bishops and deacons."

Moreover, she was a *prostatis*, which is one of the gifts mentioned in Romans 12. In fact, she was made (passive voice; perhaps appointed, Prohl) a *prostatis* by Paul. She was a leader, manager, or administrator of some sort. This is a cognate of the word Paul used to describe how bishops "manage" (*prostēnai*) the church of God in 1 Timothy 3:4 as well as leaders who "labor among you, and have charge (*proistamenous*) of you" in 1 Thessalonians 5:12. Apparently, she was a patron for Paul and others. This patronage probably included many different acts of service. For example, Walters illustrates the role of a *prostatis* in Greco-Roman culture through a contemporary patroness in Corinth named Junia Theodora. She provided hospitality, supplied financial support, and served as a diplomat for the city. Phoebe most likely had a similar function in the church at Cenchreae. *Phoebe was a recognized, even official (as we typically understand that), leader in the congregation.*

Prisca or Priscilla

Another function is *co-worker* or *co-laborer*. Paul identifies Priscilla as a *co-worker* in Romans 16. Also, Tryphena, Tryphosa, Maria, and Persis *labored* in the Lord (Rom 16:3, 6, 12). Paul often uses the term "labor" to describe his evangelistic and missionary activities (1 Corinthians 3:8; 15:10; Galatians 4:11; Philippians 2:16; Colossians 1:29; 1 Thessalonians 3:5). Further, Paul tells the Thessalonians to "respect those who work hard (labor) among" them (1 Thessalonians 5:12). Those who "labor in preaching and teaching" are worthy of honor (1 Timothy 5:17).

Further, "co-worker" describes Timothy (Romans 16:24; 1 Thessalonians 3:2; Philemon 1), Apollos (1 Corinthians 3:9), Titus (2 Corinthians 8:23), Epaphroditus (Philippians 2:25), Aristarchus (Colossians 4:10; Philemon 24), Mark (Colossians 4:10; Philemon 24), Justus (Colossians 4:10), Epaphras (Philemon 24), Demas (Philemon 24), Luke (Philemon 24), Euodia (Phil.

4:2) and Syntyche (Phil. 4:2). Paul does not hesitate to call women his co-workers or co-laborers (Byrd). In fact, in Paul's letters almost twenty percent of those so named are women (Scholer).

When we see a male name so designated we tend to think evangelist, missionary, or church leader but dismiss such designations for women. In 1 Corinthians 16:16 Paul instructs those in the house of Stephanas to *submit* to *every*, yes, "every fellow worker *(panti sunergounti)* and laborer *(kopionti)*." He did not exclude women from that category. In fact, Romans 16 identifies *five women* who fit that description. If there were female co-workers who labored in the congregation at Corinth, the house church was to *submit* to them. We have no reason to think women were not "fellow-workers and laborers" in Corinth since we know women served in these capacities in *both Philippi and Rome.*

Yes, submit—the same word that appears in Colossians 3:18 ("wives, be subject to your husbands") and Titus 3:1 ("subject to rulers and authorities"). If women were Paul's co-workers who labored in the Lord, what prevents us from acknowledging that house churches *submitted* to these women? *Only 1 Timothy 2:12 hinders us.*

Junia

Junia, along with Andronicus, was an apostle (Epp, Bauckham, Belleville, Walters's). The church has historically acknowledged this, though I had not until I was forced to think about it after reading Walters' article. I admit I was originally disturbed by this possibility. I found myself, however, unable to escape its significance, especially in light of the history of its interpretation.

The Greek Orthodox Church has always esteemed her as an apostle. She is commemorated every year on May 17 as "Apostle Junia." This is consistent with early Christian Greek writers from Origen (d. 254) to Chrysostom (d. 407). They understood the name designated a woman who was an apostle. In fact, this understanding was not questioned until Giles of Rome (d. 1316) suggested Junia was Junius, but Giles still regarded Junius as an apostle.

What does it mean to say that Junia was "outstanding (or prominent) among the apostles"? While some suggest it means "outstanding in the eyes of the apostles" (Burer, D. Wallace), it is the unanimous consensus of the early church (including those who spoke, read, and wrote Greek), the medieval church, and practically all ancient and modern commentators that it means *an outstanding member of the apostolic group.*

Paul does not mean "apostle" in any sense that would confuse Andronicus and Junia with the Twelve. The term apostle ("one who is sent") has a broader meaning analogous to missionaries, itinerant evangelists, or messengers from one church to another (2 Corinthians 8:23; Philippians 2:25). For example, Barnabas is called an apostle (Acts 14:14) as well as James, the brother of Jesus (Galatians 1:19).

Andronicus and Junia were probably husband and wife whose roots were deep in the Christian faith. They were Christians before Paul. Their story is intriguing—early believers, relatives of Paul, fellow-prisoners with Paul, and apostles (perhaps missionaries). I wish we knew more about them.

Yet, an objection emerges. All these descriptions and functions are appropriate for women, it is often argued, *as long as* their work is understood in a way that is consistent with 1 Timothy 2:12. While the diversity and breadth of these functions is extensive, whatever we say about how women served in these capacities is *delimited* by 1 Timothy 2:12. *That becomes the crux.* Perhaps we can't fully hear Romans 12 or 16 because we have already decided what 1 Timothy 2:12 means. Therefore, we impose it on Paul's letter to the Romans. I know I did for many years.

NEW HEAVEN AND NEW EARTH

The future state of humanity in the new heaven and new earth is a fixed hope, but its precise nature is unknown, especially the exact nature of our resurrection bodies. We too easily project our own desires on to it and shape it with our own speculative imaginations. Nevertheless, we are not clueless.

This glorified community is not a static accomplishment as if we attain perfected inertia and thus there is no more work, no more loving, no more growing, no more knowing, or no more connecting. Rather, the fullness of the kingdom of God involves a dynamic growth into the heart of God as well as a dynamic growth among the people of God. Similar to how God created in the beginning, the Triune God will recreate a dynamic reality that invites the redeemed community to pursue growth, intimacy, fellowship, and relationship within the new creation. We do not become identical Stepford human beings. Rather, the oneness, like the original creation, includes a diversity and a dynamism that reflects the reality of God who is loving Trinity.

Given our embodied existence in the resurrection, it seems *likely* that we will live as male and female in the new creation just as in the present good creation. However, the nature of our intimacy is deeper and more profound than what is experienced in sexual intimacy now. Presently, sexual intimacy is a window into our union with God and each other. In the new heaven and new earth, intimacy is a glorified union with God and each other. In this way, we will be like the angels (Matthew 22:30). Though male and female in body, we will not live as married persons for procreation and sexual intimacy. Rather, we will experience relational intimacy with the whole family of God analogous to what God experiences in God's own Triune life.

This is intimacy without fear, love without suspicion, and trust without doubt. There are no more barriers, no more tension between male and female, no more ethnic bigotry among peoples, no more snobbish class wars, and no more alienation or marginalization. The kingdom of God will experience community in a way that images the community of God's own life and participates in God's own communal life.

This new community constitutes the *eschatological assembly of God*. It is the church triumphant gathered around the throne of God for eternity in the new heaven and new earth. It is a multitude no one can count from every language, tribe, ethnicity, and nation (Revelation 7:9–17). There the whole assembly of God is gathered for praise and service upon the new earth.

Are women silent in that assembly? If they are silenced in the *here and now* in the assemblies of God, are they silenced in the *eschatological assembly*? Will women sing or offer a new song? Will they speak words of praise, testify to God's goodness to the assembly, or speak to God in the presence of the assembly? *Will women have to speak through men to God in that assembly?* Whatever the nature of our bodies upon the new earth, is it imaginable that women are silent in the eschatological assembly? Is it imaginable that women would not have direct, unmediated, and intimate access to God in the assembly?

I find that difficult to believe.

On the contrary, the future envisions men and women—however that differentiation is maintained and to whatever purpose—gathered around the throne without hierarchy sharing in the praise of God as each gives voice to their gratitude and awe before God. Each one will bring a hymn, a testimony, a praise, or whatever it might be before the throne of God as we worship and serve together throughout eternity.

I don't think women will be silent then, and if they are not silent then, why are they silenced now? As I, Melton, and Valentine have argued elsewhere, our present assemblies *participate in that eschatological assembly through the Spirit of God*. If they are not silent in the new heaven and new earth, there is no reason to silence them in our present experience of new creation as we participate in that eschatological assembly. The assemblies of Christ—the churches of Christ—worship in the eschatological assembly according to the order of the new creation and not according to the disorder of the present evil age. There is no reason . . . *except for 1 Timothy 2:12.*

PART 6

My Firewall

*I desire, then, that in every place [assembly?] the men should
pray, lifting up holy hands without anger or argument; also
that the women should [pray and?] dress themselves modestly
and decently in suitable clothing, not with their hair braided,
or with gold, pearls, or expensive clothes, but with good works,
as is proper for women who profess reverence [godliness] for
God. Let a woman learn in silence [quietness?] with full
submission. I permit no woman to teach or to have authority
[domineer?] over a man; she is to keep silent [quiet?]. For
Adam was formed first, then Eve; and Adam was not deceived,
but the woman was deceived and became a transgressor. Yet
she will be saved through [the?] childbearing, provided they
continue in faith and love and holiness, with modesty.*

1 Timothy 2:8–15

In the Fall of 1989, I gave two presentations about women in
the New Testament to two different groups. One was a Ladies
Day in Mississippi. The other was a University campus group in
Alabama. When I turned my attention to the assembly, I *began*
with 1 Timothy 2:8–15.

I thought it expressed a *timeless and universal command.* All
women were forbidden to teach and lead men because no woman

should have authority over any man. This was rooted in the order of creation and the negative effects of Eve's assertive rather than submissive behavior. Since there was nothing in the immediate context that limited it and the rationale was based on Genesis 2–3, I concluded it was a timeless statement of the principle of male authority. I regarded 1 Corinthians 14:33a–35 and 1 Corinthians 11:2–16 as *applications* of that principle. 1 Timothy 2:8–15 stated the principle, and the Corinthian texts applied it.

1 Timothy 2:8–15 was *my firewall*. Whatever the Corinthian texts mean, their meaning was bounded by 1 Timothy 2:8–15. As Winters observed, "Whatever may be concluded [about 1 Corinthians 11:5–6], Paul is not here approving what he else-where prohibits." 1 Timothy 2:12 was a bulwark against the *full participation* of women in the assembly because it *prohibited women from teaching and exercising authority over men* in any group gathered to worship or pray.

Moreover, I thought it prohibited *any form of leadership* in the assembly, including passing communion trays while stand-ing, singing on a praise team whether standing or sitting, making announcements, sharing a report from the mission field, offering a word of thanksgiving, a testimony, or confessing sin. It excluded women from leading singing, leading prayer, making comments at the table of the Lord, preaching, reading Scripture, and even saying "Amen." Yes, I remember that last one.

In other words, this text *carried a lot of freight*. When I advo-cated *no participation* in the assembly, 1 Timothy 2:8–15 supplied the principle that excluded women from *any* participation. In 1990, I become convinced that 1 Corinthians 11 authorized the participation of women and 1 Corinthians 14:34–35 applied only to disorderly conduct. Yet, 1 Timothy 2:12 *still barred* women from authoritative preaching and teaching in the assembly, though they may pray, lead worship, or read Scripture (see my presentation at Madisonville, Kentucky; also Archer). 1 Timothy 2:12 was the *sole text* that hindered the *full participation* of women in the assembly. That interpretation is a heavy load for 1 Timothy 2:8–15 to bear, especially given the balance of the Bible (Part 5).

In 1995, my eight year old daughter participated in a Christian event where children and teenagers gave speeches, led singing, were quizzed in Bible Bowls, and performed in puppet shows. My daughter competed in the speech category. When the time came for her to speak, I went to the designated room. I was barred entry. Men, including fathers, were not allowed to listen to pre-teen girls talk about God. When I inquired about the rationale, the organizers quoted 1 Timothy 2:12. Even though I had heard my daughter's lesson many times, she was not allowed to speak in front of me because she was not allowed to "teach men." If she did, she would, even as an eight year old, exercise authority over me. I regard that application of 1 Timothy 2:12 as terribly mis-guided. *Something is wrong with any reading of 1 Timothy 2:12 that generates that application.* I find that as problematic as saying my daughter cannot lead me in prayer, which is how 1 Timothy 2:8 is sometimes applied. Such a reading raises questions. I wonder, too, what long-term negative impact that had on my daughter and other young girls who were denied the opportunity to talk about God when their fathers were present in the room. The potential for spiritual malformation is significant.

I once thought this text was a timeless and universal prohibition that specified a particular in the blueprint for worshipping assemblies. After a long struggle with its meaning and function throughout the 1990s and early 2000s, *I now think Paul is addressing a local situation with a temporary prohibition for a specific problem.*

TEN DIFFICULTIES IN 1 TIMOTHY 2:8-15

As we walk through these difficulties, it is helpful to remember that some aspects of the Bible are not so difficult. The fundamental drama of God's saving work through Jesus the Messiah in the Holy

Spirit is neither obscure nor hidden. It is summarized, confessed, and repeated in so many ways in the Bible through history, songs, epistles, poems, and sermons (see my *Searching for the Pattern*). Though that story is profound in its meaning, it is accessible to every reader no matter their background or education. At the same time, there are difficult texts. They are difficult primarily because they were not written *to* us. They are embedded in an ancient culture and in specific situations occasioned by specific problems.

When reading Paul, *difficulties should not surprise us*. We saw quite a few in 1 Corinthians, and Peter thought Paul wrote some things that were "hard to understand" (2 Peter 3:15–16). The history of the interpretation of 1 Timothy 2:8–15 reveals how difficult its meaning and application is. For example, it has been used to oppose women's suffrage, women CEOs, and even women teaching children in Bible classes.

The difficulties are varied. Some are grammatical (how do we translate this?), some lexical (what does this word mean?), some situational (what was really happening in Ephesus?), and some conceptual (what is the principle, what is its rationale, what does it mean, and how do we apply it?).

While there are more difficulties than ten, these are sufficient to make a point: *there is significant uncertainty about the meaning and application of this text*. How one applies Paul's words to the contemporary church depends on how these difficulties are resolved. Given these ten and that there are more than ten, this provides substantial space for disagreement, varied applications, and incessant discussion. This calls for humility. At this point, my purpose is simply to note the ambiguities without necessarily attempting to resolve them.

1. Who is Praying?

The chapter opens with a call to prayer (2:1–2). Paul wants "the men" to pray "in every place" (1 Timothy 2:8) and the women to dress modestly (1 Timothy 2:9–10). But at least two difficulties are present.

First, what is the nature of this praying? We assume it is audible and has something to do with "leading" prayer, but the text does not identify the precise nature of this praying. While some assume lifting hands indicates prayer leaders, this is not necessarily the case. Lifting hands is something all worshippers were encouraged to do (Psalm 134:2) or a personal practice (Psalm 141:2). More likely, all the men are praying at the same time much like we see at the Western Wall in Jerusalem. "Anger and argument" may reflect a circumstance where people are disputing with each other while they are engaged in prayer. Nothing in the text *explicitly* says anything about leadership or leading prayer.

Second, whom does Paul encourage to pray? Some believe the grammar dictates only men (Towner, Knight, Schreiner, Cukrowski). Others believe women are included (Barrett, Witherington, Hutson, Marshall, Nichol).

1 Timothy 2:9 *may* read: "Likewise, *I desire women to pray* dressed modestly." The main verb is unstated in 1 Timothy 2:9. The text literally says: "likewise women in suitable clothing with modesty and decently to dress themselves . . ." Translations often supply the main verb as "Likewise, *I desire* . . ." It is grammatically possible as well as contextually appropriate to supply "to pray"—"Likewise, *I desire the women to pray* in suitable clothing . . ." Men should pray without argument, and women should pray dressed modestly. This is how John Chrysostom, the ancient Greek bishop of Constantinople, understood Paul's language. In this way, verses 8–10 form a unit on prayer's proper decorum. Most likely, as "likewise" suggests, Paul wants both men and women to pray—the former without arguing and the latter dressed modestly.

Whatever we might say about the grammar and context, even *if* Paul only *explicitly* identifies men as the ones who pray, this does not exclude women from praying in the assembly any more than the fact that Paul only *explicitly* identifies women as the ones who should dress modestly excludes men from modest dress in the assembly. Paul tells men to pray without arguing, but this does not imply they are to pray *instead of* women any more than women are to dress modestly *instead of* men. As Nichol wrote in 1938, "No one should conclude that the passage is antithetic, and that because Paul says men are to pray in every place, the teaching is that women are never to pray."

Is not the exhortation to prayer in 1 Timothy 2:1 directed to all, both men and women? If we include women in 1 Timothy 2:1, it seems problematic that Paul excludes women from praying in 1 Timothy 2:8–10.

2. Assembly or Everywhere?

Paul encourages prayer "in every place." Ferguson makes a good case for "in every assembly." A synagogue was known as a "holy place," and "every place" may refer to the gatherings of house churches (1 Thessalonians 1:8; 1 Corinthians 1:2; 2 Corinthians 2:14). While this seems reasonable, *the language is open to other meanings.* Bartlett extends it beyond public assemblies to *every location* where people are gathered to pray. This is not restricted to assemblies, according to Westfall, but addresses how men and women live in the broader culture peacefully, including modest dress and the practice of good works. Lipscomb (1913) thought it applied in every situation, including social venues like public lectures and political gatherings.

More precisely, would this language ("in every place") include the activities of 1 Corinthians 11:2–16 where both men and women prayed in a gathering? Does 1 Timothy 2:8 apply to the gathering envisioned by 1 Corinthians 11:2–16? If one distinguishes between the assemblies of 1 Corinthians 11:2–16 and 11:17–34, does 1 Timothy apply to both or only 11:17–34? It seems best, at a minimum, to hear "in every place" as in "every house church" *and* wherever men and women are gathered to pray. This would include gatherings like 1 Corinthians 11:2–16 (however characterized) and contemporary gatherings in small groups at home and Bible classes at the church building as well as public assemblies. The people of God constitute an assembly when two or three are gathered together because Christ is present (Matthew 18:19–20). In other words, "in every place" *at least* applies to *all* gatherings of believers to pray (Guy). Women not only dress modestly in the public assembly but everywhere believers are gathered or every public venue. Moreover, the text's principles may apply broadly to a *modest and peaceful lifestyle* in addition to assemblies.

3. What is the Nature of the Problem Regarding Women?

Is Paul talking about men/women in general or husbands/wives in particular? Interpreters are divided. In 1 Timothy 2:12, *gunaiki* (woman) may mean either woman or wife, and *andros* (man) may mean either man or husband. If it means wife and husband, the limitation—whatever it is—only applies to marriage where wives respect and honor their husbands (Burke, Westfall, Rowland, Guin, Spurgeon). Most interpreters, however, believe it refers to men and women in general.

The behavior of the women in 2:9–10 is a second difficulty. Not *every woman* was accessorized with gold, pearls, braided hair, and expensive clothes because only a few would have had that kind of wealth and leisure. Consequently, a *particular group* of women was disrupting the community by their immodesty. The exact nature of the problem is uncertain.

Perhaps some wealthy women had embraced the lifestyle of the "new woman" in Roman society (Winter). In general, they were high-minded, aggressive, and seductive. Perhaps they had taken up ascetic practices such as denying their husbands conjugal rights and rejecting childbirth (Westfall). Perhaps they were recent converts from the Artemis cult who continued to dress in particular ways and expected to lead the community as they had in the Artemis temple (Hoag). Others expand this possibility to include Greco-Roman cults such as the Dionysius Cult where women had a prominent role in the rituals (Morton). Perhaps the women, influenced by pagan myths, were spreading false teaching and seducing men (Bartlett). Perhaps the women were called to conform, for the sake of the gospel, to standards of Roman modesty reflected in contemporary moralists (Hutson). The options reveal the uncertainty.

4. Submission to Whom?

"Women are to learn in silence with full submission." There are, at least, two difficulties in that sentence.

First, the text does not say to whom or to what women are to submit. Is it submission *to men generally or only in the assembly*? Does it refer only *to husbands*? In that case, the language fits the Roman household codes of the time and apply only to the marriage relationship (Westfall). Others understand it as submission *to church bishops*, the next topic in 1 Timothy 3:2–7. Still others think it refers *to God* or *sound teaching*. Paul does not tell us. Every conclusion is inferential. Whatever one decides, Paul seems focused on a woman's peaceful and respectful demeanor.

5. Silence or Quietness?

The second difficulty is the word translated "silence" or "quietness." The word is used three times in 1 Timothy 2—verses 2 (peaceable), 11 (quietness or silence), and 12 (quiet or silent). Elsewhere the term describes believers who "work quietly" rather than causing a disturbance (2 Thessalonians 3:12) or godly women who reflect the "beauty of a gentle and quiet spirit" (1 Peter 3:4). However one translates it, the silence is not the same as in 1 Corinthians 14:34–35, which means the total absence of sound. Here "silence" describes a peaceful demeanor, a learning posture. All believers should embrace this peaceable lifestyle, not just women. But there was a disturbance among the women in Ephesus. *Paul wants the women to learn with a submissive spirit that is neither disruptive nor boisterous.*

6. What Kind of Teaching?

The meaning of "teach" in 1 Timothy 2:12 is debated. Some give it a narrow focus. It refers to the transmission and preservation of the apostolic deposit or teaching out of an official or publicly appointed role in the community. Thus, it primarily refers to pastors, elders, or bishops (Dickson, Jones, Grudem, Moo, Schreiner). Others think teaching refers to any situation where women are instructing others from a position of authority in public or private settings, including Bible classes or small groups (Guy, F. LaGard Smith, *Woman's Role in the Church*). Still others believe, combined with *authent* (to have authority or domineer; the second verb in 1 Timothy 2:12), it has a negative meaning such that Paul does not want "a woman (a wife) to persuade and domineer" (Kidson). (I have adopted Bartlett's style of leaving *authent* untranslated for the sake of discussion.) For others, teaching is sufficiently broad enough to include any kind of instruction, persuasion, or encouragement (Bartlett). Does "to teach" have a *technical* meaning like the teaching function of elders with pastoral authority, or is its meaning more *general* so that it refers to any form of instruction in any number of different circumstances?

There is also a grammatical ambiguity in 1 Timothy 2:12. The Greek construction is "not X and/or not Y but Z." Paul does not want a woman "to teach and/or *authent* a man but to be quiet." On the one hand, Köstenberger argues for this meaning: I do not want a woman to teach (a man), and, *in addition*, to *authent* a man. Both verbs, according to Köstenberger, are either positive or negative. Consequently, because he believes teaching is a positive activity, *authent* is also positive. Therefore, it means to "have authority" in a healthy sense similar to a bishop's authority over a congregation. On the other hand, Payne argues that the grammatical construction means: "I do not want a woman to teach a man *in a way* that *authent* him." Both teaching and *authent*, according to Payne, contrast with a quiet demeanor. *Authent* modifies teaching; it is the manner of teaching. Thus, Paul does not prohibit women from teaching but from teaching in a particular way. Grammatically, either is possible.

There is an additional grammatical ambiguity. It is possible Paul's sentence means something like this: "I do not permit a woman to teach," *period*. This would forbid a woman to teach anyone, which is how many in the non-Sunday School movement among churches of Christ understood it. The vast majority of interpreters reject this option because Paul instructs some women to teach other women (Titus 2:3–4).

7. Authenteō?

Authenteō is a much disputed word. It is *rare* in Greek literature and *only occurs here* in the New Testament.

Some suggest it means something like "to have authority" or "to exercise authority" (Grudem, Baldwin), or at least it has no inherently negative meaning (Wolters). Joined with "teaching," this refers to church authority or male authority over women. However, this positive meaning does not *clearly* appear in Greek literature until *after* 1 Timothy is written.

Others suggest it means something like "to domineer" or "to lord it over" (Peshitta in Syriac) another (Osburn, Westfall, Wilshire, Mowczko). Consequently, the word itself prohibits an aggressive, bossy, and potentially abusive action. Bartlett suggests the meaning "overpower." A good example of this negative meaning is found in the Greek bishop Chrysostom. In his homily on Colossians 3:19, while directing wives to submit to their husbands, he warned husbands to not *authent* their wives.

8. Why Write "First Formed"?

"Adam was first formed" does not appear difficult, but the ambiguity lies not in its *chronology* but in the *reason why* Paul employs it. Some believe it grounds the instruction of 1 Timothy 2:12 in the order of creation as a transcendent norm (Grudem, Schreiner, Morton). Women should not teach men in certain circumstances because God invested men with teaching authority rather than women by virtue of Adam's status of *primogeniture* (firstborn of the human race). That rationale, however, is not *explicitly* stated by Paul. Interpreters move from (1) Adam was created first as a chronological fact to (2) *primogeniture* as an implied theological principle with an embedded meaning to (3) male authority over women as the implication. Interpreters supply the middle step and infer the nature of the authority envisioned.

Others see a different rationale. The chronological fact begins the narration of creation ("formed"), fall ("transgressor"), and redemption ("saved") in 1 Timothy 2:13–15. God *formed* Adam then Eve, then Eve *transgressed*, but God will *save* her through "*the* childbearing" if "they" continue in faith with modesty (Bartlett, Padgett, Peppiatt). Paul narrates Genesis 2–3 in order to respond to the false teaching in Ephesus rather than rooting his application in an unstated principle of primogeniture.

Paul may also stress chronology because some myths circulating in Ephesus probably taught that women were created first, or, as in the Artemis cult, woman were responsible for the origin of man (Kroeger). "Adam was first formed" might be a direct response to a false teaching. Thus, Paul opposes women teachers who promote such myths.

9. What is Eve's Function in the Rationale or Illustration?

Because Eve was deceived, some have thought women are *more easily* deceived due to their supposed emotional nature, natural instability, or weaker mind (Lipscomb, Bell and many others until quite recently). Therefore, they should not teach men. But Paul does not explain *why* Eve was deceived. Interpreters have surmised these dubious rationales. Men are deceived as often as women are. In fact, everyone is warned about deception (Ephesians 5:6). Moreover, if women were so gullible and ill-equipped for teaching due to their nature, why does Paul direct older women to teach younger women (Titus 2:3–4)? If an emotional nature disqualifies women from teaching men, would it not disqualify them from teaching *anyone* (especially children) since men, presumably, would have greater emotional stability?

Why does Paul refer to Eve's sin? Paul does not, of course, think Eve alone is responsible for moral chaos. Adam shares responsibility (Romans 5:12). Grudem suggests Eve usurped Adam's leadership. Paul, then, uses this example as an illustration of the dire consequences of undermining male authority or subverting male leadership. However, this is not stated but inferred. Paul does not *explicitly* state that Eve subverted male authority.

Others suggest that Paul uses Eve typologically for deceived women in 1 Timothy 2:14, just as he did in 2 Corinthians 11:3 for deceived men *and* women (Payne, Padgett). What Eve has in common with the women who are causing the disturbance in Ephesus is *deception*. As deceived women, Paul does not permit them to teach.

Bartlett believes Paul's compressed narrative points to how Eve listened to the serpent and then Adam listened to Eve. In other words, somehow Eve persuaded Adam, and some deceived women were persuading (teaching) and *authent* (overpowering) men. The problem, then, was not so much that Eve subverted male authority as much as Adam was persuaded by a deceived Eve and ate the forbidden fruit with her.

The only certainties are mere chronology, Eve was deceived, and Eve sinned. Why Paul says this or how it serves as a rationale for or illustration of 1 Timothy 2:11–12 is a matter of *inference.* Significantly, Paul's narration includes *both* creation *and* fall narratives.

10. Saved Through Childbearing?

Paul wrote, *"she* will be saved through childbearing—if *they* continue in faith and love and holiness, with self-control."

Paul shifted from "she" to "they." Who is the "she," and who are the "they"? Further, what did he mean by "saved"—physical healing, spiritual healing, both, or something else? To what does "childbearing" refer? There are numerous approaches to this difficult sentence. Yet, as part of Paul's response to the problem, it shapes how we understand his previous statements. Because of its difficulty, it raises the bar once again on the uncertain meaning and application of 1 Timothy 2:8–15.

Spurgeon, for example, suggests that "she" is Eve and "they" refers to Adam and Eve as husband and wife. Consequently, in response to disruptions among husbands and wives, Paul invites them to continue in faith, holiness, and prayer in contrast to false teaching about marriage. Others believe the Artemis cult lurks in the background because it claimed the goddess could bring women safely through childbirth (Westfall, Hoag). Consequently, Paul is counseling women to trust God rather than Artemis. Moo suggests women are saved through childbearing in the sense that domesticity is their proper sphere of activity. Or, as Lipscomb wrote in 1907, "This means she is to work in the sphere of childbearing and training, and her work in the church should be in a private and quiet manner." Schreiner believes bearing children was a response to false teaching that discouraged marriage and childbearing. Hutson suggests the saying reflects Jewish anxieties about dying in childbirth where faith and modesty are appropriate responses.

Still others think "she" is Eve and "they" are the women who were causing the disturbances in Ephesus (Bartlett, Padgett,

Knight III). By stressing *the* childbearing, Paul identifies the Christ child as the one through whom the women disturbing the church will find salvation provided they continued in faith.

The Difficulties

- Are only the men praying or are women praying as well?
- What is the meaning of "in every place"?
- What is the problem regarding women in Ephesus?
- To whom or what are the women to submit?
- Are the women to be completely silent or peaceable?
- From what kind of teaching are the women prohibited?
- What is the meaning of *authenteō*?
- Why does Paul use "Adam was first formed" as a rationale or illustration?
- What is Eve's function in the rationale or illustration?
- What does "she will be saved through childbearing" mean?

TWO APPROACHES TO 1 TIMOTHY 2:8-15

These difficulties lead to two *primary* strategies for reading 1 Timothy 2:8–15 in its context. There is a continuum of readings between and beyond these. However, for the sake of brevity, I have focused on two *broad* approaches that include, *in substance*, most other alternatives. Whether one thinks the text is about husbands and wives or about men and women in general, the two general strategies still work for either.

One reading, Option A, goes *something like this*. The Ephesian church is disturbed by the behavior of some women in the public assembly. Some, influenced by years of leadership in the Artemis temple or Greco-Roman cults, brought their practices into the Christian assembly. They asserted themselves in conjunction with a seductive and/or wealthy style of dress. That style was consistent with their previous temple and/or cultic activities. Consequently, in response to this disturbance, Paul insists that *only* men lead the prayers and *only* men teach and exercise authority in the assembly. Women must learn in silence and submit to the men. In this sense, Paul's desire is actually *counter-cultural* as it opposed the practices of the Artemis temple and/or other cults. Paul's rationale, however, is *not* rooted in culture but in God's act of creation *and* Eve's transgression. As firstborn, Adam was *invested* by right of primogeniture with responsibility and authority, and Eve *illustrates* what happens when male authority is subverted. Paul's rationale includes both a creation rationale and an illustration from the fall of humanity. In contrast to Eve's presumptive exercise of authority over Adam, Paul reminds women that their primary sphere is domestic. Women will find security, peace, and influence through their domesticity rather than through public leadership in the assembly.

The other reading, Option B, goes *something like this*. Since the church is disturbed by false teaching and living in a hostile cultural environment, Paul attends to the church's gospel teaching and calls for incessant prayer. As the church learns to embody sound doctrine, men should pray without quarrelling and women should pray exhibiting a godly piety through good works. Some women were involved in the spread of false teaching in the Ephesian house churches and disrupted the church through their immodesty. These women, deceived by false teachers, needed to learn and submit to the gospel rather than promote pagan myths and practices learned from the Artemis temple, Greco-Roman cults, and/or proto-Gnostic teachers. Consequently, given that situation, Paul restricted their opportunities to persuade men until they had learned how to proclaim and embody the mystery of godliness, which is the gospel. This restriction is grounded in Paul's midrashic reading of the Genesis narrative. While Adam was first created and instructed by God, Eve was deceived and persuaded her husband. Adam listened to his wife, and Eve listened to the serpent. Just as Eve, however, was saved through the promise of the Christ child, so too the deceived women in Ephesus will be saved in the same way if they continue in the kind of piety into which God calls both men and women rather than following pagan myths that deny Christ.

Schreiner, Grudem, Moo, Morton, and Knight represent a form of Option A. Peppiatt, Payne, Hoag, Padgett, McKnight, and Bartlett represent a form of Option B.

Option A No or Limited Participation	Option B Full Participation
Only men pray.	Men and women *both* pray.
Some women are dressing immodestly.	*Some* women are dressing immodestly.
Some women are *asserting themselves* through teaching and *exercising authority.*	Some women are *promoting false teaching* through teaching and *usurping authority.*
All women should learn in submission to *men.*	*These* women should learn in submission to *God or sound teaching.*
All women should learn in *silence* rather than teaching.	*These* women should learn with a *quiet demeanor.*
Paul *universally* prohibits *all* women from teaching men.	Paul *situationally* prohibits *these women* from teaching men.
Paul prohibits the kind of teaching that belongs to church leaders and the exercise of *church authority* (e.g., bishops).	Paul prohibits an *aggressive* style of teaching over men or the exercise of a negative influence that *overpowers men.*
Adam has *primogeniture;* rights; therefore, men have authority over women.	In the creation narrative, Adam was created first and *instructed* by God.

Eve was deceived and *assumed authority* that did not belong to her.	Just as Eve was *deceived and persuaded* Adam to act falsely, some women in Ephesus were deceived and teaching falsehoods.
All women will be saved through their *domestic calling* if they pursue a path of piety and modesty.	Eve will be saved through *the Christ child*, and these women must pursue the path of piety and modesty if they would be saved.

While there is a general trajectory in both options, each has multiple variables where interpretations and applications differ. This is due, in part, to the difficulties present in the text. Nevertheless, the substance of each remains intact.

- Option A forbids *all* women or wives to exercise authority over *all* men or husbands through authoritative teaching and leading in the assembly or everywhere.
- Option B forbids a *particular* group of women (or wives/widows), deceived by others, from misleading the church through their ungodly teaching and behaviors.

Many doubt Option A because it decontextualizes Paul's prohibition and places it in a timeless and universal frame. It makes it about *all* women throughout time rather than the specific women who were dressing immodestly in Ephesus and teaching inappropriately. Option A has been applied in many different ways and different contexts. Its understanding of "to exercise authority" is often invested with more contemporary cultural baggage than biblical theology such that any form of leadership by women is thereby prohibited on the basis of cultural perceptions of modesty. The diverse and contradictory applications of this text by Option A raise legitimate concerns and doubts about this interpretation.

Option B, on the other hand, frightens some who fear it ignores the text in favor of some overriding principle derived from contemporary culture. They fear it relativizes the text and undermines Paul's theological point. This, too, is a legitimate concern. When the text loses its theological muscle, it is easily dismissed. Option B, however, offers a *close reading of the text* which discerns the theological story to which the *text itself* points. It does not play fast and loose with the text but pursues a contextual and detailed exegesis. A close reading illuminates how 1 Timothy 2:8–15 is an application of the mystery of Christ as Paul desires to conform lives and behaviors to the gospel, the mystery of godliness. Option B, just as much as Option A, seeks to understand what Paul *actually* teaches; *it does not dismiss Paul's teaching.*

Given these diverse options, which one makes sense of (1) the context of 1 Timothy, (2) "the balance of the Bible" (Part 5), and (3) the theological story of Scripture? Whatever our perspective, this calls for humility and wisdom.

FIVE QUESTIONS ABOUT 1 TIMOTHY 2:8-15

At the most basic level, the most important question is something like this: *how is the story of God applied in this text? What does it call Timothy to do and why?* We want to understand how the gospel was applied to the disturbances among Ephesian house churches that gave rise to this letter. Paul applied the "mystery of godliness" (1 Timothy 3:16) to the situation in Ephesus (Thompson).

What is its Context?

Paul's letters often open and close with a summary. 1 Timothy is a good example. In 1 Timothy 1:3–4 & 18, Paul urged Timothy to stay in Ephesus in order to

> instruct certain people not to *teach any different doctrine* (*heterodidaskalein*), and not to occupy themselves with myths and endless genealogies that promote speculations rather than the divine training

that is known by faith . . . so that you may *fight the good fight*, having faith and a good conscience.

Paul begins the concluding section of his letter by reiterating Timothy's commission (1 Timothy 6:2b-4a & 12).

Teach and urge these duties. Whoever *teaches otherwise (heterodidaskalei)* and does not agree with the sound words of our Lord Jesus Christ and the teaching that is in accordance with godliness (*eusebeia*), is conceited, understanding nothing, and has a morbid craving for controversy and for disputes about words . . . *Fight the good fight* of faith.

These are the only two places in 1 Timothy where Paul uses the verb *heterodidaskaleō* and encourages a "good fight." The verb means to teach something *different (hetero)*. Positioned at the beginning and the end of the letter, this language identifies Paul's purpose. Timothy is struggling against a "different" teaching that is disturbing the church (Fee). In fact, Paul names two of the false teachers whom he has already turned over to Satan, Hymenaeus and Alexander (1:20) and encourages Timothy to "fight the good fight" against Satan (1:18–20; 6:12).

Chapter divisions sometimes break the flow of thought because they subtly suggest a new topic. In this case, chapter two is directly dependent upon 1:18–20. Paul begins chapter two with "therefore." In other words, Paul's instruction in 2:1–7 is an application grounded in 1:18–20 (or 1:3–20). Because a "good fight" is going on in this church against false teaching, Paul urges prayer for everyone, including rulers. This fight will be won through prayer. We pray for rulers so that "we may lead a quiet and peaceable (*hēsuchion*) life in all godliness (*eusebeia*) and dignity." This makes sense because Paul barely survived a riot in Ephesus

(Acts 19). Such prayers are "right and acceptable in the sight of God our Savior."

Naming God as "Savior," Paul digresses to affirm the saving work of God in Jesus the Messiah who is the mediator between God and humanity. It is an illuminating digression. Paul reaffirms what is threatened by the false teaching in Ephesus which has supplanted the centrality of Jesus and undermined godliness (*eusebeia*). In other words, it directly addresses the false teaching and is, in fact, no digression at all but a reminder of the truth of the gospel.

In his closing section, Paul uses the word "godliness" (*eusebeia*) four times. It is his response to false teaching (1 Timothy 6:3, 5, 6, 11). Timothy must teach "in accordance with godliness." The gospel, summarized in 1 Timothy 2:5-6a, is "the mystery of godliness" (*eusebeia*; 1 Timothy 3:16). That mystery was revealed in the flesh, justified by the Spirit in the resurrection, and enthroned in the presence of the angels. This teaching was threatened by those who taught a "different doctrine."

Paul charges Timothy to teach "the mystery of godliness" in the Ephesian house churches. This means, according to 1 Timothy 4:6–7, that Timothy must "have nothing to do with profane myths and old wives' tales" [myths told by older women], but "train [himself] in godliness" (*eusebeia*). Paul connects this problem with the widows in 1 Timothy 5:13 where the problem is not so much gossip but their interest in myths. *Godliness* is integral to Paul's response to the false teaching. At the heart of this godliness is the gospel itself, which is God's saving work through Jesus the Messiah.

When Paul explains why he is writing to Timothy, he characterizes his purpose as instructing Timothy ("you" is singular) about how people "ought to behave in the household of God, which is the church of the living God" (1 Timothy 3:15). Paul is not detailing a blueprint for the assembly or church polity as if he were writing a church manual. Rather, in response to false teaching, he wants Timothy to remind believers to pursue godly lives as the family of God in the Ephesian culture. "Behave" is a broad term (cf. 2 Corinthians 1:12). In other words, Paul calls the church to live out its faith in opposition to false teaching. That life is grounded in the mystery of godliness, which is the gospel of the incarnate, resurrected, and enthroned Messiah.

How does this contextualize 1 Timothy 2:8–15? *It begins with "therefore."* Common themes illustrate how integrated the flow of Paul's thought is.

Theme	1 Timothy 2:1-7	1 Timothy 2:8-15
Prayer	Prayers (2:1)	Pray (2:8)
Godliness	Godliness (2:2)	Godliness (2:10)
Quietness	Quietness (2:2)	Quietness (2:11–12)
Salvation	Savior . . . Saved (2:3–4)	Saved (2:15)
Teaching	Teacher (2:6)	To Teach (2:12)

The *whole section* (2:1–15) guides Timothy's opposition to false teaching.

Fight the good fight, Timothy (1:18–20).
Therefore, I urge prayer (2:1–7).
Therefore, I want men to pray . . . likewise women to . . . (2:8–15).

Paul wrote 2:8–15 because of what he said in 2:1–7. He wrote 2:1–7 because of what he said in 1:18–20. In other words, given these causal connections, what Paul wrote in 2:8–15 is *directly* related to the false teachings about which he charged Timothy. Whatever is happening in 2:8–15 and whatever Paul meant by those instructions, *they are part of his response to the presence of false teaching and instability in the Ephesian house churches.* Read that last sentence again; it is an important one.

Some insist nothing is said about false teaching in 1 Timothy 2:8–15. This fails to recognize how the *letter flows from "therefore"* *to "therefore"* (2:1, 8) as well as how *the whole letter* is framed by the concern about false teaching. 1 Timothy 2:8–15 appears in the middle of Paul's instruction to Timothy about false teaching and how to combat it. Paul reminds Timothy of the central story of the gospel and addresses specific problems present in the congregation. The topic of false teaching is *integral* to 2:8–15.

When Paul addresses the situation envisioned by 2:8–15, he is well aware of the false teaching, who is involved, what is happening among the house churches in Ephesus, and who the excommunicated protagonists were (e.g., Hymenaeus and Alexander). Far from a digression about prayer and public worship or an intentional blueprint specification, 1 Timothy 2:1–15 develops the letter's theme—opposition to the presence of false teaching and associated behavior in the Ephesian house churches.

Who are these Women?

1 Timothy 2:8–10 continues the topic of prayer, which began in 2:1 where Paul prays for a "quiet and peaceable (*hēsuchion*) life in all godliness (*eusebeia*) and dignity." Forms of both *hēsuchion* (quietness) and *eusebeia* (godliness) appear in 2:8–15. What Paul says applies to "every place." The call to prayer and godliness is how one fights the good fight (1:18–20), which happens in more places than a public assembly.

Paul wants the men to "pray, lifting up holy hands, without anger or argument" (2:8). What were these angry arguments about? Why does Paul stress holiness? Reading this in the context of Paul's general purpose, we may imagine men were quarrelling about some of the issues surrounding the presence of false teaching. We don't know the specifics, but it signals a disruption in the house churches as angry men quarrel among themselves in unholy ways.

Paul wants women to pray in ways that testify to their devotion to good works and their profession of godliness (*eusebeia*). By calling women to *eusebeia* in place of their disruptive accessories, Paul associates these women with the ungodly conduct of false teachers in Ephesus. In other words, some women were engaged in practices that promoted immodest behavior consistent with false teaching (ungodliness, 2 Timothy 2:16). The verbal and conceptual links between the women of 1 Timothy 2:9–15, the false teachers, and widows (1 Timothy 5:3–16) are illuminating.

Women in 1 Timothy 2:9-15	Women in 1 Timothy 5-6
Women are to *pray* (2:1, 9–10)	Widows devote themselves to *prayer* (5:5)
Women encouraged to *godliness* (2:10)	Widows encouraged to *godliness* (5:3)
Women should *learn* (2:11)	Some women *learned* to be idle (5:13)
Women should *profess* godliness (2:10)	Some *professed* false knowledge (6:20–21)
Wearing *wealthy* accessories (2:9)	*Wealth* and love of money (6:9–10)
Women should learn in *quietness* (2:11)	Widows are *assertive meddlers* (5:13)
Wearing *seductive* clothing (2:9)	Some widows pursue *sensual desires* (5:6, 11)
Devoted to *good works* (2:10)	Idle, not devoted to *good works* (5:9, 13)
Not permitted to *teach* (2:12)	Saying what they *should not say* (5:13)
Eve was deceived by the *serpent* (2:14)	Some have turned to follow *Satan* (5:15)

Bartlett and McKnight rightly suggest that we learn *more* about the women of 2:9–15 by looking closely at 5:3–16. Together, these are two of the most extensive sections in Paul's letters that specifically discuss women. The whole letter is about false teaching, and thus Paul discusses women in relation to that false teaching in both chapters. *The similar language of chapters two and five connects both of them to the false teaching and the ungodliness present in the Ephesian house churches.*

Paul consistently refers to the purveyors of this false teaching with gender neutral language, which is the function of the Greek indefinite pronoun *tis* (1:3, 6, 8, 19; 4:1; 6:3, 10, 21). It is translated "anyone, someone, a certain, or simply a(n)" (Daniel Wallace). While no women are named, some women are included in this *tis*. This is evident from 1 Timothy 5:15: "some (*tines*) have already turned away to follow Satan" (similar use of *tines* in 6:10, 21). Women are included in the "some" (*tines*) that characterizes false teachers. We also know Hymenaeus, according to 2 Timothy 2:17 (cf. 3:6), was still targeting women and spreading myths among the Ephesian house churches (Bartlett).

The widows are not "gossips" and "busybodies" (5:13) in a *stereotypical* sense, that is, idle women who wile away their days in superfluous behavior. Rather, these widows "talk nonsense" (*phluaroi*; NIV 2011), which is similar to the language that describes false teachers in 1:6 ("meaningless talk") and 6:20 ("profane chatter"). *Phluaroi* (only used here in the New Testament) is derived from the verb *phluareo*, which means to "talk nonsense" or to talk about things out of ignorance (cf. 3 John 10). In other words, this is not secret "gossip" but something more like the "profane chatter" that characterizes some women in 2 Timothy 2:16 and 3:6 (women captured by deception). In addition, the word for "busybody" (*periergos*) is only used elsewhere in Acts 19:19 where it refers to the practice of magic and sorcery. Perhaps some widows were still engaged in some of the practices of Greco-Roman cults or the Artemis temple.

Moreover, these widows are "*saying* (*lalousai*) what they should not" (1 Timothy 5:13). In other words, they are spreading mythic nonsense as they "went around" (*perierchomai*) from house to house. They are *speaking*, which is a form of teaching or persuasion. Paul, for example, told Titus to "speak (*lalei*) what is consistent with sound doctrine" (2:1) and "speak (*lalei*) these things" (2:15). Their "house to house" activity is analogous to Paul's own activity in Ephesus as he taught from "house to house," which probably refers to house churches in Ephesus (Acts 20:20). Further, the verb "going around" (*perierchomai*) describes the practice of sorcerers in Acts 19:13. Apparently, some widows were engaged in similar activities.

Wealthy women in the Ephesian church reflected some of the cultural mores of the new Roman woman through their dress (Winter). The love of material possessions (1 Timothy 6:5, 17) and sexual immorality (1 Timothy 1:10) were also part of the ungodliness in the community. Both are reflected in the accessories Paul names in 1 Timothy 2:9–10.

The widows were significantly influenced by and promoted false teaching. Given these connections with the widows, *the women of 1 Timothy 2:9–10 are involved in that same agenda.* Paul's corrective addresses women influenced by *ungodliness*.

What is Affirmed and Prohibited?

1 Timothy 2:11–12 is important for what it *affirms* as well as for what it *prohibits*.

Women are encouraged *to learn* though education was inaccessible to many women in the Greco-Roman world. Paul affirms the privilege and duty of women to learn as part of the Christian community. This stands in general contrast to Greco-Roman culture. This is *specifically* directed to the particular women who are causing the disturbance in the Ephesian house churches described in verses 9–10.

What do they need to learn? They should learn how to devote themselves to good works as women who profess *godliness*. They must learn "the mystery of godliness" and how to live out their profession. In other words, they must learn how to combat the agenda of the false teaching that is reflected in their own immodest behavior.

In light of this struggle against false teaching, women should learn in quietness and in full submission, just as the whole church is to live peaceably and quietly in the Ephesian culture. In contrast to their present behavior, they should stop spreading myths from house to house and quietly *submit to God's sound doctrine*, which is the mystery of godliness.

But why should they learn? On the one hand, they should learn so that they will no longer spread pagan myths. Once they have learned, on the other hand, they may teach and lead others into the mystery of godliness instead of spreading pagan myths as they are now doing. Perhaps this is why Paul's prohibition is in the present tense as if Paul is saying, "*At the moment* or *in the current situation*, I do not permit a woman to teach." Whether the present tense can bear that weight is debated, but it is not unreasonable. It is another ambiguity that depends on a contextual reading in light of the whole letter. I don't think we can be sure. It may mean, "Given the present situation, this is what I want to do: these women, who dress immodestly, should not serve as teachers in Ephesian house churches and don't let them persuade (dominate, *authent*) the men." That would, of course, be true for men as well, but *in this situation* a group of women were intensifying the disturbance in Ephesus.

Like men, women learn so they can teach. 2 Timothy 2:2 reflects this Pauline agenda—people learn so they can teach. Paul wants Timothy to entrust the gospel with "faithful people" (*anthrōpous*) who are "able to teach others." Paul uses *anthrōpous* (people) rather than *aner* (male as in 1 Timothy 2:8). *Anthrōpos always* refers to men *and* women in the Pastorals when used in the plural (1 Timothy 2:1, 4; 4:10; 5:24; 6:5, 9, 16; 2 Timothy 3:2, 8, 13, 17; Titus 1:14; 2:11; 3:2, 8, 10). Since women are commanded to learn, they are also empowered to teach once they have learned.

But exactly what is forbidden? Scholars debate the meaning of the grammatical construction in 1 Timothy 2:12. Whatever its precise meaning, it forbids teaching and *authent*. There is some kind of relationship between the two activities. Whether they are two different activities (teach and *authent*) or one activity done in a particular way (teaching in a way that *authent*), the critical questions are the meaning of "teach" and "*authent*."

Paul wants to stop the women of 2:9–10 from spreading myths among the Ephesian house churches. The widows are engaged in just that activity. Just like Eve was deceived by the serpent, so the activities of these women are Satanic themselves (1 Timothy 5:15). The women of verses 9–10 are linked to the widows who are going house to house saying things they should not (1 Timothy 5:13). *The prohibition is not based on the fact that they were women but on what the women practiced.*

In what ways do women *authent* men among the Ephesian house churches? This is the only place where the word occurs in the Greek New Testament. Most likely, *authent* has a negative connotation. Recent studies have advanced the research significantly (Hübner, Westfall, Wilshire). Most probably, the term means to domineer or to "usurp authority" (KJV). In other words, this authority is abusive, overwhelming, or self-assertive. This explains why Paul did not use his ordinary term for positive authority (*exousia*). Instead, he used a rare word, a word with strong pagan associations. It was known in Jewish communities through its use in 3 Maccabees 2:29 and Wisdom of Solomon 12:6 where it evokes images of abuse and violence. The Wisdom of

Solomon, for example, describes "parents who murder (*authentas*) helpless lives" in pagan cults.

Paul does not use this word for mere stylistic variation as if drawn from an ancient Thesaurus but uses a word that evokes the milieu of *pagan myths* that promoted violent or abusive action. Paul's choice of *authent* is directly related to the practices and beliefs of these the women in 2:9–10 and the widows who are engaged in cultic practices. Moreover, one of the most common contexts for the use of *authent* in the second century is astrological and cultic (Mowczko).

Hübner's article tabulates how major studies of the word recognize every known use of *authent* before 1 Timothy refers to an abusive exercise of authority. For example, a letter from Tryphon around 27 B.C. describes how one person exerted a controlling influence over another.

Authent is not the exercise of legitimate authority but a dominating or imposing influence. Bartlett believes the "contextual meaning of *authenteō*" is that Eve's "bad teaching overpowered him;" it persuaded Adam and moved his will despite his knowledge to the contrary. In support, Bartlett cites a passage from Ptolemy's *Tetrabiblos* (mid-second century A.D.) where he describes the fact that the god Saturn has "taken sole house-control (*oikodespotei;* a despot over the house) of the soul and has gained mastery (*authenteō*) . . . of Mercury and the moon." The combination of these terms indicates how Saturn overpowered or took control of Mercury. This is the behavior Chrysostom forbids. Commenting on Colossians 3:18, he advises that husbands should not *authent* their wives. Chrysostom forbids spousal abuse. Analogously, Paul forbids women to abuse or control men (Westfall).

What Paul forbids is either (1) teaching in such a way that women take control of the situation in an authoritarian and domineering manner, (2) teaching and overpowering men in such a way that they persuade them of false teaching, or (3) both. These women promoted myths and immodest behavior by word and deed in the Ephesian house churches. Their domineering behavior is integrally connected with their house-to-house activities and immodesty. These women should stop teaching ("saying what they should not") and learn the gospel anew because their influence in the community is leading others, especially men who are the object of their desires (5:11), into myths and false teachings.

Why does Paul only identify women as false teachers? Bartlett suggests Paul had already excluded the primary male leadership involved in the false teaching (Hymenaeus and Alexander among others). But they had deeply impacted some women who continued to spread their teachings and myths. He does not name any of the women (T. Foster), but Paul does not always name false teachers (e.g., Galatians; 2 Corinthians). Paul wants to limit the influence of the women in 2:9–10. Men were the objects of their desires and interests. Having alienated themselves from Christ through their "sensual desires," they were seeking to marry as well as regain wealth and status rather than pursuing godliness (5:11–12). Paul specifically, even if temporarily, prohibits these women from teaching men because by their dress and activities they are seeking to involve men in their interests.

The generic woman ("a woman") encouraged to learn and forbidden to teach in 2:11–12 belongs to the group identified in 2:9–10. Some women (including widows), who dressed immodestly and pursued sensuality through drawing attention to themselves, were going from house church to house church practicing their astrology and magic as well as promoting myths. For example, the Artemis cult promoted seduction, sexual fulfillment, and safe childbearing, and the clothing described here reflects the practices of women in the Artemis cult (Hoag). They apparently had some success and were overpowering men in some way, which may have resulted in quarreling among the men. Paul wants to stop this. Therefore, he insists the women submit to the gospel by learning the mystery of godliness. Women should not teach until they learn sound doctrine. Consequently, Paul forbids *these women* (not every woman)—the women of 2:9–10—from teaching and overpowering men with their influence.

In other words, 1 Timothy 2:12 is *not a timeless principle but a specific application of the gospel story* in the context of women who were teaching false doctrine, just as the prohibition against wearing gold and pearls was an *application* rather than a statement of a timeless principle. Read that sentence again; it is an important one.

Why is Teaching Prohibited?

The idea that "Adam was first formed" stated a trans-cultural creation norm was deeply embedded in my psyche. I did not think it could be understood in any other way. To me, the sentiment was clear: "Adam was created first;" *therefore,* Adam had authority over Eve. At some point, it dawned on me that I was drawing an inference based on (1) my positive understanding of "authority" in 1 Timothy 2:12 and (2) the function of Adam's status as primogeniture. But the word for "authority" is not a positive one in 1 Timothy 2:12 and the principle of primogeniture was inferred rather than explicit. Recognizing this, it became possible to hear "Adam was created first" in a different framework. Perhaps it was not about creation order as a *metaphysical principle* but about the *sequence of events* within the Genesis 2–3 (T. Foster).

However we answer the question that introduces this section, we *infer* something. *Whatever principle Paul has in mind is not explicitly stated.* We infer the principle from (1) the content of Genesis 2–3, (2) what was happening in Ephesus, (3) the specific literary context of 2:8–15, and (4) the purpose of the letter. *This is the heart of the debate* about whether 1 Timothy 2:11–12 is universal and timeless or situational and temporary.

*If the debate turns on an **inference** for its universal intent, is this the **single text** around which the whole discussion about the participation of women in worshipping assemblies should revolve?* Should this be the text that becomes a premise in syllogisms that decides where women may serve and where they may not serve? *Is an inference going to determine how women use their gifts?* Does that not overstate our confidence in understanding this text and its application? Whichever view one finds convincing, humility is important.

This chart summarizes how Options A and B read 1 Timothy 2:13. They identify two different principles grounded in two different hermeneutical moves. *Neither the ground nor the principle are explicitly stated in 1 Timothy but are inferred from what both **think** is going on in the text.*

	Option A	Option B
Text (2:13)	Adam was first formed.	Adam was first formed.
Ground	Invests Adam with the rights of primogeniture (firstborn) between the sexes.	Appeals to the narrative where Adam, first created, was first instructed but listened to his deceived wife.
Principle	Primogeniture entails the principle of male authority over women.	Eve functions as a typology for deceived women in order to warn the Ephesian church.
Application	No woman should teach men or have authority over men.	Deceived women must first learn before they teach; let them learn in quiet respect.

Option A imports a positive notion of male authority (as if Paul used *exousia* instead of *authent*) into the text from a disputed understanding of headship in 1 Corinthians 11:2–16 (Moo). Interpreters assume male authority is rooted in creation. However,

Paul does not use his normal positive word for authority (*exousia*). In fact, the "authority" (*authent*) Paul names carries a more negative meaning than a positive or neutral one. If "headship" or a positive male authority is implicit in 1 Timothy 2:8–15, then why does Paul not use his *typical* term or the *language of headship*? On the contrary, he uses a word for "authority" that is negative and abusive. *He never uses it anywhere else.*

Further, if male authority (the supposed meaning of headship) is applied here, why does it not have the same import as in 1 Corinthians 11:2–16? Women are authorized to pray and prophesy in whatever situation 1 Corinthians 11:2–16 envisions even though men are the "head" of women. *If headship means women should not pray or teach in 1 Timothy 2:8 & 12, why wouldn't that same principle prohibit women from praying or prophesying in 1 Corinthians 11:2–16?* Does not 1 Timothy 2:8 apply to "every place" women and men are gathered to pray?

Moreover, *the principle of primogeniture is neither named nor applied in Genesis 2*. Rather, the narrative highlights the formation of the woman as the apex of creation with the result that man and woman are united as *one flesh*. No authority relationship is *explicitly* named in Genesis 2. If anything, in Genesis 1 animals are created *before* humans, but this says nothing about authority. Even in Genesis 2, animals are created *before* the woman, but the women is not subject to animals. In addition, *the Genesis narrative as a whole subverts the privilege of primogeniture*. God chose Isaac over Ishmael, Jacob over Esau, Joseph over his brothers, and Judah over Rueben. *The rights of the firstborn are not absolute in Genesis*. Indeed, the supposed rights of primogeniture are typically reversed or subverted in the Genesis narrative.

Further, *if primogeniture grounds male authority over women or wives, then it proves too much*. If the ground of male authority is God's act in creation, then why does not male authority—with all of its attendant injunctions, limitations, and requirements—apply to society as well as to the home and church? If man is the head of woman in the sense of male authority or if male authority is grounded in the rights of the primogeniture, then why is it permissible for women to *have authority over men* in business, education, and politics? One must either narrow this headship to the husband-wife relationship, or one must find some reason why it applies to the home and church but not to society. But restricting a theology of creation to only one aspect of human life raises additional questions. For example, what aspects of creation theology are universal and which are not?

Lipscomb believed the principle of male authority was universal (church, home, *and* society) *precisely because* Adam was created first. Why does the narrative of male leadership not apply to social relationships when it is based, according to some, on Adam's primogeniture, the corresponding purpose for which Eve was created, and Eve's assumption of leadership when it did not belong to her? Why is it restricted to the home and church?

To avoid this universal application, the blueprint hermeneutic suggests that it is *only specified* for the home and church. There are examples of women in Scripture ruling over society (Deborah and Esther), which is a different sphere of activity. We do not apply male leadership to that area because the examples in Scripture indicate otherwise. *But both Deborah and Esther exercised **religious** as well as political authority.* Moreover, since we have examples of women in Scripture leading worship, prophesying to men in an assembly, and exercising authority over men, are not these also *specific exceptions* to the rule in 1 Timothy 2:12? This restriction to only the home and church is more a function of cultural dynamics and a blueprint hermeneutic than biblical theology. If we make an exception for society, other exceptions are also possible in light of how women participated in the *religious* life of God's people. These exceptions, in turn, raise considerable doubt as to Option A's application of 1 Timothy 2:12.

Whatever we say about its universal or restricted application, nowhere in Scripture is the principle of primogeniture explicitly explained and then applied to the relationship between men and women as a trans-cultural norm. *It is not explicit in this text.* It is simply *assumed* that Adam's temporal priority *entails a primogeniture principle* that gives Adam authority over Eve. *That is an inference.* There is, however, a credible alternative for *why* Paul said, "Adam was first formed then Eve."

Option B understands 1 Timothy 2:13–14 as a telescoped or compressed retelling of Genesis 2–3 analogous to midrashic readings by Jewish interpreters. Paul's statement, "Adam was first formed, then Eve," begins the narration. Adam was created first, instructed with the task in the Garden, and then Eve was formed. However, Eve was "tricked" (deceived) by the serpent (Genesis 3:13) and followed the serpent, just like some women in Ephesus were ensnared by Satan and followed others into false doctrine (1 Timothy 5:15). She persuaded Adam who sinned with his eyes wide open. She *authent* him; she overpowered him with her persuasion and influence. Adam followed Eve; he "listened to the voice of his wife" (Genesis 3:17). This is the progression.

The italicized lines are *explicit* in 1 Timothy 2:13–15 in the chart below while the parenthetical statements are the background story *explicit* in Genesis. This flow contains *no inferred principle* but intersects the *text* of 1 Timothy 2 with the *text* of Genesis 2–3—this is an example of intertextuality within the biblical canon. This flow, in fact, reflects the broad biblical drama of creation, fall, and redemption.

Creation *Adam was first formed (1 Timothy 2:13).*
(The man was formed from the ground, Genesis 2:7.)
(The woman was formed from the man, Genesis 2:21–22.)

Fall	*Adam was not deceived (1 Timothy 2:14).*
	(He knew the command of God, Genesis 2:15–17.)
	(But he listened to Eve, Genesis 3:17.)
	Eve was deceived (1 Timothy 2:14).
	(The serpent tricked her, Genesis 3:13.)
	Eve became a transgressor (1 Timothy 2:14).
	(She ate the fruit, Genesis 3:6.)
Redemption	*She will be saved through the childbearing (1 Tim. 2:15).*
	(God promised a seed to crush the serpent, Genesis 3:15.)
	If they continue in faith, love, and holiness, with modesty (1 Timothy 2:15).

Eve is only named in two passages in the New Testament: 2 Corinthians 11:3 and 1 Timothy 2:13–14. In *both texts* Eve functions as a *type* of deceived people, including *both* men and women in 2 Corinthians. In 1 Timothy, she is a *type* of the deceived women ("they" in 2:15) who were teaching false doctrine (going from house to house "saying" nonsense). Because they were deceived by others, they were teaching pagan myths and behaving immodestly.

Paul may have had an additional reason for retelling the Genesis narrative in this way. The false teaching and its myths were probably influenced by what the Artemis cult or proto-Gnostics taught about the origin of men. Some Gnostics, for example, taught that Eve had some kind of priority. In the *Apocryphon of John* (120 A.D), *Gospel of Philip* (200 A.D.), and *On the Origen of the World* (300 A.D.) Eve awakens and teaches Adam, and in this sense gives Adam "life." These ideas were probably present in oral form long before they were written. They led to myths about Eve. If so, Paul's statement is *not* about primogeniture but a *corrective* to false teaching (Barron).

Why is Adam's sin not mentioned? Eve was deceived and transgressed, but the text is silent about Adam's wrongdoing. In fact, Paul states Adam "was not deceived." Clearly, Paul does not absolve Adam of any responsibility in the drama of Genesis 3 since he names Adam as a sinner in Romans 5:12. But he ignores Adam's sin here because the problem he was addressing involved teaching by deceived women rather than men. Deceived women were overpowering men and leading them into Satanic practices and pagan myths.

Significantly, the only word repeated in 1 Timothy 2:14 is "deceived." *That underscores the point*—it is a *deception problem, not a male leadership or authority problem.* Eve represents the women in the Ephesian house churches who had been deceived by false teachers. She illustrates the danger of listening to deceived women. The *specific situation* in Ephesus involved deceived women, not deceived men. Paul is neither describing every woman nor the nature of women but identifying one woman from the Biblical story who was deceived in order to highlight the local problem in Ephesus. Deceived women were going house to house teaching pagan myths and cultivating relationships with men. *It is not a universal statement about women* any more than some who had been, similar to Eve, deceived by Satan in the Corinthian church is a universal statement about men and women (2 Corinthians 11:3–4). Just as some Corinthians had been deceived by some who taught a different (*heteron*) gospel, these Ephesian women had been deceived by those who taught a different (*heteron*) doctrine.

How does Childbearing Fit into This?

Whatever the precise nature of the false teaching, Paul's response to immodest women (2:9–10) is to arrest their behaviors because *they were promoting ungodliness.* Paul responds with the narrative story of creation, fall, and redemption. God created; Eve was deceived; and God redeemed her through the Christ child. This is the true story; *it is the mystery of godliness.* If the women of 2:9–10 "continue in faith and love and holiness, with modesty," they, too, will be saved.

This reading depends on understanding "she shall be saved through *the* childbearing" as a reference to Eve's role in bringing the Messiah into the world. The text stresses *the* childbearing; the Greek article appears before childbearing. Many interpreters throughout Christian history have seen the Christ child in this text (Padgett, Bartlett). It echoes the promise God made in Genesis 3:15 that the offspring of the woman would crush the serpent (cf. Romans 16:20).

Eve, "the woman" of 2:14 ("she" in 2:15), will be saved through *the* childbearing, and the women of 2:9–10 ("they") will also be saved if "they continue in faith and love and holiness, with modesty." The term "modesty" only occurs twice in 1 Timothy—in verse 9 and verse 15. It bookends the discussion of women. The *immodest* women of 2:9–10 will be saved by the Christ child (the mystery of godliness) if they pursue *modesty* in faith, love, and holiness. Each of those values are themselves a response to the false teaching in Ephesus. This is Paul's corrective for the women who are disturbing the church. If they continue in faith with modesty, learn the true mystery of godliness, and practice godliness, then they will be saved, which is what God wants for all people (1 Timothy 2:4).

THE CONTEMPORARY CHURCH AND 1 TIMOTHY 2:8–15

A version of Option B is the most plausible reading of 1 Timothy 2:8–15. Therefore, it offers no hindrance to the *full participation* of women in the assembly. Though several of its contours are open to question and difficulties remain, it is a more credible interpretation than Option A.

If we adopt Option A, it opens a pandora's box of uncertain applications and unknown boundaries. Exactly what, in our contemporary setting, does the text prohibit? For example, in 1986 the new editor of the *Firm Foundation*, William S. Cline, invited female writers to contribute but asked "that the articles be directed to the needs and interest of Christian women." In other words, women should only teach women and address women's topics, *even in print*. May women teach men through the printed word? May we sing songs written by women who thereby teach us?

At the end of Part 1, I asked twenty-six questions about the relationship of men and women. Those conundrums were created precisely because we have interpreted 1 Timothy 2:8–15 in a timeless and universal way. Below is a reminder of some of them.

- Does 1 Timothy 2:8–15 *only* apply to the public assembly of the church? Or, does it apply to Bible classes, small groups, or even the relationship between a husband and wife?

- If 1 Timothy 2:12 only applies to the public assembly (and we might add 1 Corinthians 14:34–35 as well) when the whole church is gathered, does this empower women to teach men and lead men in prayer in every other setting, including lectureships, Bible classes, Wednesday devotionals, college classrooms, and small groups? How does one define what is a "public assembly" and what is not?

- Does it also apply to social, economic, and political relationships between men and women since the principle is rooted in creation?

- Does it restrict the voices of women or public leadership in every way? What are the distinctions between acceptable and unacceptable voices in the assembly?

- May a woman make announcements, report on a mission trip, or speak to the children gathered at the front in the assembly? May she do so "after the closing prayer" when the assembly is officially ended?

- If "exercise authority" has a positive meaning, what does it mean? Does it include voting in a business meeting or leading a ministry in the church? Does it only refer to functioning as a bishop or preaching? How do we decide? Or, does it only identify activities in the assembly itself?

- Does "exercise authority" mean women may not pass communion trays up and down the aisles because they exercise authority over the men present when they do so? May pre-teen girls take up attendance cards?

- What does the prohibition against teaching mean? What kind of teaching is it? Does it involve a particular kind of content, manner, or setting?

- How does one define "man" in 1 Timothy 2:12? Does it include baptized pre-teen, adolescent, and teenage Christians? Is this only an adult Christian? Does it include non-Christians?

I could go on. It gets complicated quickly. For example, in 1995 (revised in 2006), Grudem identified *nine* governing activities, *ten* teaching activities, and *one* "public visibility or recognition" position that are restricted to men, while he detailed *nineteen* governing activities, *twenty-five* teaching activities, and *nineteen* activities related to "public visibility or recognition" that are open to women. This is primarily based on his understanding of 1 Timothy 2:12. The vast majority of churches of Christ would not agree with his distinctions. We have our own, and we have a wide diversity among ourselves—both now and historically.

When we seek to apply the text to the contemporary church, there is little consensus. We make distinctions that are not rooted in Scripture but in cultural perceptions and traditioned habits.

Option A dies the death of a thousand qualifications and distinctions that do not *explicitly* appear in Scripture. Option A is problematic because the uncertainties, inferences, and fine distinctions *make a coherent and consistent application of Option A not only difficult but practically impossible.* Is the story of God regarding women and the assembly really that complicated? Moreover, we might consider the negative impact a misapplication of this text has on women as men debate where the line is for women and where it is not. The ministry of women is left to the quirks, indecisiveness, and inconsistency of empowered male leaders! (*That is **my** only exclamation mark in this whole book.*)

Option B, however, does not have these conundrums because it recognizes the temporary and circumstantial nature of Paul's instruction in 1 Timothy 2:12, just like the instruction about pearls, gold, and clothing in 2:9. Instead, Option B draws on the resources of Paul's teaching about gifts and mutuality. Each one, whether male or female, brings their gift to the assembly, and the assembly is edified through those gifts. Instead of a hierarchy of authority within the assembly, there is a mutuality rooted in the "one another" nature of relationships within the body of Christ. Instead of male authority, there is the mutual recognition of the other's value, worth, and giftedness. *The authority (exousia) is mutual rather than positional.*

Another solid reason for embracing Option B, other than its *credible* understanding of the text in its context and the *clarity* of its application, is how it *coheres* with the balance of the Bible (described in Part 5).

- Men and women share the *same identity* (Genesis 1:27) and the *same vocation* (Genesis 1:28).
- Miriam, a prophet, *led* Israel in worship and along with Moses and Aaron *led* Israel through the wilderness.

- Deborah *exercised authority* in Israel as a judge, prophet, and military leader.
- Huldah *exercised authority* as a temple prophet in Judah over both the king of Judah and the high priest and *sanctioned* the authority of a biblical book.
- Esther *authorized* the Feast of Purim.
- God became human through the discipleship and faith of a woman, *Mary*.
- Anna, a prophet, publicly *heralded the good news* of the Messiah's arrival in the courts of the temple.
- Jesus called women into *discipleship*.
- Mary Magdalene was the first to *proclaim* the resurrection of Jesus.
- God poured out the Spirit at Pentecost and *gifted* women with visions and the ability to prophesy.
- Women *prayed* and *exercised the gift of prophecy* by which they edified the assembly in Corinth.
- Women were *co-workers and co-laborers* with Paul in his missionary activity.
- Phoebe was a *deacon* of the church at Cenchreae as well as a patron and leader in Paul's ministry.
- Junia was a well-known and effective *apostle* along with Andronicus.
- Priscilla, Nympha, and Chole *hosted* congregations in their homes.

If Option B is correct, *none of these are surprising*, but with Option A they are problematic texts. Option B does not have to explain, decontextualize, or minimize them. It does not make fine distinctions to harmonize them with some inferred principle of male authority and definitions of assemblies where male authority applies and where it does not. *There is no text that delimits the gifts of women in the assembly of God.* Instead, we relish the accounts of these women and use them to highlight the giftedness of women throughout the story of God. *The theological herme-neutic embraces the relevance of the whole Bible, and the supreme importance of its central theological story moving from creation to new creation.*

Because I once believed 1 Timothy 2:12 forbade women to have a "position of authority" over men, I made distinctions so that this text did not, for example, contradict what God did through Miriam, Deborah, Huldah, or Anna.

I might have said those are Old Testament examples under a different covenant. But if the principle of male authority is grounded in creation, did God violate the intent of creation by empowering and authorizing these women? No sanctioned example in the Hebrew Bible can undermine creation theology.

I might have said they did not speak in public assemblies. But does not the principle of male authority apply in private as well as public? Are not some of these examples obviously public (Miriam, Deborah, and Anna)? These women edified men through their prophetic activity.

I might have said the *blueprint pattern* needs a *specific* com-mand, example, or necessary inference of a woman praying or teaching in a public assembly when the whole church is gathered.

Searching for the blueprint forces us to minimize, decontex-tualize, reframe, or even ignore *the balance of the Bible* because it is limited by searching for specific authorization in Acts and the Epistles. This is why, in part, *Woman's Role in the Church* only addressed questions related to Acts and the Epistles. This approach does not read the Bible theologically. Instead, it looks for positiv-istic requirements that identify church practices as marks of the true church. It is unable to hear the story of women from creation to new creation because it is limited by its own assumptions.

But what does 1 Timothy 2:12 actually say, some might question. Does it not forbid women to teach men? Yes, it does.

In the same way, does not 1 Timothy 2:9 actually forbid women from wearing braided hair, gold and pearls, and expense clothes? Yes, it does. That is as clear and plain as 1 Timothy 2:12.

But the problem is this: *which* women, *what* about their behavior or teaching is problematic, and *why* did Paul issue these prohibitions? Was it Paul's intention to provide a universal rule for all churches across time? If 1 Timothy 2:12 is universal and timeless, why is not 1 Timothy 2:9? In other words, these texts must be *interpreted* and understood in their *specific context*. Otherwise, we lift these sentences out of their context, place them in a syllogism, and make them say something Paul never intended them to say. That is what a blueprint hermeneutic often does as *Searching for the Pattern* argued.

A theological reading of Scripture, in conjunction with Option B, opens windows into the story of God to see how women *partnered* with men in the mission of God, *participated* in the assemblies of God, *led* the people of God, and *embodied* the wisdom of God. God's story is *one story*. A theological hermeneutic adopts that story as its hermeneutical framework and interprets specific biblical texts in the light of that story. Option B is not only the best contextual reading of 1 Timothy 2:8–15, it coheres with *the balance of the Bible*.

Option B may not be correct—I could be wrong. But it is, at least, *plausible* to read 1 Timothy 2:8–15 in this way. I believe it is the *best* reading. Nevertheless, if we take seriously the uncertainties of this text and continue to disagree, humility calls us to recognize the honesty, sincerity, and devotion of the other in our attempt to understand this word from God through Paul. In our disagreement, it would be wise to hold our interpretation of this text gently and cautiously rather than rigidly and absolutely. As we do so, perhaps we can love another even though we disagree.

At the same time, *the balance of the Bible speaks loudly.*

CONCLUSION

The problem with some women in Ephesus was not that they were teaching *per se*, but that they were *promoting ungodliness*. They spread the ideas of a *different doctrine*. Their dress, behaviors, and words brandished that *ungodliness*.

Paul responded with the gospel. He denied the women of 1 Timothy 2:9–10 an opportunity to teach not because women are too emotional, inherently gullible, or simply because they are women. On the contrary, he denied them opportunity because they did not understand and practice *godliness*, just as Paul had earlier opposed Alexander and Hymenaeus for the same reason. He stopped these women from teaching just as he had stopped Alexander and Hymenaeus. These women did not know, teach, or practice the "mystery of godliness" (1 Timothy 3:16). They had been deceived by others.

The gospel is the central value for Paul, which is the story of God's saving work through Jesus the Messiah in the power of the Spirit. It is the counter-story to the myths of ungodliness present in the Ephesian church. Sound doctrine "conforms to the glorious gospel of the blessed God" (1 Timothy 1:11). The gospel, or the mystery of godliness, is the appearance of God in the flesh who descended from David as the Messiah, suffered as a ransom to mediate salvation for all people, and was raised from the dead to bring immortality to light (1 Timothy 2:4–6; 3:16; 2 Timothy 1:8–10; 2:8). This story saves us from ungodliness and trains us in *godliness* (Titus 2:11–14; 3:2–8). This lies at the heart of Paul's concern. This is why he strongly opposed the pagan myths and sorcery that characterized the false teaching in Ephesus.

In other places in Scripture, women participated in the defense and spread of the gospel as apostles, prophets, evangelists, teachers, co-workers, co-laborers, and ministry leaders or deacons.

When Jesus ascended and was enthroned at the right hand of God, *he gave gifts to the church* (Ephesians 4:8–16). Women were not excluded from these gifts. *God gifted women as well as men for the edification of the body.*

But what are women to do when God calls them to use their gift (1 Peter 4:7–11) and male leaders prevent, hinder, or discourage their use? Their gift is muzzled. Consequently, many leave for other communities where their gift is honored. Neither of the above options reflects honorably on male leaders who have erected or maintain barriers that have no *explicit* sanction in Scripture.

It is time to honor all the gifts God has given to women and for male leaders to recognize those gifts, share God's mission with the other half of the church, and hear the gospel through the faithful voices of our sisters.

ADDENDUM: INCLUSIVE ELDERSHIP?

This is the obvious next question. I did not address it in this book because I focused on the assembly. *No matter what one believes about church polity or male headship, God has gifted women with the authority to fully participate in the assembly.* There are no timeless blueprint restrictions that exclude women from *full participation.*

God has poured the Holy Spirit on all the children of God, both male and female. God has gifted women as well as men for ministry in the body of Christ. Paul lists some of these gifts in Ephesians 4:11, Romans 12:6–8, and 1 Corinthians 12:7–10, which include, for example, prophets and teachers as well as ministry and leadership. There is no indication that any of these gifts belong exclusively to men.

One of these gifts is "shepherds" (pastors in Ephesians 4:11—synonymous with bishops and elders). Are women excluded from this role in the body of Christ?

I hope to address that question in another book. It will serve as the third in a trilogy: (1) *Searching for the Pattern* about hermeneutics, (2) *Women Serving God* about the assembly, and (3) a book on church polity and leadership. *Nothing in this book, however, excludes women from this function, and this book provides evidence that supports their inclusion.*

Whether the eldership is gender inclusive deserves a separate treatment where the evidence might receive a full hearing in order to draw a credible conclusion.

Afterword

With all the difficulties of 1 Timothy 2:8–15, 1 Corinthians 11:2–16, and 1 Corinthians 14:34–35, should we not do what is *safe*? Some might say, "Let's do what we have always done. That is *safe*." When uncertain, do the *safe* thing, right?

I understand that instinct. It was mine for many years. It is part of the DNA of churches of Christ. But what is *safe*? And what have we *always* done?

We have not *always* agreed on how to read and apply these texts. We have disagreed over a wide range of applications and practices. Our sense of history is often too limited by our own experience, but our traditions are not the way they have always been. Historical awareness reminds us that there has never been *uniformity* except perhaps in the 1950s.

More importantly, *what is safe*? Is it *safer* to impose an uncertain application of these texts that exclude women from audible and visible leadership in the assembly or to listen to the "balance of the Bible" on this topic from creation to new creation? Is it *safer* to use a dubious interpretation of 1 Corinthians 14:34 to silence women than to embrace the gifts the Spirit has given to women for the edification of the body? Is it *safer* to absolutize a particular understanding of 1 Timothy 2:12 despite its difficulties or to heed Paul's warning about despising another's gift? Is it *safer* to practice the received conventions or to welcome Spirit-gifted women to edify the body? Is it *safer* to use *two* highly disputed and controversial texts to exclude half the church from full participation in the assembly?

If we have misapplied biblical texts and *illegitimately* silenced women, *that is far from safe*. In fact, it would despise and depreciate the gifts God has distributed for the sake of the body. This not only harms the body of Christ for whom these gifts were shared with women, but it harms (1) the church's public witness as people are shocked to see only men lead the assembly and (2) women who are denied the use of their gifts in obedience to the call of God on their lives. When a congregation excludes women from leadership in the assembly, they *deny* God the glory that comes through those gifts, *deprive* the church of the benefit of those gifts, *wound* women called to use their gifts, *shame* the church in the eyes of contemporary culture, and *subvert* the obedience of women called to use those gifts (1 Peter 4:7–11). How many Miriams, Deborahs, Huldahs, Annas, Phoebes, and Junias have been lost to the body of Christ because male leaders did not recognize and affirm the gifts God has poured out on women?

To deny women the exercise of their gifts in the assembly, if what I have argued is correct, is a *dire and damaging abuse* based on two problematic, misunderstood, and misapplied texts. *That is not at all safe*. It is risky. It risks denying what God empowers in the lives of God's servants. It harms the congregation, scandalizes the public witness of the church, deeply wounds women, and dishonors God.

May God have mercy.

A Note for My Mother

Mom,

I wish I had heard your hurt more clearly in the past, sympathized with it more deeply, and done something about it sooner. This book is for you, Mom.

Please forgive my foolish ways and the slowness of my heart. For years, I did not believe the witness of the women in my community.

Now, Mom, I will listen to the women whom God has called to proclaim the good news of Jesus the Messiah, just as God commissioned women on resurrection day almost two thousand years ago.

Love, your son,
John Mark

Responses

AN INTRODUCTION TO RESPONSES

"I imagine I was as thoroughly socialized and spiritually formed by churches of Christ as a person could be, though I was not alone. I shared this ethos with many friends and family. This was my home, and I felt at home. I still feel at home." So I wrote in *Searching for the Pattern*.

Why do I stay within this historical tradition known by the signs on their buildings as the churches of Christ and influenced by people like Campbell, Lipscomb, and Hardeman? Given what I have concluded in this book, why do I stay when women are not permitted to speak or lead in the assemblies of most churches of Christ?

I love my home despite its flaws, some of which are quite significant and harmful. I love the shared confession of the Creator who sent the Messiah into the world and then sent the Spirit into our hearts. I love the relationships. I love my historic heritage. I could say more.

Nevertheless, I understand why some leave and find community elsewhere. Some have left because they have been silenced, excluded, and/or abused. Some have left because they are simply exhausted from the stress and tension. May God bless them, and may God use them wherever they find community.

I stay to encourage the journey toward communal sanctification in love, kindness, and hope. I want to participate in the process by which churches of Christ are increasingly conformed to the image of Christ and to advocate for God's new creation among them. I pursue this hope because I believe in the God of hope and the potential of this community.

My journey from *no participation* to *full participation* took me over thirty years of study, discussion, meditation, and prayer. For those who are still on that journey, do not agree with me, or live in situations they cannot change, I have the deepest love for you and want to live among you in kindness, gentleness, and grace. Most, in my experience, are doing their best to bear witness to the gospel of Jesus the Messiah. At one level, I believe our most basic unity is found in a common confession of the love of God, the grace of Jesus the Messiah, and the communion of the Holy Spirit. Grounded in that unity, we must also struggle, by the power and grace of God, to embody a more fully sanctified life in a more fully sanctified community.

Many women, however, are leaving the churches of Christ wounded and distraught. Their departure makes sense to me, though I lament both their wounds and departure.

When I asked Claire, Jantrice, and Lauren to share their stories and perspectives as women who grew up in churches of Christ, I committed that I would not censor their words. I did not know exactly what they would say. I only knew I wanted to listen. I hope you will listen as well because these women are dedicated servants who love God, their families, their congregations, and the churches of Christ. At the same time, they see the obstacles women face among churches of Christ.

Let those who have ears to hear, listen well.

RESPONSE BY
Claire Davidson Frederick

Claire is a faculty fellow in the College of Bible and Ministry at Lipscomb University. She serves as Program Director for the ENGAGE Youth Theology Initiative and lives in Mt. Juliet, TN with her husband Kyle. They have two daughters, one son-in-law, and one granddaughter.

YOUR SONS *AND DAUGHTERS* SHALL PROPHESY: THE FUTURE OF WOMEN IN CHURCHES OF CHRIST

The year is 1990, and I have just completed my sophomore year at Lipscomb University. It's becoming clear that I won't be able to stay here much longer, because: (1) They have an anachronistic curfew, rigidly imposed upon the young women, but allowed to slide among the young men; (2) I am a singer-songwriter, regularly playing in the bars and night-clubs around Nashville, which will eventually get me kicked out anyway; (3) I am in love with a Belmont graduate, a blues drummer from New Jersey, who is about to move back home and open a recording studio five minutes outside of New York City, and would I like to come? Age twenty, religious rebel, resourceful enough to get into Rutgers and complete the transfer—sign me up! Farewell Nashville. Farewell Lipscomb. Farewell Churches of Christ!

Why do we leave? Why do women like me leave? Women whose spiritual and musical gifts should have led to vocations in worship leadership, public teaching and preaching in the Churches of Christ? We leave because there is still, some thirty years later, no place for us here.

And when we leave—to the loss of the church and to the detriment of God's reconciling kingdom agenda—our voices are not even missed, because, in the words of preaching minister Katie Hays, "The majority of our voices were never heard anyway" (Hays, 2009 Christian Scholars Conference).

Looking back, my calling to ministry was present, although latent, in my youth. It was there in the early years of Sunday school, when I wanted to respond to every single Bible question my teachers posed. "Claire, give someone else a chance to answer now," I was told. It was there in the fifth and sixth grade girls' class where we were encouraged to memorize large portions of Scripture, and I was determined to earn more stickers on my chart than anyone else in the room. It was there during the Sunday night singings, where "anyone who wanted to" (translation—"anyone who was male") could "get up and lead a song." I loved music and singing more than anything else, and I had to literally sit on my hands to keep from volunteering for my elusive turn to lead, which never came, because I was a girl.

I knew better than to ask for that opportunity. You simply knew you would *never have* the opportunity. It did not matter if you had a gift for song leading and had been allowed to do it in Sunday school as a child under the tutelage of a woman teacher. By the time you reached middle or high school, you were never allowed to lead anything at a youth meeting or on a youth retreat ever again. Why? Because you were a girl. Unlike John Mark's daughter, I never got the chance to practice the gift of preaching as a "leaderette," not even behind closed doors. That program did not exist at our church, but we did have something similar.

During the 1986 "Young Men's Development Class," the young men were taken aside once a week for eight weeks and were trained in the skills of public prayer, public reading of Scripture, song leading, and the presentation of a lesson or sermon from the pulpit. During this same time, the "Young Ladies' Development Class" learned the art of needlepoint, baking casseroles, babysitting, and writing thank you notes and notes of encouragement. It was sort of like "finishing school" for Christian young ladies.

Let me be clear here: there is intrinsic value in all of these tasks, and the skill sets we were given were things that the church needed and still needs. However, the issue for me was that the division and training was rigidly conducted along traditional gender lines, according to traditional gender roles. There was no overlap. The recognition, development, and cultivation of our talents according to our spiritual gifting was never even considered.

My father was an elder in my home church for twenty-six years; my mother was the church secretary for half that time. My parents are loving and nurturing people. They cultivated my talents at home. They supported me with piano and voice lessons. They even came to my first songwriter's night when I was eighteen at the stinky little, smoke-filled bar on Elliston Square, wearing their Sunday best. They had always told me I could be "anything I wanted to be when I grew up," and I believed them. The unspoken part of that was "anything you want to be...except in the church."

It did not matter how the Spirit of God had gifted you. The list of things that a good "Church of Christ" girl might aspire to when she grew up did not include preaching, worship leading, or vocational ministry. Those things were off the table. In fact, they were off the radar screen. If they did exist outside the walls of our church in "the denominations," it was kind of like life on Mars. I for one had never seen it. And we can't become what we don't see.

So I put my gifts to use in the country music business. Here my gifts were welcome. Here they had a place. I signed two major publishing deals as a songwriter, recorded vocals in big studios in Nashville and New York, and performed on arena stages, in theatres, even the Grand Ole Opry. One song I co-wrote was actually inspired by a long-winded preacher in Churches of Christ, who used to wrap up his sermons with the phrase: "I Said All That to Say All This." This song was recorded by George Jones in 1998. In all this activity, my call to ministry was not actualized. It was sublimated. I would spend twelve years in this industry, before I discovered what God truly had in mind for me.

A RETURNING

God has a way of redeeming our pasts. I know this, because after I returned to the Churches of Christ in my thirties, I began to discern my call to ministry more clearly. And the discernment of that call led me—providentially—back to Lipscomb University where I enrolled in the Master of Divinity program on a full scholarship in 2010. Maybe there would be a place for me here, after all!

My very first semester at the Hazelip School of Theology, I took a course called "Gender in Ministry," co-taught by Rhonda Lowry and John York. I took this class, first, because I needed the "woman question" to be answered first, right at the beginning of my program. If I could not articulate a theological rationale on which to base my call, then why go any further? Why complete the eighty-two hour degree if it was "wrong" to be doing what I sensed God wanted of me?

One of the first things I learned in this class (which frustrated me then) was that it is not so much about "what" is in Scripture, but about "how" we read it. I pushed back against Dr. York: "What do you mean? 'How' we read it!?! We just read it and do what it says." (I was still operating from the blueprint hermeneutic). However, as Scholer famously quipped: "All biblical interpretation is socially located, theologically and ecclesiastically conditioned, and individually skewed." We all read and interpret Scripture based on the socio-cultural, personal, theological, and denominational lenses we have inherited. We wear these lenses on our face like a pair of glasses, looking through them to ascertain meaning and to arrive at an acceptable application of the biblical text. Most of the time though, like an absent-minded grandmother, we are not even aware, or we forget, that the glasses are sitting right there on our noses.

As time went on, I discovered that not only is our theology of women in ministry based primarily on our hermeneutics (or how we read and apply the text), but it is formed largely on *where we begin in Scripture.* In Churches of Christ, we historically, have begun with Paul because of our dispensational approach, which taught that the "Christian dispensation" did not even begin until Acts 2. Consequently, we paid more attention to Paul and his instructions to first-century congregations than we did to Jesus and the Gospels. This is unfortunate, because in doing so, we downplayed the radical ways in which Jesus interacted with women throughout his ministry and continually brought them from the margins of God's story to the center. Moreover, this emphasis on Paul seems counter-intuitive to Paul himself, since we are not "of Paul" but "of Christ" (1 Corinthians 1:12–13).

Paul was a missionary and a church planter. Through his letters, Paul pastored young churches from a distance and frequently issued temporary, localized injunctions to some out-of-control congregations for the sake of their growth and flourishing. Paul was also a "culturally directed" evangelist (Liefield). To the Jews, Paul became as a Jew; to the Greeks, Paul became as a Greek, so that by "all possible means" he might win people to the gospel (1 Cor. 9:19–23). Paul knew what it would take to get the gospel heard in his particular time and place and that the gospel is flexible enough to be culturally contextualized without losing its core commitments. Often, Paul's guiding principle was that he wanted to "give no offense" (1 Cor. 10:32) in the culture in which he was evangelizing, so that his "ministry would not be discredited" (2 Cor. 6:3). In fact, Paul gives "social perception" as a reason for the submission of both slaves and women in Titus 2:5, 10, "so that in every way they will make the teaching about God our Savior attractive."

Let us apply this Pauline principle to the present. By excluding women from the visible leadership and public ministry of the church today, are we not discrediting the ministry and mission of Jesus in our Western culture where a woman is more likely to become president than she is to become a preacher among Churches of Christ? Have our interpretive choices led to a faithful cultural contextualization of the gospel and to the growth and flourishing of Churches of Christ? Or is our practice of taking a few specialized, situational prohibitions from Paul and applying them universally to every woman in every congregation, contributing to the twenty-first century church's decline? Maybe we need to "become all things to all people" in our time and place, so that "by all possible means [including women preachers, we] might save some." Maybe we need to remove our blueprint lenses and exchange them for a new pair of glasses.

I believe a *theological* hermeneutic gives us a more faithful reading of Scripture, one that takes into account the "whole counsel of God" (Acts 20:27) or, as Holman said, "the balance of the Bible." Often, egalitarians are accused of not valuing the text, of wanting to throw out Paul completely. I have come to my egalitarian conclusions, not because I *don't* value Scripture, but because I *do*. As John Mark already noted, a "theological hermeneutic recognizes how the gifts of women throughout Scripture echo God's intent in creation and serve as signposts for new creation itself." It pays close attention to the activity of women in the earthly ministry of Jesus, the ways in which God has used women throughout both testaments, and the interesting reality that nearly twenty-percent of Paul's "co-laborers" in his own gospel ministry were women (Scholer; Romans 16).

A theological hermeneutic asks us to consider the rich tradition of female Hebrew prophets, including Miriam, Huldah, Deborah, Anna, Philip's four daughters, the women of Corinth, and Mary, the mother of Jesus who prophesies in Luke 1:46–55 what God is doing in her and through her to the glory of his name. It calls us to reflect upon the fact that Jesus is the first rabbi in early Judaism to have female disciples, including Mary of Bethany, who studiously sits at the feet of Jesus in Luke 10:38–42, shirking the traditional female role of kitchen duty in order to bask in the Savior's words.

This hermeneutic hears afresh Jesus' praise for the "woman of the city" in Luke 7:36–50, who ironically teaches the teacher of Israel (Simon the Pharisee) about what it means to "love much." It highlights for us the women who bankrolled Jesus's itinerant ministry (Joanna, Susanna, Mary Magdalene and "many others" in Luke 9:1–3) and recovers the names of those who were financial patrons of the early church, hosting congregations in their homes: Priscilla (Acts 18:26, Romans 16:3–4), Lydia (Acts 16:14–15, 40), Mary the mother of John Mark (Acts 12:12), Nympha (Colossians 4:15), Apphia (Philemon 2), and Chloe (1 Corinthians 1:11).

A theological hermeneutic moves us to learn how the Samaritan woman of John 4 is canonized by the Orthodox Church as "St. Photine, the Enlightened One," and that she should be remembered, not for her five failed marriages, but for the fact that she is the first person in John's Gospel to whom Jesus reveals his Messianic identity. She then takes this extraordinary testimony and evangelizes her entire town, bringing many to Jesus, whom they then confess as the "Savior of the world" (John 4:39–42).

A theological hermeneutic recovers the great commissioning of Mary Magdalene in John 20:16–18, where Jesus speaks her name and gives her a direct command to "go" and "tell" the male apostles the good news of his resurrection. She is the first to preach the gospel on that Sunday morning, proclaiming: "I have seen the Lord!" She is often called "the apostle to the apostles." A theological hermeneutic ultimately became the liberating lens through which I could both see myself in these women and operationalize my call. Their stories and this faithful way of reading Scripture gave me theological language for what I knew to be true about myself all along.

BETTER THAN SAFE

One argument I have heard from leaders in Churches of Christ regarding the silencing of women in the assemblies is that to adhere to this exclusionary praxis is "safe." They dare not make the mistake of Nadab and Abihu, lest God also find our worship unacceptable. However, as John Mark rightly notes, "If we have misapplied biblical texts and silenced women inappropriately," we are far from safe. In fact, we have done harm to women and to the body of Christ.

A decade ago, as I interrogated the "safety" of my choice to remain silent, I found that it was damaging my body, heart and soul; and it was no longer a faithful option for me. Reading the "Parable of the Talents" one day, the truth hit me like a ton of bricks (Matthew. 25:14–30). I was the servant who was afraid. I had buried my gifts and talents in the ground out of fear. Christians are to be good stewards of everything with which God has entrusted us—our time, talents, money, opportunities, etc. When Jesus returns, I could picture him asking me: "What did you do with those musical gifts, those speaking and teaching gifts I gave you? Did you bury them in the ground because you were afraid? Because you thought I was a hard man, ready to strike you down at a moment's notice?" No, when Jesus returns, I will not have to answer to members of the Churches of Christ for how I have used my gifts. I will have to answer to Christ and Christ alone, and I want to hear him say, "Well done, good and faithful servant . . . enter into the joy of your Master" (Matthew. 25:21).

RECLAIMING A HERITAGE—WHY DO WE STAY?
AND HOW DOES GOD MAKE A WAY?

Some of you may be asking at this point, "Why don't you just leave (again)? Why does this faith community continue to claim your commitment?" First, the Churches of Christ are my family— my sweet, infuriating, and sometimes dysfunctional family. For better or worse, it has both formed and malformed me. Churches of Christ taught me to love the study of Scripture and theological inquiry. I appreciate Alexander Campbell's confidence in the capacity of common people to interpret the Bible for themselves, even as my hermeneutical conclusions regarding the role of women differ from his. Through our practice of congregational acapella singing, the Churches of Christ taught me a rich hymnody, the melodies and lyrics of which are deeply woven into my DNA, with certain songs bringing me to tears. Moreover, I take seriously the egalitarian impulses embedded in the theology of the Stone-Campbell Movement, which advocate for a "priesthood of all believers." However, for me, "all" has to mean "all."

As Richard Hughes noted in a recent essay for *Vocation Matters*, leaving the Churches of Christ is always an option, but not one he himself could embrace: "Somehow I knew that turning my back on this tradition would amount to turning my back on myself." Indeed. To leave the Churches of Christ would be like leaving a part of myself behind; and there is a sense of homelessness and longing when one leaves, a "C-of-C" imprint eternally carved on one's heart. I felt it during my ten-year exile, and I have heard the same sentiment from other women ministers who left (or were forced out) to go fulfill their pastoral vocations in other religious contexts. Being "Church of Christ" reminds one of the song "Hotel California"—"You can check out anytime you like, but you can never [really] leave."

Second, if all women like me leave, then nothing will ever change. As I said earlier in my essay, "we can't become what we don't see," and I intend to be a visual representation of what a woman in ministry in Churches of Christ can look like for the generations coming behind me. Some of us stay and do women's ministry and preach or lead singing for all-female audiences. Some of us stay and do children's ministry, organizing spiritual formation activities for families and students. Some of us stay and teach theology or Bible courses at our universities and preach at lectureships or egalitarian congregations when we are invited to do so as a guest. In the past twenty years, I have done all of these things. Women who are called to ministry in Churches of Christ find various ways to plow in difficult ground and walk through the doors that God (and human leaders) open for us with grit and grace.

Some of us have even planted new churches that retain the best parts of our heritage, while also creating space for the full participation of women: Tiffany M. Dahlman serves as the preaching minister for Courtyard Church of Christ in Fayetteville, NC. Cheryl Russell serves as the pastor of New Heritage Fellowship in Fairview, TX. Naomi Walters serves as lead minister for the River of Life worshiping community in Rochester, MI.

In August of 2016, when John Mark Hicks asked me if I would like to be part of a liturgical church plant, the words coming out of his mouth were like streams of water in the desert to my parched and weary soul. My family and I had just exited a congregation where I had served as children's minister from 2011–2015. We left because the senior minister had committed sexual abuse against one of our women members and the fall-out was mishandled by the all-male leadership. This was the *fourth* congregation among Churches of Christ I had attended where sexual misconduct by a male minister had occurred; and at the time, I was "done with Churches of Christ." For about six months, we visited a Methodist church near our house while I gave my heart time to heal.

Then in October 2016, we helped plant All Saints Church of Christ, a liturgical, egalitarian, ecumenical congregation formed by twelve lifelong members of the Churches of Christ. We decided to root ourselves in The Great Tradition of the church universal and in foundational aspects of our Stone Campbell Movement. However, for us, the "priesthood of all believers" would be more than mere theology. It would become our weekly practice. Following the liturgical calendar, our congregation moves through a three-year cycle of lectionary texts. Each week we hear an Old Testament reading, a Psalm, an epistle, and a gospel. We do not have any paid ministers or staff; we believe that every baptized Christian is called to ministry. The task of worship and preaching is to "equip the saints for the work of ministry" (Ephesians 4:12). We meet in a borrowed space, and since we have no overhead costs, we give away 100% of our contribution each week to a different faith-based charity.

At All Saints, I am finally experiencing a place where all my gifts are used. I write and assemble liturgy, curate poetry, and lead us in songs of praise and prayers of confession. I have officiated communion, preached, and distributed funds to the faith-based charities we support. However, my most important task is this: I invite, invite, invite others to use their gifts in ways they have previously not been permitted. At All Saints, we get to hear from the whole body of believers on the whole counsel of Scripture, as all who feel called may preach, teach, pray, present a reading, or lead singing. We have heard sermons from different ages, different races, and different genders.

Why do we need so many perspectives on the gospel and on how God is working in the world? Since humans are the image bearers of God, I believe we need all these voices and a multiplicity of perspectives to get at *all* of who God is. The church's experience and witness is impoverished without them. Is the picture of the God whom we worship big enough and diverse enough to contain and be imaged by all ages, all races, all classes, and all genders (Acts 2:17)? I believe so.

Therefore, I am grateful for sermons like we heard from Annette, a widow who asked to preach for the very first time at the age of eighty-two, a mere ten weeks after her husband's passing. I'm also grateful that over the past three years, we have heard sermons and songs from Jan, Becky, Melanie S, Brittany, Kaitlin, Carly B, Gayle, Jackie, Micki, Falon, Mackenzie, Jenny, Christine, Denver, Paula, Melanie C, Jennifer, Emily, Carly K, Beth, Anna Caroline, Rylee, and Jessica.

There is freedom and a sense of shalom that is experienced, when one doesn't have to fight anymore to be "allowed" to use one's gifts and live into the spiritual calling that God has clearly placed on one's life. Paul writes in Galatians 5:1—"It is for freedom we have been set free...do not let yourselves be burdened again by a yoke of slavery." I for one do not want to be the cause of any person remaining in bondage to a system of biblical interpretation that may very well be quenching the Spirit and diminishing the witness and power of the gospel in our world. "How long, O Lord, how long" (Psalm 6:3)?

RESPONSE BY
Jantrice Johnson

Jantrice is a Real Estate Agent and Adjunct Professor at Concordia University Chicago. She lives in Smyrna, TN with her husband, Justin. They share two daughters and are members of the Hwy 231 Church of Christ.

> *Thank you to my Mom,*
> *Felita Smotherman, and*
> *Ira Booker*
> *for teaching me how to serve,*
> *praise, and*
> *teach through my wounds and questions.*

As an African American woman within Churches of Christ, I hesitated to give my response to this work. I wondered what so many people would perceive, predict, theorize, and what I would ultimately lose. Looking back, I had already lost so much for holding onto "1 Timothy 2" hurt from years ago (that is, how people have abused and used 1 Timothy 2). A call to have a voice in this book has helped me to heal in some areas that I thought I had buried. By journeying through this book with Claire, Lauren, and John Mark for several months, I realized that I not only buried my hurt, but deviating from my calling has affected so many others as well.

THE CALL

calling (n.): a strong inner impulse toward a particular course of action, especially when accompanied by conviction of divine influence (Merriam-Webster).

As an African American leader, while dealing with racial issues in the church, the late Humphrey Foutz, stated that "You want me to lift myself up by my own bootstraps, but you are standing on my boots." I understand that feeling of stagnancy, but as a woman, I felt like the boots were never my size to even try on.

At age eleven, I vividly remember how my Dad complimented my male cousins and friends for reading Scripture and leading songs in a morning worship service. I also recall seeing them fall asleep (ten minutes later) during the sermon. They were uninterested in true worship but more interested in when the worship would be over. Yet, they were lavishly praised for their work. I often sat trapped on the pew with excitement about the Word of God that I couldn't explain to a lot of my peers.

When I was fourteen, I signed up to teach during the week of VBS. Honestly, I didn't even think they would allow me to teach, and I had prepared my heart to be the best assistant I could be to my cousin, Pam. Fortunately, we had a teachers meeting, and she suggested that I should teach for a few days and volunteered to be my assistant. It was a microscopic gesture to a child, but a token that would change the trajectory of my life. Eloquently, I taught children of 4 to 5 years old every lesson I had been pondering and assimilating as I sat on the pews wondering when I would be permitted to share it or allowed to participate in the church.

It has been over twenty-five years, yet, I still remember how I painstakingly dramatized to these little children how Naaman had to put his pride aside to dip himself in the muddy River Jordan in obedience to the Prophet Elisha's instruction. Interestingly, I had no idea that God would call me to do likewise.

Calling is frequently associated with males being ordained to serve in the church, while their female counterparts are often deemed unfit. However, John Mark's view has encouraged me to discuss this subject that I've always been apprehensive to address. He wrote, "Women participated in the defense and spread of the gospel as apostles, prophets, evangelists, teachers, co-workers, co-laborers, and ministry leaders."

John Mark also wrote, "When Jesus ascended and was enthroned at the right hand of God, *he gave gifts to the church* (Ephesians 4:8–16). Women were not excluded from this divine provision. *God gifted women as well as men for the edification of the body*." Realistically, I am specifically called to teach teenagers. I say this with all sense of humility and responsibility. This is my calling, and here lies my divine purpose.

In my twenties, I was not officially appointed to function as a youth minister, but I was the youth teacher, director, van driver, and literally filled any available vacuum. During this time, the youth group was growing, not just numerically but also spiritually. I had a great affinity and an indescribable passion for God's Word, so it was given priority in everything we did as a group. In *Searching for the Pattern,* John Mark takes us on this journey of how to read the Bible and how commands, examples, and necessary inferences play a part in this orchestration of interpretation.

As a young person in charge of the youth, my focus was on getting the teenagers to listen, enjoy, assimilate, and apply the Word of God to every area of their lives. The key was finding exciting ways to drown out the chaos of their own lives so that they can experience the pattern that could be life-changing for them. I discovered the melody that led them to certain music and genres. The Word also has the same beat, rhythm, and drawing power. Helping them to identify questioning tones and sequences excited me, and we learned together.

During this time of growth, I was called into a meeting with a parent that vehemently opposed my appointment "over" the youth. This stiff opposition was neither caused by my actions nor erroneous teachings. Surprisingly, my only offense was inaccurate gender (because I was a woman), and 1 Timothy 2 was the supporting evidence to justify why I shouldn't continue. This subordination within the church can be forceful, and oftentimes goes unquestioned. I was crushed. My calling was enervated, but my only desire was to serve God with my gift. My boots didn't fit even though they clearly had my name on them.

Jeremiah 20:8–9: "But if I say, 'I will not mention his word or speak anymore in his name,' his word is in my heart like a fire, a fire shut up in my bones. I am weary of holding it in; indeed, I cannot."

THE CRIES

Cry (v): an inarticulate utterance of distress, rage, or pain (Merriam-Webster).

In my hurt, I retreated and came to the same conclusion Mansfield noted, "When we've been hurt by the church, we often tell ourselves that we are going to keep on loving Jesus but that we no longer want anything to do with His people. We say this to ease our pain, but we are fools when we do."

John Mark's "firewall" use of 1 Timothy 2 to prohibit women from leading in any way has bruised more women than advanced the gospel the apostle Paul passionately preached. A firewall establishes a barrier between a trusted internal network and untrusted external network, such as the Internet. As a woman and lover of God, should I be seen as an untrusted network?

Curt Thompson challenged me with a statement in his book, *Anatomy of the Soul*. He wrote about finding himself amidst past struggles and hurt. His breakthrough came when he was honest about his cries, "I decided it was time to wade into that sea of feelings and hoped that this excursion would somehow save me."

Although my hurt was initiated by someone else, I had to dig deep and take a trip to the young girl that resented the praise showered on young men who didn't have the desire to serve. I had to go back to the anger that I felt towards someone that only repeated a pattern of taking a portion of the Scripture out of context and subsequently enacting it. It was necessary for me to nurse and transform my heart that bled for so many years. My pain had festered and hindered me from serving maximally in my calling to the extent that I missed many opportunities where I could have actually bloomed. On this note, I held my anger for gender equality to the extent that I forgot my true position and posture to God and God's people. I needed an internal healing and an appropriate avenue to express my feelings.

In my community, you may not see women take leading roles, but *you can always hear their praise*. My cry of worship continues to save me over and over again. You can disagree with it, but you can never take me from my posture of praise. The psalmist says, "He turned to me and heard my cry" (Psalm 40:1). My cry has no barrier when it reaches God's ear. He has no gender bias. He knows me, and I know Him.

Ephesians 2:13–16: "*But now in Christ Jesus you who once were far away have been brought near by the blood of Christ. For he himself is our peace, who has made the two groups one and has destroyed the barrier, the dividing wall of hostility, by setting aside in his flesh the law with its commands and regulations. His purpose was to create in himself one new humanity out of the two, thus making peace, and in one body to reconcile both of them to God through the cross, by which he put to death their hostility.*"

THE COMPETITION

Competition (n): a contest between rivals (Merriam-Webster).

When you enter a shoe store and turn to the athletic section, you're hit with a clear line of distinction. The female choices for shoes have always been below par, and because of the low numbers, it's a battle to find your desired style, size, or color. If surveyed, a lot of women have chosen to shop on the male side because of the variety of selections.

I recently remembered riding in the car with my Mom when she looked at me and said, "I understand that you're different, and you struggle with fitting in." Like me, many women within the church have callings in certain areas, but the limitations have often been stringent with no freedom of choice. We cry about our frustrations but are usually appeased with one position for which twenty women contend. This causes a disruption in the growth of the body because it's no more about calling but a competitive advantage.

In 2009, many famous shoe companies relied on health findings and medical research to determine how they could help women with their athletic shoes. These studies concluded that women's feet are different; hence, their shoes couldn't be the same. It resulted in the companies putting the same care to developing a women's line of shoes at the engineering stage (Cummins). I'm grateful for the opportunities given to women to serve; however, I would be doing a disservice to others to say it is adequate or at a pace that I find respectful to women who have been called.

I'm thankful that God sees us as women and understands the disparity but still finds us worthy of receiving the shoes. I'm grateful that God is the one that gives the shoes that fit us perfectly. You can't give me the same shoes as my husband, but I still deserve a pair that suit me.

Galatians 5:6–9: "*For in Christ Jesus, neither circumcision nor uncircumcision has any value. The only thing that counts is faith expressing itself through love. You were running a good race. Who cut in on you to keep you from obeying the truth? That kind of persuasion does not come from the one who calls you.*"

THE CHOICE

Choice (adj): selected with care (Merriam-Webster).

Dallas Willard wrote, "Those gifted by God for ministry should serve in the capacities enabled by their gifts, and human arrangements should facilitate their service and provide them with opportunities to serve."

I believe this statement is very true, but I had lost sight of what was really important. If my fight for the human arrangements for women was bigger than the grace, support, and love that I showed to those who still struggled with the traditional views and theology of women in ministry, then I have lost the battle. My calling and cries are obsolete.

John Mark wrote, "Paul responded with the gospel in 1 Timothy 2:9–10. He denied the women of 1 Timothy 2:9–10 the opportunity to teach not because women are too emotional, inherently gullible, or simply because they are women. On the contrary, he denied them opportunity because they did not understand and practice *godliness*."

I've always been a student of the Word. As much as I have studied about the type of women that Paul was addressing, I started to become one in my heart. For years, I debated that he never excluded women from serving in their gift but that he was admonishing behavior that wasn't beneficial to the kingdom. Ouch, I was becoming the very thing the Word opposed. My perspective on what women should be given the freedom to do in the local assembly and outside of the assembly means nothing if my heart does not align with God. So, my service is to God, and that's what I've been called to do.

My decision to stay is for my daughters that will come after me and for the students who are now adults. As I have made the decision to stay, God has given me hope along the way. Watching my former students grow in the Word, hearing them recite exact bible lessons from years ago, and listening to the young men who still consider me as a mentor.

In staying, I'm asking God to mend my heart, not to merely choose to stay but to stay with a heart of unity. I don't know if I will personally see the changes that I believe need to be made, but maybe the people after me will experience it. The love I have for them transcends everything. I want them to understand the melody of the Word for themselves but to see it in me, a woman that zealously serves God.

RESPONSE BY
Lauren Smelser White

Lauren is Assistant Professor of Theology at Lipscomb University. She and her husband Jason live in Nashville, Tennessee and have two children. They attend the Otter Creek Church of Christ.

If you've carefully worked through this book, then you might be feeling the weight of its central argument: that excluding women from leadership in corporate worship settings runs contrary to God's purposes for the church. John Mark has certainly provided ample textual evidence and sound theological reasoning to that end.

Of course, all of John Mark's main supports open into further conversation and analysis; but, in an afterword to the book, I am unlikely to add much to their substance. This is not particularly easy for me, admittedly. I am in familiar territory when pursuing some point of theological exposition and constructing formal arguments. Diving into the realm of personal reflection on this topic, however, feels far more unwieldy. It is a bit like trying to choose a few pages from a private travel journal to show someone who has asked you to describe a life-transforming journey that you've taken.

Rather than worrying about offering the perfect representation of my journey, I decided that it might work best if I were simply to write as if you, dear reader, had engaged me in a post-book conversation. I've found that such conversationalists tend to pose thoughtful questions, which may go something like:

> *"What was it like for you, growing up in Churches of Christ?"*
> *"Is it hard for you to remain in Churches of Christ?"*
> *"How can we move forward without sidelining women who aren't where you are?"*

When offering answers to such questions, I am always mindful of the fact that my past experiences are still unfolding in my awareness and understanding (as is always true for all of us). But conversations must begin and end somewhere before they can begin again. So I do my best here to offer what I believe I have learned at this stage in my ongoing evolution, with hope that my reflections suggest something worthy of the faith-community's ongoing discernment.

WHAT WAS IT LIKE FOR ME, GROWING UP IN THE CHURCHES OF CHRIST?

There is far too much that could be said here, because there is no separating out my raising in Churches of Christ from the rest of my childhood or young adulthood. My family's "Church-of-Christness" was the overarching feature that either tinged or defined nearly all other aspects of our shared life. It was the stuff of the everyday, woven into the fabric of my burgeoning sense of selfhood. A great many of those memories and associations are beautiful, comforting, and valuably formative. Many others are quirky or comical, unremarkable or commonplace; some seem a bit bizarre, in hindsight. But not one of those memories and associations is, for me, overtly painful as it concerns the issue of gender roles.

Perhaps you find that last point surprising? It is hardly everyone's experience. But it is a fact that seems worth noting: not all women who were raised in Churches of Christ, and have come to hold egalitarian beliefs, associate deep pain with their upbringing. While I am lucky in this regard, I know many other women in Churches of Christ who would say they had the same good fortune. We are those who did not consciously experience the restrictions placed upon girls as tyrannical or belittling. We felt we belonged to an interesting and extensive network of good, faithful people in our little world; and the gender roles were just one aspect of what it meant for us to be a part of things.

It is also important to note, however, that although I did not experience our gender norms as demeaning, I never felt at home with them. As I aged into adolescence, I recall numerous points at which I had difficulty reconciling my internal spiritual experience with what I was being taught about a female's God-given role and dignity in her family, church, and society. The unifying feature of those struggles might best be described as cognitive dissonance: a nagging sense of being ill-at-ease with the conflict between what I *wanted* and what I was *supposed to want*. I was generally drawn to and good at activities for which boys were ultimately intended—namely, in my case, theological discernment and discussion—far more than I was drawn to and good at the things for which girls were intended (which, to my young mind, came down to the proficiencies of being "good" yet skilled at prompting male adoration).

I dealt with my cognitive dissonance as most adolescents deal with their errant desires: I wrote myself off as a far cry from the feminine ideal (which I nonetheless sought to perform); I found back-channel outlets for my interests; I rebelled against adult expectations, just enough to assert myself without seriously rocking the boat. I also loved being in the youth group, going on mission trips, and having late-night conversations about God with my friends. I never questioned what our community believed about gender roles. I just figured that we all had to adapt to Scripture's clear indications, and I found much else to capture my attention.

This cognitive scaffolding held up until I was twenty-two years old. I had entered a graduate program in English at Abilene Christian University and began attending a congregation near the university. I loved the hospitality of its people, its rich range of ministries in the community, the ways that its preaching and teaching opened up Scripture in all of its theological texture—but I was thrown back on my heels when I witnessed women visibly and audibly assisting in leading its worship services. Wasn't this congregation associated with Churches of Christ? How did they justify this biblically?

All the more befuddling to me was the fact that nothing detrimental seemed to occur as a result of the women's participation. These women did not seem to be "attention-seeking" types, nor did their contributions dial down the content quality of what was presented; in fact, and in spite of my skepticism, I found myself feeling that their perspectives and presence enriched the worship experience.

Standing in the parking lot one evening after a Wednesday night service, I mentioned my inner conflict over all of this to my rhetoric professor, who was a member at the congregation. I remember saying something like, "I actually kind of enjoy the part that women play here. But I just don't know how this congregation reconciles it with the commands in the New Testament." I clearly remember his response: "Well, Lauren, have you ever studied the issue from all angles? This group only made this shift because of a long period of serious study."

Of course, I had *not* ever studied the issue from all angles. And, as I did so over the following months, I was surprised to find that I had a harder time building a biblically based argument in support of the conservative position than the egalitarian one. I have always counted that time of discernment immensely important, because I could see advantages to either outcome (and if anything, I "leaned conservative," hoping I could find good reason to stay in the realm of the familiar).

By the end of that academic year, my old scaffolding had fallen, and an overwhelming yet rather enthralling range of possibility lay before me as a woman serving God. Only three years later, I found myself enrolling in another master's program—this time to pursue a degree in theological studies. I really had no idea what I would do with such a degree. I only knew I had a thirst for knowledge that always seemed to land me in theological matters. And I no longer believed that this was a desire God wanted me to suppress.

IS IT HARD FOR ME TO REMAIN IN CHURCHES OF CHRIST?

During my first year of master's work in theology, I seriously wondered if God was calling me to leave Churches of Christ. I had begun finding it increasingly difficult to reconcile what I had learned, and who I was becoming, with our community's beliefs and practices. So I spent much of that year visiting other denominational or non-denominational fellowships, praying about what to do, and trying to sort through all of my hang-ups.

I was graced with two important discoveries that year, both of which turned me back to the fellowship of the Churches of Christ, and both of which have been reiterated at later stages in my journey. The first occurred late that spring semester when, for an assignment in a reader-response hermeneutics course, I wrote a reflection on the book of Jeremiah from the perspective of an oppressed woman in Churches of Christ. My heroine bravely railed against her community's rigid faithlessness with concern for gender roles. My professor, very patient with my high-and-mighty approach, jotted in the margins of my essay: "Remember, even if you think it misguided, that your community's practice is born out of deep respect for the biblical text."

The impact of his words opened the door to a second discovery. This one did not come as a one-time event but rather was afforded via my communing with Christians of all stripes in divinity school, and during my Sunday morning visits with other ecclesial fellowships: I learned that *all* denominational groups have nettlesome issues to resolve, and that there are also real goods unique to my own context—elements I loved and would miss, were I to leave. I also realized that I know how to move in the circles of Churches of Christ in ways that I cannot elsewhere. In fact, it occurred to me, it may be incumbent upon me to stay—if only so that God might use me to carve out different imaginable possibilities for girls who love to talk about God.

Perhaps the most important aspect of these two discoveries is how they reoriented my sense of theological vocation in the context of Churches of Christ. I continued on with a graduate school training that would set me increasingly at odds with the usual expectations of women in this community, but my inner life was cut free from the roots it had been burrowing into toxic soils of misgiving and resentment. Granted, those feelings can still rear their ugly heads at times. But they are not definitive of my participation. I was graced with realizations that enabled me to stay with a sturdy sense of purpose in doing so, a sense which is not dependent on anyone pursuing me to use my aptitudes in a particular way—and which is grounded in my valuing the many gifts that come with belonging to this community, not because I've discovered the ideal fellowship.

This might paint a rather too-rosy picture of my sense of place in Churches of Christ. The real picture is certainly sullied by dark stripes of various sorts: by my exhausted wishing that there were more women in our fellowship pursuing theological studies; by my feeling hacked off at the stubborn resistance some leaders display in the face of sound evidence that our tradition had it wrong on "the women's issue"; by my frustration at the fact that numerous years of academic study isn't enough to lend my voice credibility in many of our circles. I have learned, the hard way, how human I am: that I very much need a community of fellow believers to encourage and orient me in my work.

But I have also learned that same lesson in ways that are infused with inestimable grace: in the hospitable interest my fellow congregants take in my Sunday school teaching; in the ways my male colleagues and bosses at Lipscomb University have advocated for my place on faculty, and have been true friends to me; in the notes of appreciation from my students (worth their weight in gold); and in the countless other ways my community has loved me and my family into being: in baby showers, nursery care, and now teaching my children about God; in opened homes, shared meals, and attentive prayers; in checking in on us when times are hard, and celebrating with us when times are good; in beautiful new friendships forged, and beautiful old friendships maintained; and in all the acts of care that keep the church and its ministries going, that teach us how to love in new ways. All of this is grace.

HOW CAN WE MOVE FORWARD WITHOUT SIDELINING WOMEN WHO AREN'T WHERE I AM?

In venturing to answer to this final question, I'll step away from personal narrative and into more of a prescriptive mode, because I think there are take-aways from my experiences (both those mentioned above and many not mentioned) that are relevant here. In what follows, I've organized these as bullet-pointed summary statements, with an eye to the practical import for communities working to move towards egalitarian practices. A few of my recommendations include the following:

- *It does no good to tell women how they ought to feel about how they were taught, concerning gender roles.*

Some women in Churches of Christ describe experiences of great heartbreak or of distressing bullying before they found their way out of traditional fellowships. Others, like me, do not identify with those experiences of acute pain but certainly felt out of place growing up, and, in hindsight, feel sincere grief in view of lost opportunities. And many women say they still feel completely at home in complementarian or traditional contexts.

Telling anyone how she ought to feel about her experience is, to my mind, not only barking up the wrong tree; it could be a serious misstep into the role of colonizer. (And, as an aside: for these reasons, I believe it best that we not frame movement on this issue as demanded by *justice*—which, in effect, sets one set of women's experiences over another's—but rather as warranted by *God's will for the church.*)

- *Hermeneutical/scriptural discernment at the communal level is the key to healthy movement on this issue.*

There are two sub-points here.

First, I believe it is vital that, before moving into close analysis of this or that passage, Christians' interpretive work should always begin with seeking hermeneutical awareness (asking, "How are we reading Scripture? What drives us to do so? Are we reading the text as Scripture itself invites us to read?"). After all, unless we inspect the construction of our reading lenses, we cannot evaluate the pictures they deliver. (In short: I highly recommend starting with John Mark's precursor to this book, *Searching for the Pattern*!)

Second, I'd want to emphasize the *communal* point here. Conservative women (like conservative men) will remain skeptical of top-down policy changes concerning women's roles, however much their elders insist that they have carefully studied the issue. The surest way forward as a community is by equipping every member of the body to understand *why* the elders believe that faithfulness to God warrants a new set of practices. This is a long, generally tedious, and sometimes messy process that calls for much patience from all participants. The unity of the body is well worth it.

- *Even if our congregations move toward change, our social histories and long-standing habits live within us; these bear deep-seated gender-related expectations.*

The grave side of this situation is that congregations that have reached egalitarian arrangements can still traffic in old guard gender-related expectations, which operate beneath the surface of awareness. This is surely why we tend to be harder on women who lead in various ways than we are on men, for example; and this is surely why women who would otherwise feel quite comfortable leading find themselves intimidated to do so in ecclesial settings.

Just as importantly, however, is the fact that—given how deeply formative our social histories and habits are—there simply may be fewer women who feel called to serve publicly than there are men. And, as much as I would love for my children to witness as many women leading in worship as men, this must not become a numbers game. There is far too much value in the quieter ways that women in Churches of Christ have traditionally served their congregations for us to do anything but celebrate those avenues of service. The key, it seems, is that we take pains to root out the old biases; and that we work to enculturate our children to serve, not according to gendered expectations, but rather according to gifting. And this leads to my closing point, which is to acknowledge the slipperiness of the notion of "calling."

- *The church community should be, and remain, profoundly influential in its leaders'—male and female, alike—discerning a calling to public service.*

When those who are wary of female leadership hear of a woman saying she feels "called to preach" (or otherwise lead), they often protest that Christians ought not seek positions of high status. Of course, one hopes such persons are willing to turn the critique back upon their protest, to consider their own motives in offering it—that is, have they considered their own personal investment in the status quo, as a matter of comfort and privilege? And, regardless of motive, they ought to be aware that calls for women to squelch their hopes ring a little hollow when those calls come from people well suited for the present way of doing things.

On the other hand, however, there must be something correct in the reminder that Christians are not called to set their sights on acquiring prestige. Otherwise, I'm not sure what it means to follow a Lord who bids us take up our crosses, giving over our whole lives to God's purposes, rather than working to retain the rights to our stories. How are we to proceed in supporting women in ministry, with all of this on the table? I propose that we attend closely to three concerns:

Concern one: There is the obvious necessity of our working to reach communal agreement that God gifts women and men alike for public service to the church. Nonetheless, as I mentioned above, even after we reach this agreement we must remain aware of the inevitable baggage of our past lives. Women who can be perceived as "prestige hungry" sometimes prove to be divisive figures, even in egalitarian congregations (and however loudly we note the unfairness of tendencies to label women this way, when few of us bat an eye at the same behavior coming from men).

Concern two: Critiques of "prestige-hungry" women raise pressing questions concerning our general treatment of congregational leadership—for surely we want to encourage humility in *all* leaders, male and female alike? Let us ask ourselves, then: To what extent have we unthinkingly made church leadership roles into positions of *too much* status, or the *wrong sort* of authority, and how can we guard against this in our teaching and practice? What systems could we put in place to support all church leaders in cultivating humility, a collaborative spirit, and the disciplines of lifelong learning? When we identify and encourage young persons who strike us as gifted for leadership, are we considering the wide range of virtues they will need for effective ministry, or are we simply taken by their talent or charisma (and thereby setting them up for a hard road)? The list could go on.

Concern three: How ought we proceed in the meantime? My hunch is that one vital remedy to our internalized biases, and our unwitting tendencies towards cults of personality, is this: that the women who have long been with our congregations—who have served consistently and generously, and have live with evident wisdom and humility—should be the ones we hear and see most often. These women are hardest to dismiss as they move into this role. They will be those most likely to steer our attentions towards God.

Of course, these women may be among those most hesitant to "take the mike." So, in conclusion, *male leaders*: please ask, and continue asking, such women to serve publicly. (One woman at my congregation—who has all of the above attributes, and wonderful gifts for preaching—says that she was asked to lead publicly somewhere between fifteen to twenty times before she finally agreed to do so.) And, to these *female leaders*: please consider that God is calling you through these invitations to serve in new and perhaps uncomfortable ways. The people of God need to hear your voice, to benefit from your wisdom, and to see your form before us, reflecting Christ by calling our hearts to God.

A WORD FROM A
PREACHER'S DAUGHTER
Bethany Joy Moore

Many parents in the churches of Christ begin to have new questions when raising daughters. They ask—how do I raise my daughter in a congregation that differs from me concerning the way she could or should be in the life of the church?

I can't speak as a parent of a daughter in such a position, but I can speak as a daughter with only sisters raised in mostly traditional churches of Christ with my father as the preacher. My first advice is to encourage your daughters to lead at home. One way is to give them assigned times to pray. My parents set up a rotation so that each of my sisters and I led the prayer before meals and at bedtime. Because of this we grew up comfortable praying aloud, a gift not offered to many women in our tradition.

Another way to prepare her to engage and lead is to read the Bible aloud and discuss what the passages mean. As a family we set aside time 5 days a week to read the Bible out loud and discuss the text. This time was not always peaceful and sometimes we girls were bored or the discussions got heated, but this practice developed some specific skills. The first is our great ease and comfort in reading the scriptures out loud. Many women don't receive practice at this and find themselves scared of genealogies or Hebrew Bible city names. Because of years of practice and correction I can happily offer to read a passage aloud in class or church. The second skill is the ability to look for themes in passages and see direct application to my world. The last skill came from the dialogue afterwards where the responses of my parents taught me how to discuss differences and refine my Biblical ideas.

Another place we were encouraged to lead was on the rare winter Sundays when the snow canceled services. On these days my mom and dad would assign each of us girls a role—song leading, communion, or sermon—and we would each be given the chance to do that in our little family worship.

The final way my parents offered us space to lead is that as we grew older my parents treated us as spiritual equals and sisters in Christ. They confessed sins to us and us to them; they allowed us to change their mind about scriptures; and they asked our interpretation and listened. My parents made great effort to make our home one of egalitarian faithfulness and that space, where I could lead and be heard, sustained me even when the church wouldn't hear me.

Equally important to making space for your daughters to learn and lead at home is the effort you make to champion, advocate, and protect them at the congregation. When you can, publicly praise your daughter's faithfulness, mention from the pulpit that she asked you a wise question, and choose her to read a few verses aloud in Wednesday night Bible class. Advocate for her gifts to be used in any capacity they can be used. If she wants to teach, help her find a space to teach children or peers. Finally, protect her. When, and in my experience it will be "when," she is criticized for her voice, ideas, or faithfulness, defend her. Make sure your daughters know they are more important to you than smooth sailing with the elders, popularity with congregants, and your sense of job security. Your daughters have one life and one soul—value it appropriately. I never doubted that my father valued me and my faith more than his job, and that made all the difference.

Despite making space at home, questions come up. Daughters want help understanding what quiets them at church. Daughters want to know where to do what activities. Daughters long to know what God thinks and for what they were designed. My parents handled this with great grace. They always explained the verses that are used in these discussions and as we brought up questions they did their best to answer them. I remember asking questions that were pretty vulnerable like, "Why is braiding our hair okay but not speaking in church?" or "Does God like boys more?" These questions were addressed like other sticky subjects with age and maturity in mind.

Another way this situation was handled, was that by implying if not stating that home is not church, we learned that when at home, the rules are different. I knew I was not allowed to volunteer to pray in the assembly, but I could in my children's Bible class and I could at home. It also helped that we visited churches more "conservative" or specific doctrine focused (with preaching time spent on no instruments, cessationism, and women's roles). These provided a sharp contrast to our more midline congregation. Occasionally we would also visit churches that had women serving in public and this caused us girls to be able to see that some things were interpreted in a wide variety of ways. That was helpful to my developing mind.

My final advice to someone raising daughters in a congregation that does not allow the participation of women to the degree that you desire is to either advocate for change or move to a new congregation. In the end, despite my parent's work and the love the congregation gave me, it hurt me to be raised in a church where women were silent in the hour and half of service and the leaders and powerhouses behind the other one hundred and sixty-seven and a half hours of the week. I keenly remember feeling less valuable, wishing I was a boy so I could serve like my best friends, and secretly wondering if God just loved men more. If you can, advocate space for your daughters and the other women in your church. If you can't, pray for somewhere to minister that has that space. Being raised in a church where the ways I was permitted to serve (communion preparation, teaching pre-k, nursery duty, and seasonally changing the bulletin boards) were undervalued and seemed undesired by the men of the church caused me to feel like my worth was in question. If your only option is to raise your daughters in a space such as this, be intentional to create a culture of leadership, equality, value, and openness at home. This will help off-set the potentially damaging feelings church can create.

Works Referenced

Allen, C. Leonard. "Silena Moore Holman (1850–1915), Voice of the 'New Woman' among Churches of Christ." *Discipliana* 56 (Spring 1996): 3–11.

Allen, James A. "The Woman's Christian Temperance Union." *Gospel Advocate* 49 (December 19, 1907): 812.

Allison, Robert W. "Let Women Be Silent in the Churches (1 Corinthians 14:33b-36): What Did Paul Really Say, and What Did It Mean." *Journal for the Study of the New Testament* 10 (January 1988): 27–60.

Almlie, Gerald L. "Woman's Church and Communion Participation: Apostolic Practice or Innovative Twist?" *Christian Brethren Review* 33 (March 1982): 41–55.

Archer, Timothy. "Women in the Assembly." Available at http://www .timothyarcher.com/kitchen/women-in-the-assembly-of-the-church/

Atkins, Ben. "The Woman Question." *Christian Leader* 11 (February 2, 1897): 2.

Bailey, Fred A. "The Cult of True Womanhood and the Disciple Path to Female Preaching," 485–517. In *Essays on Women in Earliest Christianity, Volume Two*. Edited by Carroll D. Osburn. Joplin, MO: College Press Publishing Co., 1995.

———. "The Forgotten Controversy," 9–12. In *The Church of Tomorrow: Horizons and Destiny*. Edited by Winford Claiborne. Henderson, TN: Freed-Hardeman College, 1983.

Baldwin, Henry Scott. "An Important Word: *Authenteō* in 1 Timothy 2:12," 39–52. In *Women in the Church: A Fresh Analysis of 1 Timothy 2:9-15*. Edited by Andreas J. Köstenberger and Thomas R. Schreiner. 2nd Edition. Grand Rapids: Baker Academic, 2005.

Banks, Robert J. *Paul's Idea of Community: The Early House Churches in Their Cultural Setting*. Grand Rapids: Baker Academic, 1994.

Barrett, C. K. *The Pastoral Epistles*. Oxford: Clarendon, 1963.

Barron, Bruce. "Putting Women in Their Place: 1 Timothy 2 and Evangelical Views of Women in Church Leadership." *Journal of the Evangelical Theological Society* 33 (December 1990): 451–459.

Bartlett, Andrew. *Men and Women in Christ: Fresh Light from the Biblical Texts*. London: Inter-Varsity Press, 2019.

Barton, Sara G. "A Biblical Example of a Sexually Healthy Woman for a World Where Unhealthy Sexuality Makes Headlines." *Priscilla Papers* 32 (2018): 10–14.

Bauckham, Richard. *Gospel Women: Studies of the Named Women in the Gospels*. Grand Rapids: Eerdmans, 2002.

Bell, R. C. "Woman's Work." *The Way* 5 (August 6, 1903): 775–777.

Belleville, Linda. "*Iounvian . . . episēmoi en tois apostolois*: A Re-Examination of Romans 16:7 in Light of Primary Source Materials." *New Testament Studies* 51 (April 2005): 231–49.

Bilezekian, Gilbert. *Beyond Sex Roles: A Guide for the Study of Female Roles in the Bible*. Grand Rapids: Baker, 1985.

Bird, Michael F. *Bourgeois Babes, Bossy Wives, and Bobby Haircuts: A Case for Gender Equality in Ministry*. Grand Rapids: Zondervan, 2012.

Bird, Phyllis A. *Missing Persons and Mistaken Identities: Women and Gender in Ancient Israel*. Minneapolis: Fortress Press, 1997.

Birt, Robert G. *Prophetical Preaching in the Twenty-first Century Addressing the Role of Women in the Glass City Church of Christ*. D.Min. thesis, United Theological Seminary, 2013.

Black, Allen. "Women in the Gospel of Luke," 445–468. In *Essays on Women in Earliest Christianity, Volume I*. Edited by Carroll D. Osburn. Joplin, MO: College Press, 1993.

Black, Mark. "I Corinthians 11:2–16," 191–218. In *Essays on Women in Earliest Christianity, Volume I*. Edited by Carroll D. Osburn. Joplin, MO: College Press, 1993.

Brown, W. J. "Notes of Passing Interest." *Christian Leader & the Way* 18 (August 16, 1904): 5.

Burn, Harry. For the story about Harry and Phoebe Burn, see http://teachtnhistory.org/File/Harry_T._Burn.pdf

Burer, Michael. "*Episēmoi en tois apostolois* in Romans 16:7 as 'Well Known to the Apostles': Further Defense and New Evidence." *Journal of Evangelical Theological Society* 58 (December 2015): 731–755.

Burer, Michael and Daniel B. Wallace. "Was Junia Really an Apostle? A Re-Examination of Romans 16:7." *New Testament Studies* 47 (January 2001): 76–91.

Burke, Gary T. God's Woman *Revisited: Women and the Church*. Eugene, OR: Luminare Press, 2019.

Byrd, Aimee. *Recovering From Biblical Manhood & Womanhood: How the Church Needs to Rediscover Her Purpose*. Grand Rapids: Zondervan, 2020.

Carr, O. A. "Woman's Work in the Church, What She Should Do in Public Worship. No. 3." *Christian Leader & the Way* 19 (May 30, 1905): 1.

Carson, D. A. *Showing the Spirit: A Theological Exposition of 1 Corinthians 11–14*. Grand Rapids: Baker, 1987.

Casey, James. "In Defense of Girls Praying." *Firm Foundation* 92 (April 1, 1975): 201.

_____. *In Defense of Girls Praying*. Baytown, Texas: Casey Publications, 1975.

Cervin, Richard S. "Does *Kephalē* ('Head') Mean 'Source' or 'Authority Over' in Greek Literature? A Rebuttal." *Trinity Journal* 10 (Spring 1989): 85–112.

Christy, Jennifer Hale. *From Theology to Praxis: The Quest for the Full Inclusion of Women in Churches of Christ*. D.Min. thesis, Lipscomb University, 2015.

Chrysostom. *The Homilies of S. John Chrysostom on the Epistle of St. Paul the Apostle to the Romans*. See Bridget Jack Jeffries, "John Chrysostom on the Apostle Junia." Available at http://www.weighted-glory.com/2019 /01/john-chrysostom-apostle-junia/

_____. *The Homilies of S. John Chrysostom on the First Epistle of St. Paul to Timothy*.

_____. *The Homilies of S. John Chrysostom on the Epistle of St. Paul to the Colossians*.

Cline, William S. "Writer's Guidelines." *Firm Foundation* 103 (August 12, 1986): 2.

Cottrell, Jack. *Gender Roles & the Bible: Creation, the Fall, and Redemption*. Joplin, MO: College Press, 1994.

Cukrowski, Kenneth L. "An Exegetical Note on the Ellipsis in 1 Timothy 2:9," 232–238. In *Transmission and Reception: New Testament Text Critical and Exegetical Studies*. Edited by J. W. Childers & D. C. Parker. Piscataway, NJ: Gorgias Press, 2006.

Cummins, Eleanor. "As Women's Running Takes Off, the Shoe Industry is Racing to Keep up." Available at https://www.theverge.com/2019/12 /23/21035009/running-shoes-women-sneakers-design-injuries-data -foot-pain.

Cutler, Caroline Schleier. "New Creation and Inheritance: Inclusion and Full Participation in Paul's Letters to the Galatians and Romans." *Priscilla Papers* 30 (Spring 2016): 21–29.

Davis, John Jefferson. "1 Timothy 2:12, the Ordination of Women, and Paul's Use of Creation Narratives." *Priscilla Papers* 23 (Spring 2009): 5–10.

Deaver, Roy. "Women–And 'Chain Prayers'." *Spiritual Sword* 6 (July 1975): 20–21.

_____. "Women and Prayer." *Spiritual Sword* 6 (July 1975): 13–16.

Deaver, Roy and Lester Hathaway. *Debate on the Bible Class Question.* Abilene: Chronicle Publishing Company, Inc., 1952.

Dickson, John. "'Teaching' as Traditioning in 1 Timothy 2:12: An Historical Observation," 107–119. In *The Gender Conversation: Evangelical Perspectives on Gender, Scripture, and the Christian Life.* Edited by Edwina Murphy and David Starling. Eugene, OR: Wipf & Stock, 2016.

Ellis, E. Earle. "The Silence Wives of Corinth (1 Cor. 14:34–35)," 213–30. In *New Testament Textual Criticism: Its Significance for Exegesis: Studies in Honor of Bruce M. Metzger.* Edited by Eldon J. Epp and Gordon D. Fee. Oxford: Clarendon, 1981.

Epp, Eldon Jay. *Junia: The First Woman Apostle.* Minneapolis: Fortress Press, 2005.

Faurot, R. "Shall Women Pray or Exhort in Public?" *Millennial Harbinger* 5th series 7 (August 1864): 370–371.

_____. "Shall Women Pray or Exhort in Public?" *Millennial Harbinger* 5th series 7 (September 1864): 415–8.

Fee, Gordon D. *The First Epistle to the Corinthians, Revised Edition.* Grand Rapids: Eerdmans, 2014.

_____. *1 & 2 Timothy, Titus.* Understanding the Bible Commentary Series. Grand Rapids: Baker, 2011.

Ferguson, Everett. "*Topos* in 1 Timothy 2:8." *Restoration Quarterly* 33 (Spring 1991): 65–73.

_____. *Women in the Church: Biblical and Historical Perspectives.* 2nd edition. Abilene, TX: Desert Willow Publishing, 2015.

Fewkes, John A. *As in All the Churches: A Close Look at the Call for Full Female Participation and Leadership in the Church.* CreateSpace Independent Publishing Platform, 2018.

Finger, Reta Halteman. *Roman House Churches for Today.* Grand Rapids: Eerdmans, 2007.

Foh, Susan T. "What is the Woman's Desire?" *Westminster Theological Journal* 37 (Spring 1975): 376–383.

Forehand, Garrell L. "Girls Leading Public Prayer." *Firm Foundation* 92 (May 13, 1975): 296.

Foster, Timothy D. "1 Timothy 2:8–15 and Gender Wars at Ephesus." *Priscilla Papers* 30 (Summer 2016): 3–10.

Foster, W. W. "Twelve Women and Two Men." *Christian Leader & the Way* 18 (February 18, 1904): 4.

Franklin, Benjamin. *Queries and Quandries.* Compiled and edited by Kyle D. Frank. Chillicothe, Ohio: DeWard Publishing Company, 2012.

Frazee, J. C. "Your Women." *Octographic Review* 47 (5 July 1904): 2.

Fuqua, E. C. *Woman's Place in the Church* (1950). Stone-Campbell Books . 304. https://digitalcommons.acu.edu/crs_books/304.

Glover, J. C. "Questions on the Woman Question Answered." *Christian Leader & the Way* 20 (19 June 1906): 4.

Grasham, Bill. "The Role of Women in the American Restoration Movement." *Restoration Quarterly* 41 (Fall 1999): 211–39.

Grudem, Wayne. "But What *Should* Women Do in the Church?" *Council of Biblical Manhood and Womanhood News* 1 (November 1995): 1, 3–7. Available here: http://mzellen.com/2013/04/27/but-what-shoul d-women-do-in-the-church-by-wayne-grudem/

_____ *Countering the Claims of Evangelical Feminism: Biblical Responses to the Key Questions.* Portland, OR: Multnomah Books, 2006.

_____. "Does *Kephalē* ('Head') Mean 'Source' or 'Authority Over' in Greek Literature? A Survey of 2,336 Examples." *Trinity Journal* 6 (March 1985): 38–59.

_____. *Evangelical Feminism: A New Path to Liberalism?* Wheaton, IL: Crossway, 2006.

_____. *Evangelical Feminism & Biblical Truth: An Analysis of More than One Hundred Disputed Questions.* Wheaton, IL: Crossway, 2012.

_____. "The Meaning of *kephalē* ("Head"): An Evaluation of New Evidence, Real and Alleged." *Journal of the Evangelical Theological Society* 44 (March 2001): 25–65.

Guin, Jay. *Buried Talents: In Search for a New Consensus.* Tuscaloosa, AL: Jay Guin, 2007.

Guy, Cynthia Dianne. *What About the Women? A Study of New Testament Scripture Concerning Women*. Nashville: Gospel Advocate Company, 2005.

Hairston, Andrew Jasper. *A Study of the Participation of Women in the Ministries of the Simpson Street Church of Christ*. D. Min. thesis, Emory University, 1999.

Hall, Michael. "Women and the Assembly." *Integrity* 5 (November/December 1973): 92–93.

Harding, James A. "Scraps." *The Way* 3 (March 20, 1902): 393.

_____. "Where and How Shall Women Speak and Pray?" *Christian Leader & the Way* 20 (July 31, 1906): 8.

_____. "Woman's Work in the Church." *Christian Leader & the Way* 18 (March 8, 1904): 8–9.

Harmon, F. U. "The Woman Question." *Christian Leader & the Way* 18 (September 6, 1904): 9.

Hawley, Henry. "Woman and Her Work." *The Way* 5 (August 20, 1903): 810.

Hawk, Ray. *May Women Lead Men in Chain Prayers?* Pensacola, FL: Bellview Preacher Training School, 1975.

_____. "The Role of Women in the Bible: Genesis 3:16 to Jesus's Coming! Teaching Men Outside the Public Assembly." Available at https://www.academia.edu/23829408/Women_Teaching_Men_the_Bible_Outside_the_Churchs_Public_Assembly

Hays, Katie. *We Were Spiritual Refugees: A Story to Help You Believe in Church*. Grand Rapids: Eerdmans, 2020.

Herndon, E. W. "Woman's Suffrage." *Christian Quarterly Review* 7 (October 1888): 607–9.

Hicks, John Mark. "Equal, but Subordinate." *Gospel Advocate* 120 (June 29, 1978): 405, 410.

_____. "Hermeneutics and Gender: A Seminar Conducted at the Pennyrille Church of Christ, Madisonville, KY, May 15, 2000." Available at http://johnmarkhicks.com/wp-content/uploads/sites/10/2008/06/hermeneutics-and-gender.doc

_____. "Quiet Please: Churches of Christ in the Early Twentieth Century and the 'Woman Question.'" *Discipliana* 68 (Fall 2009): 7–24.

_____. *Searching for the Pattern: My Journey in Interpreting the Bible*. Kindle Direct Publishing, 2019.

_____. "Women in the Assembly: 1 Corinthians 14:34–35." http://johnmarkhicks.com/2009/02/20/women-in-the-assembly-1-corinthians-1434–35/

_____. "Women in the Assembly: Issues and Options (First Corinthians 14:34–35)." A paper presented at the Institute for Biblical Research, Regional Meeting, Jackson, MS, December 1990. http://johnmarkhicks.com/wp-content/uploads/sites/10/2009/02/hardlec-women-1-cor-14.doc

_____. "Women Serving God: Four Bible Classes." Woodmont Hills Church of Christ, January, 2004. Available at http://johnmarkhicks.com/wp-content/uploads/sites/10/2008/04/women-serving-god-series.doc

_____. "Worship in 1 Corinthians 14:26–40: The Injunction of Silence." *Image* 5 (August 1989): 24, 26.

Hicks, John Mark and Bruce L. Morton. *Woman's Role in the Church.* Shreveport, Louisiana: Lambert Book House, 1978.

Hicks, John Mark, Johnny Melton, and Bobby Valentine. *A Gathered People: Revisioning the Assembly as Transforming Encounter.* Abilene, TX: Leafwood Publishers, 2007.

Highland Preacher. "The Modern Sunday School." *Gospel Advocate* 38 (November 5, 1896): 706–707.

Hoag, Gary C. *Wealth in Ancient Ephesus and the First Letter to Timothy: Fresh Insights from* Ephesiaca *by Xenophon of Ephesus.* Winona Lake, IN: Eisenbrauns, 2015.

Hogue, Eric. Quoted in news article available at https://www.wfaa.com/article/news/local/texas-mayor-says-women-cant-pray-at-city-council-meetings/

Holladay, Carl. *The First Letter of Paul to the Corinthians.* Abilene, TX: ACU Press, 1984.

Holman, Silena Moore. "A Peculiar People." *Gospel Advocate* 30 (May 2, 1888): 12.

_____. "Let Your Women Keep Silence." *Gospel Advocate* 30 (August 1, 1888): 8.

_____. "The 'New Woman.'" *Gospel Advocate* 38 (July 9, 1896): 438.

_____. "The New Woman. No. 2." *Gospel Advocate* 38 (July 16, 1896): 452–3.

_____. "The Scriptural Status of Woman." *Gospel Advocate* 30 (October 10, 1888): 2–3.

_____. "Women's Scriptural Status Again," *Gospel Advocate* 30 (November 21, 1888): 6–7.

Holley, Bobbie Lee. "God's Design: Woman's Dignity" [three articles].
Mission 8 (March 1975): 3–6; (April 1975): 3–7; and (May 1975): 10–17.

Hommes, N. J. "Let Women Be Silent in the Church: A Message
Concerning the Worship Service and the Decorum to be Observed by
Women." *Calvin Theological Journal* 4 (April 1969): 5–22.

Hooker, Morna D. "Authority on Her Head: An Examination of 1 Cor 11:10."
New Testament Studies 10 (April 1964): 410–16.

House, Wayne T. *The Role of Women in Ministry Today*. Grand Rapids:
Baker, 1995.

_____. "The Speaking of Women and the Prohibition of the Law."
Bibliotheca Sacra 145 (July-September 1988): 301–318.

Hübner, Jamin. "Translating *authenteō* in 1 Timothy 2:12." *Priscilla Papers* 29
(Spring 2015): 16–26.

Hughes, Richad T. "The Grace of Troubling Questions." *Vocation Matters*
(May 12, 2020). Available at https://vocationmatters.org/2020/05/12
/the-grace-of-troubling-questions/.

Hunter, Victor L., editor. "Mission: Women in Christ Today." *Mission* 8
(March 1975): 3–24.

Hutson, Christopher Roy. *First and Second Timothy and Titus*. Grand
Rapids: Baker Academic, 2019.

_____. "Laborers in the Lord: Romans 16 and the Women in Pauline
Churches." *Leaven* 4, no. 2 (1999): 29–31.

_____. "'Saved by Childbearing': the Jewish Context of 1 Timothy 2:15."
Novum Testamentum 56 (2014): 392–410.

Hurley, James B., *Man and Women in Biblical Perspective*. Grand Rapids:
Zondervan, 1981.

James, B. B. "Difficult Passages in I Corinthians No. III," 352–363. In *Studies
in I Corinthians*. Edited by Dub McClish. Denton, TX: Pearl Street
Church of Christ, 1982.

Jewett, Paul K. *Man as Male and Female*. Grand Rapids: Eerdmans, 1975.

Jones, Hefin. "Women, Teaching, and Authority: A Case for Understanding
the Nature of Congregational Oversight as Underlying 1 Timothy
2:11–12," 143–154. In *The Gender Conversation: Evangelical Perspectives
on Gender, Scripture, and the Christian Life*. Edited by Edwina Murphy
and David Starling. Eugene, OR: Wipf & Stock, 2016.

Kidson, Lyn. "'Teaching' and Other Persuasions: The Interpretation
of *didaskein* 'To Teach' in 1 Timothy 2:12," 125–137. In *The Gender*

Conversation: Evangelical Perspectives on Gender, Scripture, and the Christian Life. Edited by Edwina Murphy and David Starling. Eugene, OR: Wipf & Stock, 2016.

Keener, Craig S. *Paul, Women, and Wives: Marriage and Women's Ministry in the Letters of Paul.* Grand Rapids: Baker, 1992.

Kemp, Thomas E. "Putting Woman in Her Place." *Mission* 7 (May 1974): 4–8.

Knight, G. W. *The Pastoral Epistles: A Commentary on the Greek Text.* Grand Rapids: Eerdmans, 1988.

Köstenberger, Andreas J. "A Complex Sentence Structure in 1 Timothy 2:12," 53–84. In *Women in the Church: A Fresh Analysis of 1 Timothy 2:9–15.* Edited by Andreas J. Köstenberger and Thomas R. Schreiner. 2nd Edition. Grand Rapids: Baker Academic, 2005.

Kroeger, Catherine. "The Apostle Paul and the Greco-Roman Cults of Women." *Journal of the Evangelical Theological Society* 30 (March 1987): 25–38.

Kroeger, Catherine and Richard Kroeger. *I Suffer Not a Woman: Rethinking 1 Timothy 2:11–15 in Light of Ancient Evidence.* Grand Rapids: Baker, 1998.

Krutsinger, W. H. "Items from Indiana." *Gospel Advocate* 29 (March 16, 1887): 162.

_____. "Items from Indiana." *Gospel Advocate* 29 (May 4, 1887): 284.

Lard, Moses. "The Care of the Churches." *Lard's Quarterly* 5 (January 1868): 100–107.

Ledbetter, Hoy. "The Prophetess." *Integrity* 4 (January 1973): 11–15.

Lewis, John T. *A Review of "God's Woman."* Montgomery, AL: Sound Doctrine, 1942.

_____. "There is Death in the Pot." *Bible Banner* 1 (July 1939): 12–13.

Liefeld, Walter. "A Plural Ministry View: Your Sons and Daughters Shall Prophesy," 127–153. In *Women in Ministry: Four Views.* Edited by Bonnidell Clouse and Robert G. Clouse. Downers Grove, IL: InterVarsity Press, 1989.

_____. "Women, Submission and Ministry in 1 Corinthians," 134–153. In *Women, Authority & the Bible.* Edited by Alvera Mickelsen. Downer's Grove, IL: InterVarsity Press, 1986.

Lightfoot, Neil. *The Role of Women: New Testament Perspectives.* Memphis: Student Association Press, 1978.

Lipscomb, David. "An Answer to a Query on Woman's Work." *Gospel Advocate* 55 (February 13, 1913): 155.

_____. "Information Wanted on the 'Woman Question.'" *Gospel Advocate* 53 (January 19, 1911): 78–79.

_____. "Preachers or Teachers." *Gospel Advocate* 15 (September 25, 1873): 903–916.

_____. "Queries." *Gospel Advocate* 18 (November 16, 1876): 1110–11.

_____. "Queries." *Gospel Advocate* 28 (December 29, 1886): 818.

_____. "Queries." *Gospel Advocate* 30 (March 7, 1888): 14.

_____. "Queries." *Gospel Advocate* 49 (March 21, 1907): 185.

_____. "Queries." *Gospel Advoc*ate 49 (October 17, 1907): 662.

_____. "Should Women Sing in the Worship?" *Gospel Advocate* 52 (October 31, 1907): 697.

_____. "Should Women Teach?" *Gospel Advocate* 52 (August 25, 1910): 968–9.

_____. "Woman and Her Work." *Gospel Advocate* 34 (October 13, 1892): 644.

_____. "Woman's Station and Work." *Gospel Advocate* 30 (October 10, 1888): 6–7.

_____. "Woman's Work in the Church." *Gospel Advocate* 30 (March 14, 1888): 6–7.

_____. "Women in the Church." *Gospel Advocate* 30 (21 November 1888): 6.

MacGregor, Kirk. "1 Corinthians 14:33b-38 as a Pauline-Quotation-Refutation Device." *Priscilla Papers* 32 (Winter 2018): 23–28.

McGarvey, J. W. *Thessalonians, Corinthians, Galatians and Romans.* Cincinnati: Standard Publishing Co, 1916.

McGuiggan, Jim. *The Book of 1 Corinthians.* Lubbock, TX: Montex Publishing Co., 1984.

McQuiddy, J. C. "Mrs. Catt and Woman-Suffrage Leaders Repudiate the Bible." *Gospel Advocate* 62 (August 12, 1920): 788.

Mansfield, Stephen. *Healing Your Church Hurt: What to Do When You Still Love God But Have Been Wounded by His People.* Reprint edition. Carol Stream, IL: Tyndale Momentum, reprint 2012.

Massey, Lesly F. "Alexander Campbell and the Status of Women." *Priscilla Papers* 30 (Autumn 2016): 16–21.

Marrs, Rick R. "In the Beginning: Male and Female (Genesis 1-3)," 1–36. In *Essays in Earliest Christianity: Volume Two.* Edited by Carroll B. Osburn. Joplin, MO: College Press, 1995.

Marshall, I. Howard. *The Pastoral Epistles.* New York: T & T Clark, 1999.

May, Cecil, Jr. "Women and Prayer." *Integrity* 4 (May 1973): 182–187.

McKnight, Scot. *The Blue Parakeet: Rethinking How You Read the Bible*. 2nd edition. Grand Rapids, MI: Zondervan, 2018.

Meyers, Carol L. *Discovering Eve: Ancient Israelite omen in Context*. New York: Oxford University Press, 1991.

_____. "Gender Roles and Genesis 3:16 Revisited," 337–54. In *The Word of the Lord Shall Go Forth: Essays in Honor of David Noel Freedman*. Edited by Carol L. Meyers and M. O'Conner. Winona Lake, IN: Eisenbrauns, 1983.

_____. *Rediscovering Eve: Ancient Israelite Women in Context*. New York: Oxford University Press, 2012.

_____. "Was Ancient Israel a Patriarchal Society?" *Journal of Biblical Literature* 133 (January 2014): 8–27.

Meyers, J. B. "Should a Woman Lead in Prayer?" *Gospel Advocate* 112 (April 9, 1970): 231.

Moo, Douglas. "What Does It Mean Not to Teach or Have Authority Over Men?," 179–193. *Recovering Biblical Manhood and Womanhood: A Response to Evangelical Feminism*. Edited by John Piper and Wayne Grudem. Redesigned Edition. Wheaton: Crossway, 2012.

Morton, Bruce L. *Deceiving Winds: Christians Navigating the Story of Mysticism, Leadership Struggles & Sensational Worship*. Nashville: 21st Century Christian, 2009.

Mowczko, Marq. "The Meaning of AUTHENTEIN in 1 Timothy 2:12, with a Brief History of AUTHENT-Words." Available at https://margmowczko.com/authentein-1-timothy2_12/

Nelson, Savannah. "Christian Teen 'Unpacks' Why She Takes a 'Safe' Stand on Prayer." *Christian Chronicle* 77 (February 2020): 12.

Niccum, Curt. "The Voice of the Manuscripts on the Silence of Women: The External Evidence for 1 Cor. 14:34–5." *New Testament Studies* 43 (April 1997): 242–255.

Nichol, C. R. *God's Woman*. Clifton, TX: Nichol Publishing Company, 1938.

_____. *Nichol's Pocket Bible Encyclopedia*. Abilene, TX: ACU Press, 1949.

Nichol, C. R. and Robert L. Whiteside. *Sound Doctrine: A Series of Bible Studies for Sunday School Classes, Prayer Meetings, Private Study, College Classes, Etc.* 5 Volumes. Clifton, TX: Mrs. C. R. Nichol, 1920–1952.

Nugent, John and Sean Benesh. *The Polis Biblical Commentary, Volume 1a: Genesis 1–11*. La Vista, NE: Urban Loft Publishers, 2018.

Orbison, Jr., Guy. "Teenage Girls Leading in Prayer." *Firm Foundation* 92 (January 14, 1975): 25.

Origen. *Commentary on Romans*. See Bridget Jack Jeffries, "Origen on the Apostle Junia: A New Translation." Available at http://www.weighted -glory.com/2018/12/origen-apostle-junia/

Osburn, Carroll D. "AUTHENTEŌ (1 Timothy 2:12)." *Restoration Quarterly* 25 (Spring 1982): 1–12.

_____. "1 Cor. 11:2–16—Public or Private?" 307–17. In *Essays on Women in Earliest Christianity, Volume Two*. Edited by Carroll D. Osburn. Joplin, MO: College Press, 1995.

_____. "The Interpretation of 1 Cor. 14:34–35," 219–242. In *Essays on Women in Earliest Christianity, Volume One*. Edited by Carroll D. Osburn. Joplin, MO: College Press, 1993.

_____. *Women in the Church: Reclaiming the Ideal*. Abilene, TX: ACU Press, 2001.

Oster, Richard. *1 Corinthians*. Joplin, MO: College Press, 1995.

_____. "When Men Wore Veils to Worship: The Historical Context of 1 Corinthians 11:4." *New Testament Studies* 34 (October 1988): 481–505.

Padgett, Alan G. *As Christ Submits to the Church: A Biblical Understanding of Leadership and Mutual Submission*. Grand Rapids: Baker, 2011.

Page, Emma, editor. *The Life Work of Mrs. Charlotte Fanning*. Nashville: McQuiddy Printing Company, 1907.

Parks, Norman. "Set Our Women Free." *Integrity* 4 (January 1973): 2–10.

Payne, Philip B. "Is 1 Corinthians 14:34–35 a Marginal Comment or a Quotation? A Response to Kirk MacGregor." *Priscilla Papers* 33 (April 2019): 24–30.

_____. *Man and Woman, One in Christ*. Grand Rapids: Zondervan, 2009.

_____. "*Oude* Combining Two Elements to Convey a Single Idea and 1 Timothy 2:12: Further Insights." *Journal of the Center for Biblical Equality* (2014): 24–34.

Pendleton, W. K. "Shall Women Pray or Exhort in Public?" *Millennial Harbinger* 7 (July 1864): 325–330.

Peppiatt, Lucy. *Rediscovering Scripture's Vision for Women: Fresh Perspectives on Disputed Texts*. Downers Grove, IL: Inter-Varsity Press, 2019.

Pierce, Madison N. "Trinity without Taxis? A Reconsideration of 1 Corinthians 11," 57–84. In *Trinity Without Hierarchy: Reclaiming*

Nicene Orthodoxy in Evangelical Theology. Edited by Michael F. Bird and Scott Harrower. Grand Rapids: Kregel Academic, 2019.

Poe, John T. "Female Evangelists." *Firm Foundation* 16 (January 29, 1901): 11.

Porter, D. G., "Republican Government and the Suffrage of Women." *Christian Quarterly* 6 (October 1874): 471–496.

Prohl, Russell C. *Woman in the Church.* Grand Rapids: Eerdmans, 1957.

Pulley, Kathy J. "Gender Roles and Conservative Churches: 1870–1930," 443–83. In *Essays on Women in Earliest Christianity, Volume Two.* Edited by Carroll D. Osburn. Joplin, MO: College Press Publishing Co., 1995.

Pullias, C. M. "Preface," 3–5. In *Review of "God's Woman."* By John T. Lewis. Montgomery, AL: Sound Doctrine, 1942.

Reid, Barbara E. *Wisdom's Feast: An Invitation to Feminist Interpretation of the Scriptures.* Grand Rapids: Eerdmans, 2016.

Robinson, Thomas. *A Community Without Barriers: Women in the New Testament and the Church Today.* New York: Manhattan Church of Christ, 2002.

Rowland, Robert H. *"I Permit not a Woman—" to Remain Shackled.* Corona, CA: Lighthouse Publishing, 1991.

Ruden, Sarah. *Paul Among the People: The Apostle Reinterpreted and Reimagined in His Own Time.* New York: Crown Publishing Company, 2010.

Sandifer, J. Stephen. *Deacons: Male and Female? A Study for Churches of Christ.* Houston, TX: J. S. Sandifer, 1989.

Sattenfield, Charles L. "A Study of 1 Timothy 2:8." *The Defender* 5 (August 1976): 63–64.

_____. *The Question of Women Praying.* Fort Smith, Texas: Star Bible and Tract Corporation, 1977.

Schreiner, T. R. "An Interpretation of 1 Tim 2:9–15: A Dialogue with Scholarship," 85–120. In *Women in the Church: A Fresh Analysis of 1 Timothy 2:9–15.* Edited by Andreas J. Köstenberger and Thomas R. Schreiner. Grand Rapids: Baker Academic, 2005.

Scholer, David M. "How Can Divine Revelation Be So Human." *Daughters of Sarah* 15 (May/June 1989): 11–15.

_____. "Paul's Women Coworkers in Ministry." *Theology, News, and Notes* 42 (1995): 20–22

Scobey, James E. "Charlotte (Fall) Fanning," 147–168. In *Franklin College and Its Influences*. Edited by James E. Scobey. Nashville: McQuiddy Printing Co., 1906.

_____. "Reunion Exercises," 351–372. In *Franklin College and Its Influences*. Edited by James E. Scobey. Nashville: McQuiddy Printing Co., 1906.

Sewell, Elisha G. "The Elevation and Proper Position of Women Under the Religion of Christ." *Gospel Advocate* 30 (June 13, 1888): 8.

_____. "What is Woman's Work in the Church (Again)?" *Gospel Advocate* 39 (July 22, 1897): 432.

_____. "What May Women Do in the Church?" *Gospel Advocate* 39 (November 4, 1897): 692.

Shelly, Rubel. "Objections to Females Leading In Prayer." *Firm Foundation* 92 (May 13, 1975): 297.

Smith, F. LaGard. *Male Spiritual Leadership*. Nashville: 21st Century Christian, 1998.

Smith, F. W. "About Christian Women." *Gospel Advocate* 71 (August 15, 1929): 778–9.

_____. "The Glory of True Womanhood: A Sermon Delivered by F. W. Smith to Graduates of the Horse Cave High School." *Christian Leader & the Way* 20 (1 May 1906): 2–3.

Sommer, Daniel. "Woman's Religious Duties and Privileges in Public." *Octographic Review* 34 (August 20, 1901): 1.

Spurgeon, Andrew B. "1 Timothy 2:13–15: Paul's Retelling of Genesis 2:4–4:1." *Journal of the Evangelical Theological Society* 56 (2013): 543–56.

Stelding, Charles. "'Brothers and Sisters' (*adelphoi*) in 1 Corinthians." Available at https://drive.google.com/file/d/1X6BcMpngqV3lDd8kwcoYypQ_A2mdARvK/view

_____. "Galatians 3:28 'Nor is There Male and Female." Available at https://drive.google.com/file/d/1biDJ1waU1GU6IyuJtzfineGI5VGXLGdQ/view

Thiselton, Anthony C. *The First Epistle to the Corinthians*. The New International Greek Testament Commentary. Grand Rapids: Eerdmans, 2013.

Thompson, Curt. *Anatomy of the Soul: Surprising Connections Between Neuroscience and Spiritual Practices That Can Transform Your Life and Relationships*. Carol Stream, IL: Tyndale House Publishers, Inc., 2010.

Thompson, James. *The Apostle of Persuasion: Theology and Rhetoric in the Pauline Letters*. Grand Rapids: Baker, 2020.

Towner, Philip H. *The Letters to Timothy and Titus*. Grand Rapids: Eerdmans, 2006.

Wallace, Daniel B. *Greek Grammar Beyond the Basics: An Exegetical Syntax of the New Testament*. Grand Rapids: Zondervan, 1996.

Wallace, Jr., Foy E. "God's Women Gather." *Bible Banner* 2 (November 1939): 15.

Walters, James. "'Phoebe' and 'Junia(s)'—Romans 16:1–2, 7," 167–190. In *Essays on Women in Earliest Christianity, Volume One*. Edited by Carroll D. Osburn. Joplin, MO: College Press, 1993.

Warlick, Mrs. Joe S. [Lucy]. "May Women Teach? When? Where?" *Gospel Guide* 8 (August 1923): 2.

Warlick, Joe S. "Let Your Women Keep Silent in the Church!" *Gospel Guide* 5 (August 2920): 2.

_____. "Editorial." *Gospel Guide* 12 (May 1927): 14.

Warlick, Joe S. and George W. Phillips. *A Debate on the Sunday School Question*. Dallas: J. S. Warlick, 1924.

Weeks, Noel. "Of Silence and Head Covering." *Westminster Theological Journal* 35 (Fall 1972): 21–27.

Westfall, Cynthia Long. *Paul and Gender: Reclaiming the Apostle's Vision for Men and Women in Christ*. Grand Rapids: Baker Academic, 2016.

_____. "The Meaning of *authenteō* in 1 Timothy 2:12." *Journal of Greco-Roman Christianity and Judaism*. 10 (2014): 138–173.

Whiteside, R. L. "Should She Have Taken the Lead?" *Gospel Advocate* 77 (January 10, 1935): 34.

Willard, Dallas. "Foreword," vi-x. In *How I Changed My Mind about Women in Leadership: Compelling Stories from Prominent Evangelicals*. Edited by Aland F. Johnson. Grand Rapids: Zondervan, 2010.

Wilshire, Leland E. *Insight into Two Biblical Passages: Anatomy of a Prohibition 1 Timothy 2:12, the TLG Computer, and the Christian Church*. UPA: Amazon Services, 2010.

Winter, Bruce W. *Roman Wives, Roman Widows: The Appearance of New Women and the Pauline Communities*. Grand Rapids: Eerdmans, 2003.

Winters, Howard. *Commentary on First Corinthians: Practical and Explanatory*. Greenville, SC: Carolina Christian, 1987.

Wise, William M. *Primeval Woman*. Denton, TX: Christian Monitor
Publishing Co., 1920. Stone-Campbell Books. 410. https://
digitalcommons.acu.edu/crs_books/410

_____. "Woman's Work in the Church." *Firm Foundation* 20 (3 May 1904): 3.

Witherington III, Ben. *Letters and Homilies for Hellenized Christians: A
Socio-Rhetorical Commentary on Titus, 1–2 Timothy and 1–3 John.*
Downers Grove, IL: InterVarsity Press, 2006.

_____. *Women in the Ministry of Jesus*. Cambridge: Cambridge University
Press, 1984.

Whitmire, Charles A. "An Objection to Girls Leading Prayer." *Firm
Foundation* 92 (May 13, 1975): 9.

Wolters, Al. "The Meaning of AUTHENTEO," 65–116. In *Women in the
Church: An Interpretation & Application of 1 Timothy 2:9–15*. Edited
by Andreas J. Köstenberger and Thomas R. Schreiner. 3rd Edition.
Wheaton, IL: Crossway, 2016.

Woods, Guy N. *Questions and Answers: Open Forum, Freed-Hardeman
College Lectures.* Henderson, TN: Freed-Hardeman College, 1976.

_____. "Women and Prayer (1 Tim 2:8–12)." *Gospel Advocate* 120 (October
12, 1978): 643.

Wyatt, J. J. "Queries." *Gospel Advocate* 30 (March 7, 1888): 14.

Further Reading

Standard Anthologies

Limited Participation
Grudem Wayne and John Piper, editors. *Recovering Biblical Manhood and Womanhood: A Response to Evangelical Feminism.* Redesigned Edition. Wheaton, IL: Crossway, 2012.

Full Participation
Pierce, Ronald E., Rebecca Merrill Groothuis, and Gordon D. Fee, editors. *Discovering Biblical Equality: Complementarity Without Hierarchy.* Downers Grove, IL: InterVarsity Press, 2010.

Multi-View Books
Beck, James R., editor. *Two Views on Women in Ministry.* 2nd edition. Grand Rapids: Zondervan, 2005.

Clouse, Bonnidell and Robert G. Clouse, editors. *Women in Ministry: Four Views.* Grand Rapids: InterVarsity Academic, 1989.

General Presentations

No or Limited Participation
Foh, Susan. *Woman and the Word of God: A Response to Biblical Feminism.* Phillipsburg, NJ: Presbyterian and Reformed Publishing Co., 1978.

House, Wayne. *The Role of Women in Ministry Today.* Grand Rapids: Baker, 1995.

Kassian, Mary. *Women, Creation and the Fall.* Wheaton, IL: Crossway Books, 1990.

Keller, Kathy. *Jesus, Justice, and Gender Roles: A Case for Gender Roles in Ministry.* Grand Rapids: Zondervan, 2012.

Köstenberger, Andreas J. and Thomas R. Schreiner, editors. *Women in the Church: An Interpretation and Application of 1 Timothy 2:9–15*. 3rd edition. Wheaton, IL: Crossway, 2016.

Full Participation

Bartlett, Andrew. *Men and Women in Christ: Fresh Light from the Biblical Texts*. London: Inter-Varsity Press, 2019.

Byrd, Aimee. *Recovering From Biblical Manhood & Womanhood: How the Church Needs to Rediscover Her Purpose*. Grand Rapids: Zondervan, 2020.

Keener, Craig S. *Paul, Women, and Wives: Marriage and Women's Ministry in the Letters of Paul*. Grand Rapids: Baker, 1992.

Matthews, Alice. *Gender Roles and the People of God: Rethinking What We Were Taught about Men and Women in the Church*. Grand Rapids: Zondervan, 2017.

Payne, Philip B. *Man and Woman, One in Christ: An Exegetical and Theological Study of Paul's Letters*. Grand Rapids: Zondervan, 2009.

Westfall, Cynthia Long. *Paul and Gender: Reclaiming the Apostle's Vision for Men and Women*. Grand Rapids: Baker, 2016.

Hermeneutics:

Limited Participation

Grudem, Wayne. *Evangelical Feminism & Biblical Truth: An Analysis of More than One Hundred Disputed Questions*. Wheaton, IL: Crossway, 2012.

Reaoch, Benjamin. *Women, Slaves, and the Gender Debate: A Complementarian Response to the Redemptive-Movement Hermeneutic*. Philipsburg, NJ: Presbyterian and Reformed, 2012.

Full Participation

McKnight, Scot. *The Blue Parakeet: Rethinking How You Read the Bible*. 2nd edition. Grand Rapids, MI: Zondervan, 2018.

Webb, William J. *Slaves, Women & Hermeneutics*. Downers Grove, IL: InterVarsity, 2001.

Seeking Common Ground

Lee-Barnewall, Michelle. *Neither Complementarian Nor Egalitarian: A Kingdom Corrective to the Evangelical Gender Debate*. Grand Rapids: Baker, 2016.

American Restoration Movement

Audio Series (Podcast)

Christy, Jennifer Hale. *PreachHER: A Podcast*. Available on buzzsprout. com.

Nugent, John C., Ronald D. Peters, and Samuel C. Long. *The After Class Podcast*. 15 one hour podcasts on women in the Bible. Episodes 2.33–41, 43–48.

Hearing the Voices of Women

Love, D'Esta, editor. *Finding Their Voices: Sermons by Women in Churches of Christ*. Abilene: Leafwood Press, 2015.

Multi-View

Gilmore, Ralph, Lynn Mitchell, Robert M. Randolph, and Don McWhorter. *Gender and Ministry: The Role of Women in the Work and Worship of the Church*. Huntsville, AL: Publisher Designs, 1990.

No or Limited Participation

Archer, Timothy. "Women in the Assembly." See his many blog posts on this topic. Available at http://www.timothyarcher.com/kitchen/women-in-the-assembly-of-the-church/

Cottrell, Jack. *Gender Roles & the Bible: Creation, the Fall, & Redemption: A Critique of Feminist Biblical Interpretation*. Joplin, MO: College Press, 1994.

Ferguson, Everett. *Women in the Church: Biblical and Historical Perspectives*. Abilene, TX: Desert Willow Publishing, 2015.

Fewkes, John A. *As in All the Churches: A Close Look at the Call for Full Female Participation and Leadership in the Church*. CreateSpace Independent Publishing Platform, 2018.

Guy, Cynthia Dianne. *What About the Women? A Study of New Testament Scripture Concerning Women*. Nashville: Gospel Advocate Company, 2005.

Lightfoot, Neil R. *The Role of Women: New Testament Perspectives*. Memphis: Student Association Press, 1978.

McWhorter, Don. *God's Woman, Feminine or Feminist?* Huntsville: Publishing Designs, Inc., 1992.

Sproles, Renée. *On Gender: What the Bible Says About Men and Women—and Why It Matters*. Murfreesboro: Renew.org, 2019.

Smith, F. LaGard. *Male Spiritual Leadership*. Nashville: 21st Century Christian, 1998.

Full Participation

Barton, Sara Gaston. *A Woman Called: Piecing Together the Ministry Puzzle*. Abilene: Leafwood Publishers, 2012.

Burke, Gary T. God's Woman *Revisited: Women and the Church*. Eugene, OR: Luminare, 2019.

Coyle, Rob. *The Silencing of God's Woman: How the Bible Has Been Misunderstood and Misused to Hold Back and Oppress the Female Voice in the Church*. Amazon Services, 2017.

Guin, Jay. *Buried Talents: In Search for a New Consensus*. Jay Guin, 2007.

Osburn, Carroll. *Women in the Church: Reclaiming the Ideal*. Abilene, TX: ACU Press, 2001.

Reese, Jeanene. *Bound and Determined: Christian Men and Women in Partnership*. Abilene, TX: Leafwood, 2010.

Robinson, Thomas. *A Community Without Barriers: Women in the New Testament and the Church Today*. New York: Manhattan Church of Christ, 2002.

Rowland, Robert H. *"I Permit Not a Woman . . ." to Remain Shackled*. Corona, CA: Lighthouse Publishing Co., 1991.

Seeking Common Ground

Highfield, Ron. *Four Views on Women and Church Leadership: Should Bible-Believing (Evangelical) Churches Appoint Women Preachers, Pastors, Elders, and Bishops?* Keledei Publications, 2017.